EXCAVATING PAINTED ROCKSHELTERS

A.K. SHARMA

BHARATIYA KALA PRAKASHAN
DELHI (INDIA)

First Edition : 2006

Published by **C.P. Gautam**
BHARATIYA KALA PRAKASHAN
3421-A, IInd Floor Narang Colony, Tri Nagar,
Delhi-110035. Phone : 27393083, 32967505 (O), 32492129 (R)

ISBN : 81-8090-115-7

Laser Type Setting by
A-ONE GRAPHICS
JD-18C, IInd Floor, Pitampura, Delhi-110088

Printed By :
BDH Printer at Salasar Imaging Systems
Delhi

EXCAVATING PAINTED ROCKSHELTERS

Dedicated

to

MAA BAMLESHWARI

PREFACE

In the Indian sub-continent Central India can boast of having the richest prehistoric cultural heritage. Environmentally also, this region was favoured more from prehistoric times, and it is for this reason that almost all the river valleys in Central India have yielded relics of man through the ages.

Natural rock shelters occur in large numbers, scattered throughout the Vindhyan hills of Central India and a number of them contain habitational deposits which if systematically excavated and studied will reveal the wealth of information contained in them, about the past, in chronological order. Amongst the group of rock shelters scattered in seven hills around Bhopal, those at Jhiri were selected for detailed examination under Indo-French Rock Art Project sponsored by Indira Gandhi National Centre for the Arts. The basic aims of this project were:-

(a) To devise an international basic approach to rock art in different and complementary situations by detailed study of rock paintings in India and France alongwith their archaeological and ethnographical contexts;

(b) To do pigment analysis with an eye on chronological dating and

(c) By study of conservation problems devise means of protecting these valuable cultural wealth of bygone days. In the season 1993-94, the French team recorded the paintings and studied conservation problems in Rock Shelter No. 10, whereas the Indian team subjected the habitational deposits in Rock Shelter nos. 3, 8, 10 and 17 to detailed investigations apart from manual and photo-recordings of the paintings.

After the discovery of rock-shelters and paintings at Jhiri by late Shri Shankar Tiwari in 1975-76. these shelters were variously numbered by different agencies. Since there numberings were not done in a scientific manner, the Indian team renumbered them on the basis of their location (contourwise) starting from north to south as all the shelters are located on the western slope of the hill. In all twenty two rock shelters with paintings were recorded.

Rock paintings are known from almost all parts of the country but in the absence of any absolute methods for their dating, so far, they have been dated on the basis of "style" as one of the criterion. The chronology established on the basis of 'style' has not been accepted by the majority of scholars in toto.

Under the present circumstances archaeological approach seems to be the only answer supplemented by chemical analysis of wall pigments alongwith the pigments found in the excavations and ethnological studies of the prevailing traditions in the area. With this aim in view excavations were undertaken at Jhiri and they resulted in recovery of Mesolithic tools, wood-charcoal, pigments and coins in perfect chronological order. Here we have for the first time some material for absolute dating and chemical analysis both from the dig and from the wall. The results will definitely go a long way in establishing the chronological sequence of the rock paintings atleast in Central India and firmly dating the use of these shelters by men.

The present monograph contains the details of the excavations conducted in 1993 -94 and typological study of the Stone Age artefacts and other antiquities recovered there in. Results of C-14 samples, soil analysis and pigment analysis are awaited.

I conducted the excavations in Jhiri rock shelters on behalf of Indira Gandhi National Centre for the Arts and the credit for undertaking this project goes to Smt. Kapila Vatsyayan, the Academic Director, Shri M.C. Joshi, Member Secretary and Shri B N. Saraswati, Senior Professor, Janpada Sampada Division of the institution. I take this opportunity' to express my deep sense of gratitude to S/Shri M.S. Mani. Draftsman, Rakesh Khanduri and Anil Tiwan, Assistant Archaewologists, G.R. Verma, store keeper, Sarabjeet Singh Dhillon, photographer and Gautam D. Chowdhury who constituted the excavation team and helped me in completing the work in record time. I am also thankful to Dr. Mathpal and Dr. Malla who recorded the paintings.

In the field, almost daily, on the spot discussions on various problems, techniques, conservation methods and our findings with Dr. M. Lorblanchet and his other team mates went a longway in understanding each others point of view and resulted in mutual enrichment of knowledge It was a scene of perfect homogeneity between the two teams coming from entirely different cultural zones. The visit of late Dr. Shankar Tiwari from Bhopal to the site at regular intervals and discussions with him were most rewarding. I am grateful to him for sharing his vast knowledge about the rock shelters and environmental conditions in the area with us.

This report was submitted by me to the India Gandhi National Centre for the Arts on 22nd March, 1994, before leaving the centre with the hope that it will be published with the same speed which I showed in excavating the site and completing the report there upon. As even after twelve years, when I found that the IGNCA has not yet published the report, I thought it proper to publish it so that its importance is not lost to the academic world.

Soil samples and charcoal samples were handed over to Birbal Sahani Institute of Palaeobotany for analysis and dating respectively. While the palinological report on soil samples was received promptly and is appended here as appendix I, C-14 dating is still awaited.

Preliminary report on rock art of Jhiri by the French team forms appendix-2. Detailed report from French team is still awaited.

I am grateful to Birbal Sahani Institute of Palaeobotany, Lucknow and to the French team for their reports.

Inspite of detailed planning the entire project was abandonded halfway, which unfortunately happens with many of the projects in India. I do-not know where things went wrong and why the controlling authorities at New Delhi did not allow the project to come to its logical conclusion, which would have gone a long way in settling the lingering problem of dating the Rack-Paintings in India. In my opinion even now it is not too late. The project needs to be revived with the participation of experienced and young scholars from both the countries.

Mumbai
14th March 06

A.K. Sharma
F 8/5, Sector 3,
C.B.D., Belapur,
Navi Mumbai-400614
Mobile :09422803230

Contents

List of Figures

List of Plates

1

Introduction

In Central India the beginning of location of rock shelters and paintings contained therein was made in 1883 when Archibal Carlleyele explored some rock-paintings in the Kaimur ranges and also collected microliths and fossilized bones of wild animals from these shelters. In 1883 J Cockburn located the rock shelters of Ghormangar, Lohari and Lekhania in Mirzapur district and collected stone implements and red pigments of haematite from these shelters. In 1907 C.A. Silberrad published a paper on 'Rock drawings in the Banda district'. He visited the shelters at Sarhat, Malwa, Kuria-Kund and Karpalia where mostly hunting scenes were depicted in red ochre. In 1910 C.W, Anderson[1] discovered the rock shelters of Singhanpur in Raigarh distric of Chhattisgarh. A detailed account of the paintings was published by him in 1918. He also collected some stone implements and a lump of red ochre. In 1992 the archaeological value of Adamgarh rock-shelters were noticed by Manoranjan Ghosh[2]. A brief description was published in the *Memoirs of the Archaeological Survey of India,* No. 24 in the year 1932. E.A. D'Abreu made actual size copies of the paintings by means of tracing paper. The entire material was published in the book form in 1934 by Nagpur Museum.

In 1932 and 1933 G.R. Hunter[3] conducted excavations near some of the rock-shelters in Pachmarhi. In Dorothydeep shelter he could get deposit upto the depth of nearly 2m. The report of this excavation was published in 1936. His excavations proved that the earliest levels belonged to Mesolithic period. From 1932 to 1945 D.H. Gordon located a number of rock-shelters in the vicinity of Pachmarhi[4]. He recorded the material from the first fifteen rock shelters, classified them and published a paper titled 'Indian Cave Paintings' in the Journal of Royal Asiatic Society of Bengal in 1943[5].

After 1955 extensive survey of rock-shelters in Central India were conducted by Prehistory Branch of Archaelogical Survey of India, VS. Wakankar, Shankar Tiwari and S.K. Pandey. Excavations were also conducted in various rock-shelters to find out the culture sequence and to correlate them with the paintings. Dr. R.V. Joshi of A.S.I, conducted extensive excavations at Adamgarh rock shelters in 1961[6]. V.N. Mishra[7] and V.S. Wakankar[8] excavated in some of the shelters at Bhimbetka but their conclusions were criticised by Shankar Tiwari and K.D. Banerjee. The credit of extensive exploration in the Betwa source region termed by him as 'S' belt goes to Shankar Tiwari. This is one of the biggest areas encompassing the districts of Raisen, Bhopal and Sehore in M.P. where hundreds of rock shelters are located. Jhiri is one of them. The floors of most of the rock-shelters, in this region are filled with habitational deposits.

Jhiri hill seems to have been a much frequented site from the Mesolithic to historical periods as the archaeological evidences and paintings on the walls indicate. It's convenient situation in the vicinity of a perennial stream met the basic needs of water. The thick forested hills provided animal and vegetable food. Natural rock shelters on the hill served as shelters during fair and foul weather and also as a defence against wild beasts. Plenty of fine grained quartzitic raw material available in the area were handy for manufacturing implements required for hunting animals and digging up edible roots. In Early Historical Period and Historical Periods these shelters located on ancient piligrim and trade roots, occupying commanding positions, served as rest shelters for the piligrims and traders and occassionally also for the chieftains of the area as their temporary headquarters. The paintings pertaining to different periods clearly speak about these occupations. Thus, periodically since the Mesolithic times this area has provided the basic requirements of food, water, shelter and had been a favoured habitation site.

With a view to investigate the habitational deposits of different periods and to trace the evidence for dating the rock paintings, excavations were conducted in this site in the year 1993-94 Out of twenty two *rock* shelters four (nos. 3. 8. J 0 and J 7) were subjected to investigations. While selecting these shelters, it was kept in mind that the same could be studied by the French team from recording and conservation point of view also. Three of them (3, 8 and 10) are profusely painted whereas the fourth (17) has very few paintings as the surface available is limited, but from archaeological point of view it came out to be very important, as it was the factory site for manufacturing Mesolithic tools. The maximum depth reached in rock shelter no. 3 was 0.95m, in rock shelter no. 8 it was 1.25m, in rock shelter no. 10 it was 1.30m and in rock shelter no. 17, it was 0.98m. After these depths there was bed rock formation. The deposits in these shelters mostly consisted of redish lateritic clay mixed with weathered shale, ash and loose brownish earth. In all the trenches there were boulders scattered through out. The redish lateritic soil yielded microlithic assemblage from layer 2 downwards in rock shelter no. 3 and 8 whereas in rock shelter no. 17 the occurance of this assemblage was right from the top as this shelter was the factory site. In rock shelter no. 10 the entire deposit consisted of big boulders which were evidently deposited over the bed rock to make the surface even by people who occupied the shelter in later periods. During mesolithic period the occupation was over the bed rock itself which was clear from the presence of a grooved grinding stone. Occurance of fire places in rock shelter nos 3 and 8 were significant from the occupational point of view. The excavation yielded apart from large quantity of mesolithic tools, colour pigments of various shades, hop-scotches on stone, few pottery fragments, charred fragments of animal bones and few bone tools. From the top level of rock shelter no. 3 two uninscribed cast copper coins datable to 3rd-4th cent. B.C. were recovered indicating that the shelter was occupied as late as during this period.

From the slopes of the embankments of the newly laid road leading to the reservoir on top of the hill, large number of Early and Middle Stone Age tools were recovered (Pl. I A & B). These tools shaped out of fine grained quatzitic sand stone were conspicuously absent on the top of the hill, the slopes and inside the rock shelters. As the survey of the hill showed that this raw material is not available here, it was evident that these tools came here alongwith the lateritic earth that was brought to raise the embarkment for the road. On enquiry from the local people, I was able to locate the Stone Age site itself just 2 kms. south of Jhiri. Here in the lateritic deposit in an exposed section, these tools could be scene forming a layer just 1m, below the present surface. This was the factory site as there were plenty of out crops of quartzitic boulders all around. This indicates that Stone Age man also roamed in the area around Jhiri. Whether he occupied the rock shelters and painted the walls is doubtful as the evidences in the shelters do not point out in this direction.

Prof. Shankar Tiwari took me to a spot nearly 3 kms. south of Jhiri, winding through rocky out crops and deep jungles where he pointed out towardsd hundreds of stone alignments. This site was discovered by him nearly fifteen years back but he was not sure about it's antiquity. After clearing one of them, on close examination I found them to be megalithic burials. As they were unlike those, identified so far in other areas of the country, Prof. Tiwari could not identify them definitely to be megalithic burials. These are rectangular enclosures formed by upright stone slabs, oriented lengthwise in east-west direction, with opening towards east. On the eastern corners there are ritualistic structures (Pl.II). It is for the first time that in Central India a sprawling magalithic site has been discovered and identified. A megalithic site being so close to the rock-shelters, it is likely that the megalithic people might have also depicted their artistic ability on the walls of these shelters. The occurance of iron spears and arrowheads typical of megalithic period in the paintings indicate in this direction.

To surmise, it is now clear that Jhiri rock shelters area had witnessed the activities of man from Early Stone Age to Historical times and right from Mesolithic Period onwards he had been occupying these shelters and painting their walls, depicting activities of his life and environment. These hills and shelters, evidence of our glorious past need to be preserved from ever growing greed of the modern man for land. IGNCA's effort was a step in this direction.

The seven hills around Bhopal abound in rock-shelters. Jhiri is one of them These shelters served as ideal habitational spots for pre-historic man and his later successors, the evidence of which are recorded in the form of paintings on the exposed surfaces inside these shelters and in the form of habitational debris, forming successive layers on the floor of the shelters. Man does not require only shelters to settle down. The other pre-requisites he used to look far are perennial supply of water and plenty of food both vegetarian and non-vegetarian. It is totally a misconception to think that early man was predominantly dependent on game for his food. Tubers and fruits played equally important role. A look at the forest cover around Jhiri indicates that in ancient times there was plenty of water in the area. The dense alignments of trees in a particular line for several kms indicates that there must have been a sufficiently broad stream always full of running water. Due to deforestation and conversion of forest area into agricultural fields the drainage pattern of the area has changed. Now instead of a mighty stream there are a number of 'Finger tip" tributaries. Now instead of having a stream of 3rd order there are streams of 1st order i.e finger tip streams as per Harton's law. These scavengers of first order play a greater and devasting role in erroding the soil of the area and this is what is presently happening around Jhiri. About 30° inclination of the trees on the slopes of the Jhiri hill, just below the rock shelters indicates soil creepe. Curvature in trees growing on slopes develops if creepe movement is slower than growth rate of the trees but if creepe is faster, than the trees will be inclined as at Jhiri.

Animals intutionally search for shelters. This is more so with those species which are smaller in size and more vulnerable to fall prey to the dominant species. In the evolutionary sequence the egg laying species generally require shelters more for the protection of the eggs during hatching period than those who give birth to offsprings directly i.e. mammals. Amongst mammals man is an exception. In the evolutionary process when man started walking erect, he has powerful enough to face the onslaught of ferrocious animals, though in encounters mortality rate might have been quite high but he never felt the need for any shelter to hide. As the brain case enlarged, the number of cells in grey and piamatter increased, he observed the birds, the smaller reptiles, building shelters in the form of nest and burrows, the idea crept in his mind why not look for such safe places for ourselves This idea most probably entered his thought only when he turned from a ferocious hunter into hunter-gatherer. He was now not so wild and powerful, he required safer places for his children. While moving up and down the hills in search of game. tubers and fruits., he had noticed animals coming oult of rock-shelters and caves, an idea occurred to him, why not drive them away and occupy them? This was the beginning of the man using rock shelters for habitational purposes. Probably this started happening around the Middle Stone Age as per evidences elsewhere but at Jhiri it was first the Late Stone Age (Mesolithic) man, preparing and using microliths for hunting and fishing, who occupied these rock shelters first. During this period, as he had more sophisticated weapons to hunt and morc skill to collect food, he had plenty of time while sitting around the fire places, roasting the kill of the day and the collected tubers, to stretch his imagination to other creative aspects. Collecting the colour pigments lying in plenty around him, he dissolved them in water, added the binding material, the latex from *dhoara* (Anogeissues latifolia) and painted the daily dominant episodes of his life-the hunting scenes, the fear striken running animals etc. While collecting fruits he has observed the thick sticky milk ozing out from *dhaora* trees, which are in abundance in the slopes of the hills around the shelters (Pl. III). He was careful enough to select only such spots on the roof and walls of the rock shelters which were not affected by rain water and which were directly under his gaze. Thus the story of rock-shelters and paintings contained therein, at Jhiri began.

FOOTNOTES

1. Anderson, C.W., Rock Paintings in Singhanpur, *Journal of the Bihar and Orissa Research Society,* IV No.2, 1918.
2. Ghosh, M.R., Memoirs of Archaeological Survey of India, Vol. 24, Calcutta, 1932.
3. Hunter, G.R. Excavations at Pachmarhi, *Nagpur University Journal,* Nagpur, 1934.
4. Gordon, D.H. Rock Paintings of the Mahadeo Hills. *Indian Arts and letters,* No. 1, 1936.
5. Gordon, D.H. Indian Cave Paintings, J.R.A.S. of Bengal, Vol. DC, 1943.
6. Joshi, R.V. *Stone Age Cultures of Central India,* Pune, 1978.
7. Misra, V.N. Prehistoric culture sequence of Bhimbetka, *Prehistoric Man and his Art in Central India, Pune.*
8. Wakankar, V.S. Bhimbetka Excavations, *Indian Historical Quarterly* Vol. I & n, Trivendrum, 1973.

2

GEOLOGY AND ENVIRONMENT

Geologically Jhiri falls in the Malwa region of Central India. Majority of rock shelters in the Indian sub-continent are located in the Vindhyan system. This system is a vast stratified formation of sand stone, shales and limestone encompassing a thickness of nearly 450m. at places. It is composed of two distinct faceis of deposits- (a) marine, calcareous and agrillaceous, characteristically developed in the lower part and (b) arenaceous of fluviatile or estuarine deposition, forming the upper portion. The shale, limestone and sandstone strata show very little structural displacement of their original horizontality of deposition. The lower Vindhyans show tectonic deformation by folding movements. The lower Vindhyan is seperated from the upper by an unconfirmity that is very apparent in the north but tends to disappear south of Mewar, Chittor and Son Valley. This signifies that the earth movements supervened after the deposion of the lower Vindhyan sediments which elevated them into land in the Aravali areas of the north and put a stop to further sedimentation. When after resubmergence deposition was renewed, an interval of time had elapsed, during which the former set of conditions disappeared, and the mountains and highlands which yielded the detritus changed completely. Such earth movements, causing the cessation of deposition, are at the root of stratigraphic divisions.

Prevalance of arid, continental conditions in the Upper Vindhyan times is suggested by the perfect rounding of quartz grains in the majority of the sand stones and also by the prevailing red and brown colours of the sediments and by the occasional presence of gypsum in the Bhander shales.

The junction of the Upper Vindhyan with the older rocks of the Aravallies, at their north-west extremity reveals an extremely long fault of great throw, which has brought the undisturbed, almost horizontal strata of the Vindhyan sandstone in contact with the highly folded and foliated schists of the Aravallis. In the great Vindhyan basin the sandstones and quarzite form a series of well marked scraps while the intervening strata being soft, give rise to sloping talus. The chief members persist over large areas with fairly uniform characters. Taken as a whole the structure of the Vindhyan areas is that of a basin, the sandstones forming plateaux. Over the greater part of the area the beds are nearly horizontal but they show evidence of disturbances near the north-west and south-east margins. In the Dhar forests and near Jhalrapatan the Vindhyans are folded and show steep dips. They are thickest in the southern and south-western areas. The upper Vindhyans are 500m thick in the south-west, 1500m in the north-west. The lower Vindhyans are either their or absent in the north-west, the Kaimur overlapping them.

The margins of the Vindhyan basin show a good development of sand stones, while the shales are best-developed in the centre and east, passing gradually laterally into sand stone. The prevalence of current bedding and raffle marks marks in the strata is indicative of shallow water origin, while the red sand stone of the Kaimur and Bhander probably indicate semi and continental conditions.

The most striking feature formed by the Vindhyan rocks is the scarp which marks the northern flank of the Narmada-Son valleys; in the west this is largely formed of the Deccan Lavas, but Vindhyan rocks occur between Bhopal and Itarsi. To the north of Vindhyan range lies a wide expanse of lava landscape overlying a pre-cretaceous surface. Its general elevation is 500-600m. Erosion has succeeded during tertiary times in carving out an extensive levelled surface over the pile of lavas, drained by the headwaters of the Mahi, Chambal, Kali-sindh, Parbati, Betwa and Dhasan with gently undulating divides. Most of these river valleys are flanked by terraced slopes; the paired terraces of Kali-Sindh between Sonkatchh and Sarangpur-a distance of about 70 kms. are typical examples. Here to the east of Bhopal city- the Vindhayan sand stones are found in juxtaposition with the trap in an irregular fashion. These indicate that the trap was poured out upon very uneven surface of the pre-cretaceous age.

The younger trap hills are invariably lower in elevation because of rapid weathering of basaltic lava. The resurrected sand stone hills are higher, craggy and steep-sided, though they are often cuesta-shaped. Isolated mesas, rounded or linear, occur practically everywhere on the Malwa Plateau, whereas it is only in Bhopal and Vidisha that one comes across the sandstone hills.

The western Vindhyanas is really an escarpment which varies in character and height depending on its structure and lithology. For the first 100 kms. from its western terminous, Gomanpur peak (554m) in the Dhar district of M.P., Vindhya Range runs in a curve, its complex side facing the Narmada Valley. From Gomanpur peak broad spurs descend southwards giving rise to Bagh hills. General elevation of this scarp varies from 450m to 600m though a few points rise above 800m, Janpa and Singarchori (884 m) being noteworthy.

For the next 160km. a more open type of country prevails, and the basaltic escarpment becomes more prominent near Hoshangabad. The rock type changes, Vindhyan Range comes down very close to the Narmada river and presents a terraced slope built of hard sandstones alternating with shales.

This whole range lying in Malwa region forms the *Paripatra* upto *Rksa* (both mentioned in Puranas) eastward.

Drainage

The area lies in the drainage basins of two great rivers, the Ganga and Narmada. The main range of the Vindhyachal, for its greater length is the principal water divide. The Northern portion of Raisen district is drained by the Betwa and Bina rivers and their tributaries which ultimately flow towards north and join the Yamuna. The other series of streams is formed of those which flow southwards to join Narmada. It is fed by many tributaries in the district, of which the important ones are the Sindor, the Tendoni and the Barna. The Narmada system also extends to the north of the main Vindhyachal range and includes the narrow valleys of Barna and the Tendoni forming separate sub-water divides between separate parallel ranges of the Vindhyachal.

Climate

The main factors in the climate of Malwa region are its latitudinal location giving fairly high temperatures throughout the year. The climate in general is tropical Monsoon type, healthy. Elevated plateau is notable for its cool nights in the hot season. The two parallel ranges of the Vindhyas and Satpuras have marked effect on the climate of the region. It is characterised by a hot and dry summer except during the south-west monsoon season. The year falls into three seasons viz. the cold season (Oct-Feb), the hot weather (March-June) and the rainy season (July-Sept).

Temperature

It starts rising from February but the rise is appreciable in March (4°C-5°C) and continues till May, the hottest month throughout the region and when occasionally very high temperatures (45.6°C at Bhopal on 22.5.47) accompanied by the heat waves are also experienced. Irrespective of altitude, the cumulative increase in average monthly temperature between January and May is almost uniform (around 15°C). During May the temperature spatically varies from 29.6°C to about 35°C with the diurnal range of about 15°C. With the outburst of Monsoon in June a fall of about 8°C in average monthly temperature is noted till September. Following the withdrawal of Monsoon it again experiences slight upward trend which continues with the day temperatures of even October, though the relative nights keep the average low During the rainy season the temperature varies from 33.15°C (June) to 25.9°C (August). The temperature begins to fall again from October and continues till December which marks the coldest month on an average with average temperatures ranging between 14.7°C and 18.1°C, though occasional lowest temperature associated with cold wave are experienced in January (Bhopal 0.6°C on 18.1.38) A significant feature of the daily winter temperature is its higher range (16°C).

Rainfall

The average annual rainfall is almost 126 cm. The rainiest months are July-September, the Monsoon gives over 90% of the annual total. During post and pre-monsoon periods it varies from 3 to 7cm. Except during the Monsoon months the atmosphere is generally dry, afternoons being drier than the mornings. On the post-monsoon and winter months relative humidity ranges between 20-40% in the afternoon, while in the summer months it is still lower (10-15%).

In the summer and monsoon months winds are strong. During the monsoon they blow mainly from south-west and north-west. In the post-monsoon and winter months, morning winds are light and are mainly easterly or north-easterly. In the afternoons wind steers between south west and north west through west. Dust storms occassionally occur during the summer season. Fog occurs very rarely in the post-monsoon season.

Soil

The black soil occupies almost the whole region. It varies in depth and is usually loamy to clayey in texture. Lime concretion zone and free calcium carbonate are invariably present at different depths. Red and yellow soil is generally light and sandy though the medium and heavy varieties are also present. It is poor in phosphoric acid, humus and nitrogen.

Flora

The flora in this region is of Savana type of the plateau. Forests are of three types based on their occurance: (i) Hill forests (ii) Stream forests and (iii) Plateau forests. Hill forests are found on higher altitudes having teak associated with Saj *(Terminalia tommentosa),* Haldau, Tinsa, Salai *(Boswellia Serrata),*

Sal, dhaora, *(Anogeissus latifolia), tendu (Diospyros melanoxylon),* Bamboo *(Dendrocalamus strictus).* Stream forests occur in strips along the water courses and consist of Date palm, Babul *(Accecia arabicd), Neem, Mahua, Harra, Tamarind, Jamun, Karanj, Kusum (Schleichera Oleosa), Palas* (Butea monosperma) etc.

Plateau forests consists of mainly *Dhak* and thorny bushes are found on higher terraces.

Fauna

The forests of Raisen district are having large number of species of wild animals, birds and insects. Amongst the primates apart from Homo-sapiens, Bengal monkey *(Macacos rhern)* and the langur or *Karmuha (Semnopithecus Centullus)* are the two species that occur in large number and are always in groups. The carnivores include tigers *(Panthera tigris)* and Rendua *(Panthera Pardus).* Harbivores are Cheetal or spotted deer *(Cervus axis),* Sambhar *(Rusa unicolor),* Neel Gai (*Boselaphus traeocamelus).* Chinkara *(Gazella Bennetti), Bhekri (Tetracerous qudricornis),* Black buck (*Antilope cervicagra),* barking deer, wild boar *(Sus cristatus),* hare etc. Amongst the aves the predominant aves are house crow *(C. Splenders splenders)* sparrow, Koel *(Endynanis scolopaceus),* hawk, cuckoo *(Hierococy valius),* tailer bird *(Orthotomus sutorius),* nilkanth *(caracus bengalensis),* spotted dove *(Steptopelia Chinensis),* ring dove *(S. risori).* Apart from these there are numerous species of storks, teals, herons, cranes, ducks, eagles, kites, owls etc. The game birds *are jungli murgi (Gallus sonnerati), (Gallus ferruginous),* Pea bird or mer *(Pova cristatus),* titar *(Funacolinus pondicerannus)* bhat-titar *(Pteroles species'), baler (Conturinx commnix)* and blue rock pigeon or *kabutar (Columba linia intermedia).*

Amongst the snakes the important ones are Cobra *(Nai tripudious),* daboia *(Dobia eleyans).* Krait *(Bungarus caerulens)* common rat snake, pythons etc. In the rivers, ponds and dams plenty of fishes of Katla *(Catla catla),* rohu *(Labeo rohita),* Kalbasu *(Labeo Calbasu)* varities etc. are found.

Minerals

Amongst the minerals iron occurs in ferruginous lateritic cappings and contains high percentage of metal.

Tribes

Amongst the scheduled tribes Gonds alone constitute nearly 85% of the tribal population whereas Sahariyas 5.6%, Keer 2.8%, Korku 2.0% and Kal account for 1.3%. Gonds who were once ruling in the area have by and large preserved their pastoral and animistic culture. Their houses generally made of wattle and daub give a picture of cleanliness. They paint the walls of their houses with scenes depicting religions functions, and hunting farming activities. Some of the subjects of worship are done yearly on a particular auspicious day when rejoicing and mass feasting is also observed.

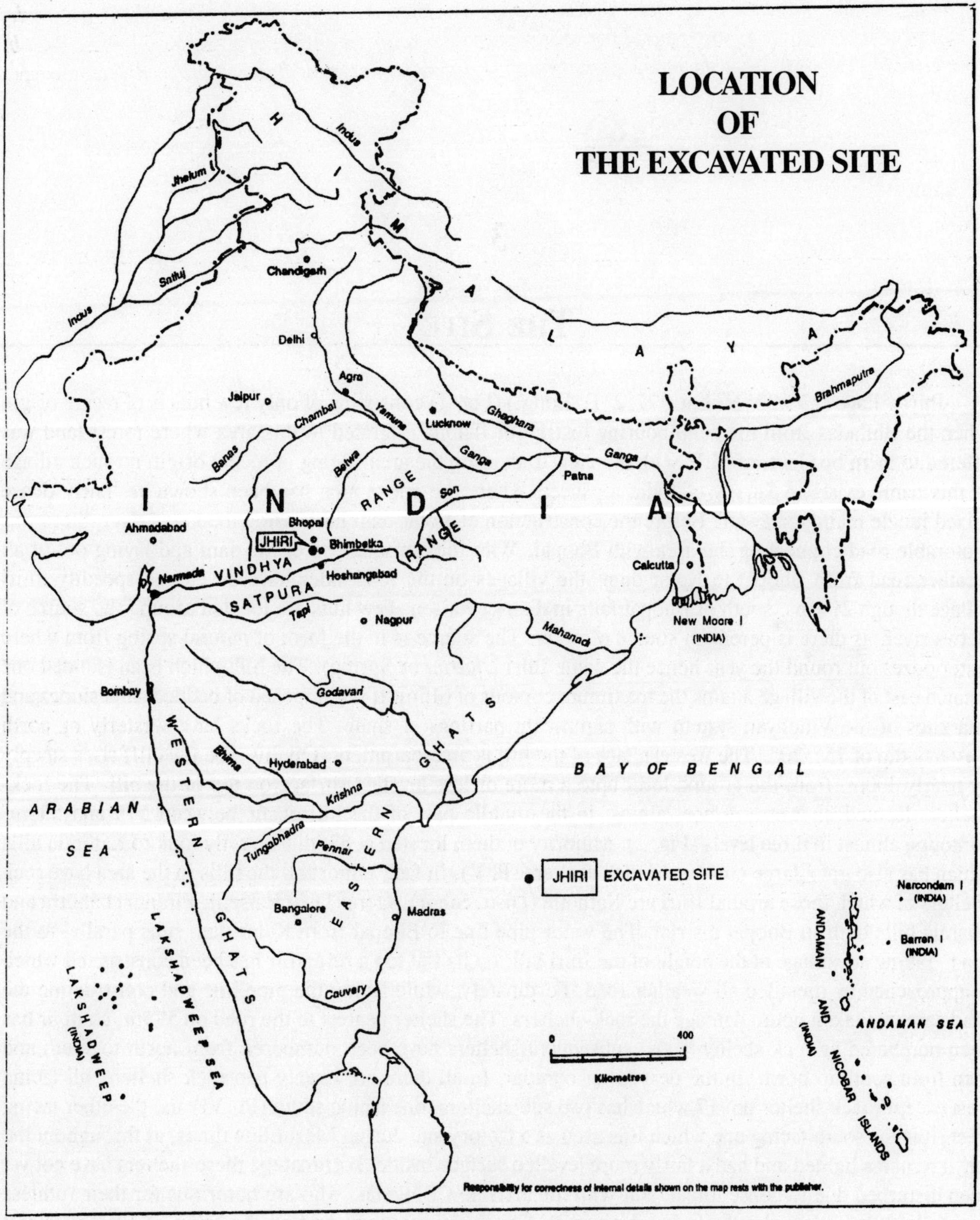

Fig. 1. Location Map

3

The Site

Jhiri village (23°.23' N. Lat., 77°2' E. Long.) (Fig. 1) consisting of only few huts is of recent origin when the Bhiladas from the neighbouring district of Jhabua migrated to this area where forest land was offered to them by Govt. of M.P. with the view to develop the area. Being of recent origin no such village of this name exists in Survey of India topsheets where the entire area has been shown as 'fairly dense mixed jungle mainly sagwan'. Before the construction of Kolar dam harnessing the kolar river, there was motorable road connecting the area with Bhopal. With the construction of the dam and laying out of all weather road from Bhopal to Kolar dam. the villages on the road sides have developed speedily. Jhiri village though 21 kms. south of Bhopal falls in district Raisen. Few huts are located around the source of Betwa river, as there is perennial source of water. The source is in the form of natural spring from where water oozes out round the year hence the name Jhiri *(Jharna* or Spring). The hill which is an isolated one located east of the village attains the maximum contour of 615m. It is composed of bedded sand stones and quarzites of the Vindhyan system with significant partings of shale. The rocks have westerly or north westerly dip of 15°-20°. The western face of the hill is an escarpment. On this side the cliff rises steeply by nearly 100m. from the ground level upto a more or less levelled surface on top of the hill. The rock-shelters located on western face, almost in the middle part of the hill occur between 575 and 535m. contours, almost in three levels (Fig. 2). Majority of them located at 575m., directly look to Kathotia hills which has also got a large number of such shelters (Pl V). In fact, almost all the hills in the area have rock shelters of which those around Jhiri are Kathotia (Distt. Sihor), Jaora (Distt Raisen), Firangi chabutra and Shamla hills both in Bhopal district. The water pipe line to Bhopal from Kolar dam runs parallel to the road. Taking advantage of the height of the Jhiri hill, on its flat top a reservoir has been constructed which is approached by metalled all weather road. Fortunately, while laying the pipe line and constructing the road care was taken not to damage the rock-shelters. The shelter nearest to the road on 575m. contour has been numbered as rock shelter 1 and subsequent shelters have been numbered from north to south and then from south to north, in the next lower contour. In all there are twenty two rock shelters, all facing west except roack shelter no. 17 which has two sub-shelters, one facing south (Pl. VI) and the other facing west. It is the south facing one which was used as a factory site during Mesolithic times, as throughout the day it remains lighted and had a fairly more levelled surface inside. Fortunately, these shelters have not yet been disturbed due to dense forest. But with the arrival of Bhiladas, who are notorious for their ruthless tree felling activities, the thick forest cover is fast thinning down, and as the town of Bhopal is fast

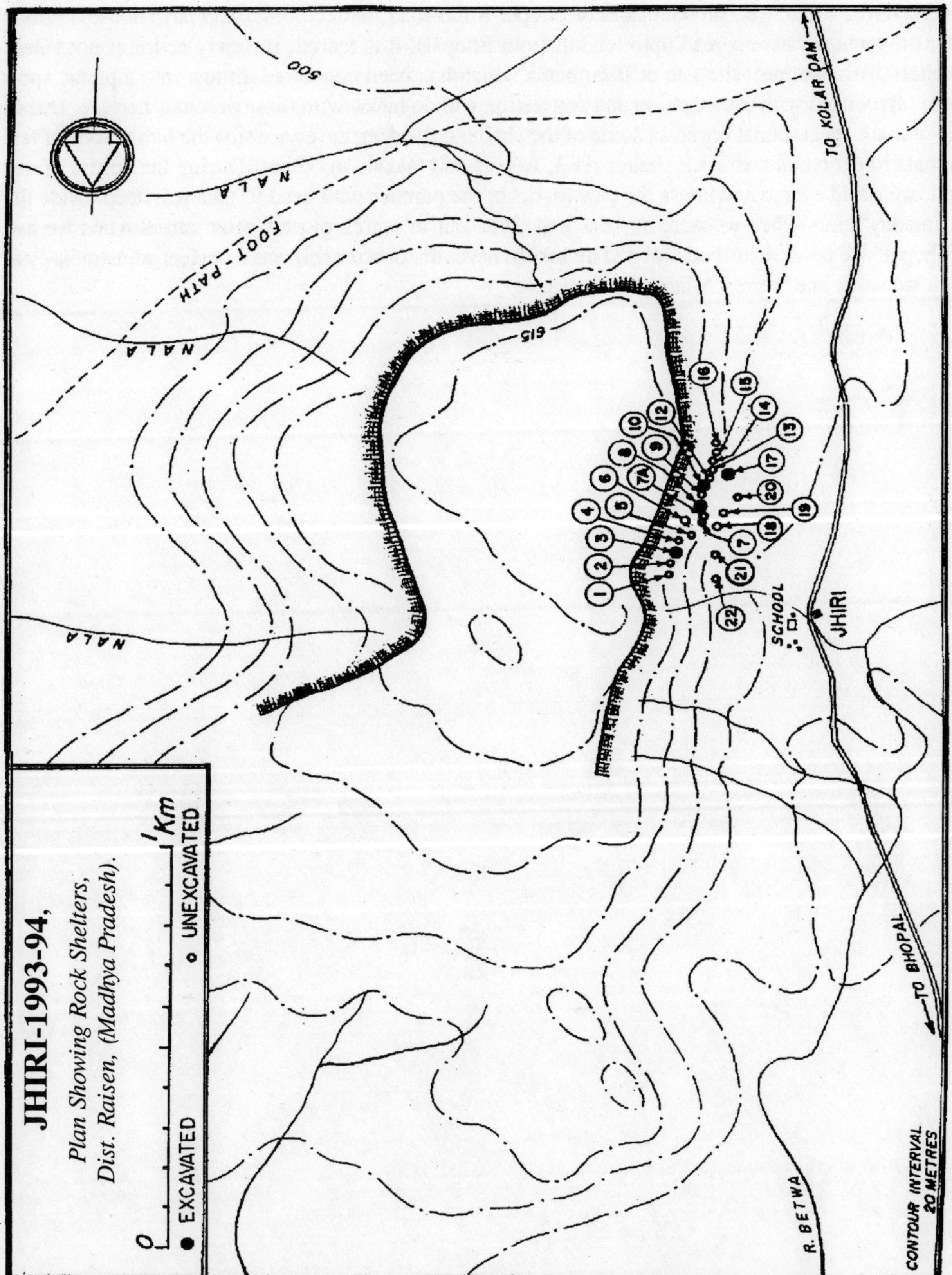

Fig. 2. Plan showing rock-shelters at Jhiri

expanding towards south, i.e., on both sides of Bhopal-Kolar road, with colonies and farm houses coming up (so far the tentacles have spread upto ten km from Bhopal), it is feared, if timely action is not taken, these shelters will also meet the fate of Bhimbetka which has been converted almost into a picnic spot. Vandalism, associated with urbanization and congestion will do havoc with these precious hertage. Due to presence of thick vegetational cover, in some of the shelters, the deep caves are still the habitations of few wild animals like a panther in rock shelter no 3, wolves and jackals in others. During the course of our operation, we could everyday witness the paw marks of the panther who used to take rest deep inside the cave during day hours when we were at work and come out in search of prey after sunset when we had left for Bhopal. We never disturbed him and he in turn never disturbed us. It was a perfect adjustment- you rest when we work and we rest when you work.

4

THE ROCK SHELTERS

In order to understand in correct perspective, the formation of rock shelters, it is more beneficial to adopt the evolutionary approach method for morphological mapping of the area under study. For this purpose conventional topo-sheets to satellite imageries have to be used supplemented by spot study of the area in question and individual rock shelters. The multi-spectral analysis using the computers alongwith other conventional methods, of the area between Bhopal and right bank of Narmada have established that the densely forested area of the Vindhyas is composed of tuff quartzite labelled as Vindhyan quartzite. These are pinkish looking rocks lying in horizontal formations. At many places these rocks show dipslopes on one side of the hills and escarpments on the opposite side. At many places this quartzitic bed is capped by highly weathered quartzitic shale. In this area quartzite also shows spheriodal weathering like basalt and granite. The rocks exposed along the scarp show differential weathering and the sand stones and shales have been most effected. In the weathering process apart from heating and cooling effect, chemical weathering has also been found to play a role. Rather the later process is more pronounced due to highly siltic nature of the shale. The process gets more momentum during rainy season when heavy monsoon showers lash these rock formations. It may be remembered that in this area erosional effect of wind has almost negligible role to play. The weathering agents mentioned above, slowly, in millions of years, eat away the more fragile areas. The quarzites, however, have resisted erosion and these beds are often left as projections when the underlying weaker sandstone and shale bed have been denuded. Once small cavities and concave patches are formed, these spots act as storage pockets for water and the process of chemical weathering is quickened resulting in formation of deeper cavities. In course of time huge chunks of quartzite and shale fall down, not able to stick to mother rock due to a thin band of patinated portion running throughout. This process results in formation of rock shelters. This process of weathering has been hastened in recent years due to removal of (a) vegetational cover which has resulted in removal of top soil thus exposing the rock surface directly to the weathering agencies, (b) unscrupulous mining activities for stone and (c) at some places by disturbing the normal equilibrium of the formations by heavy dynamiting for the purpose of dam construction, pipe line laying etc. This could be witnessed around Jhiri, few kms. from where Kolar dam has been raised and from where pipe line of huge diameter runs to Bhopal carrying drinking water for this new capital of M.P.

Central India's bio-diversity is undergoing rapid decimation. Illegal cuttings of vegetational coverings are recklessly stripping away the surviving natural richness in a region which is one of India's prestine cornucopious of timber and medicinal plants.

5

THE EXCAVATIONS

I. STRATIGRAPHY

In general the thickness of habitational deposits in the rock shelters at Jhiri varies from 1.25m to 0.75m depending on the levelled surface available inside the shelters. Some of the shelters are totally devoid of any habitational deposit. From the evidences available it appears that in such shelters the deposits got washed away by the seepage of rain water, after the cracks and fissures developed on the walls and roofs of these shelters partly due to erosional and weathering activities. The deposits go 4 to 5 layers deep. The lowest layer is composed of redish calcareous lateritic soil mixed with quatzite and sand stone nodules and chunks and chips of weathered shale lying in inclined position. Ashy patches are also noticeable. The layer above the lowest one is composed of redish latertic soil mixed with shale chips and patches of ash. The next layer is loose brownish silt and clay with tiny pieces of shale, fragments of charcoal and patches of ash. The top most layer comprises of loose greyish soil mixed with pieces of sand stones. It shows yearly deposition of fine silt and sand in the form of laminations. Due to decomposition of vegetation the top soil has acquired dark brownish colour. The thickness of these depositions vary from rock-shelter to rock-shelter. One interesting point to note is that only those portions of wall surfaces and in some cases roofs have been painted which lie directly in front of and over the habitational area (Pl. VII & VIII). In almost all cases neither the entire floor area of the shelters have deposits nor all the available wall and roof surfaces have been painted. While selecting surfaces for execution of paintings painters were careful to select only those depressions or flat and smooth surfaces where there was no percolation of water and where patination had not set in (Pl. IX). This tendency indicates that they were concious about the durability of their artistic creations.

II. THE TRENCHES

A. Rock Shelter No. 3 (Pls, X to XV, Figs. 3 to 6)

This rock shelter located at the height of 575m. from sea level is spacious enough with its eastern wall and a part of roof richly painted (Pl. VIII). Atleast five layers of paintings in different colours, superimposed one over the other, could be noticed. This shelter was nick named by us as the 'Panther Cave' as a gentleman 'panther' was still residing in the deep cave on the southern corner of the shelter (Pl. XI).

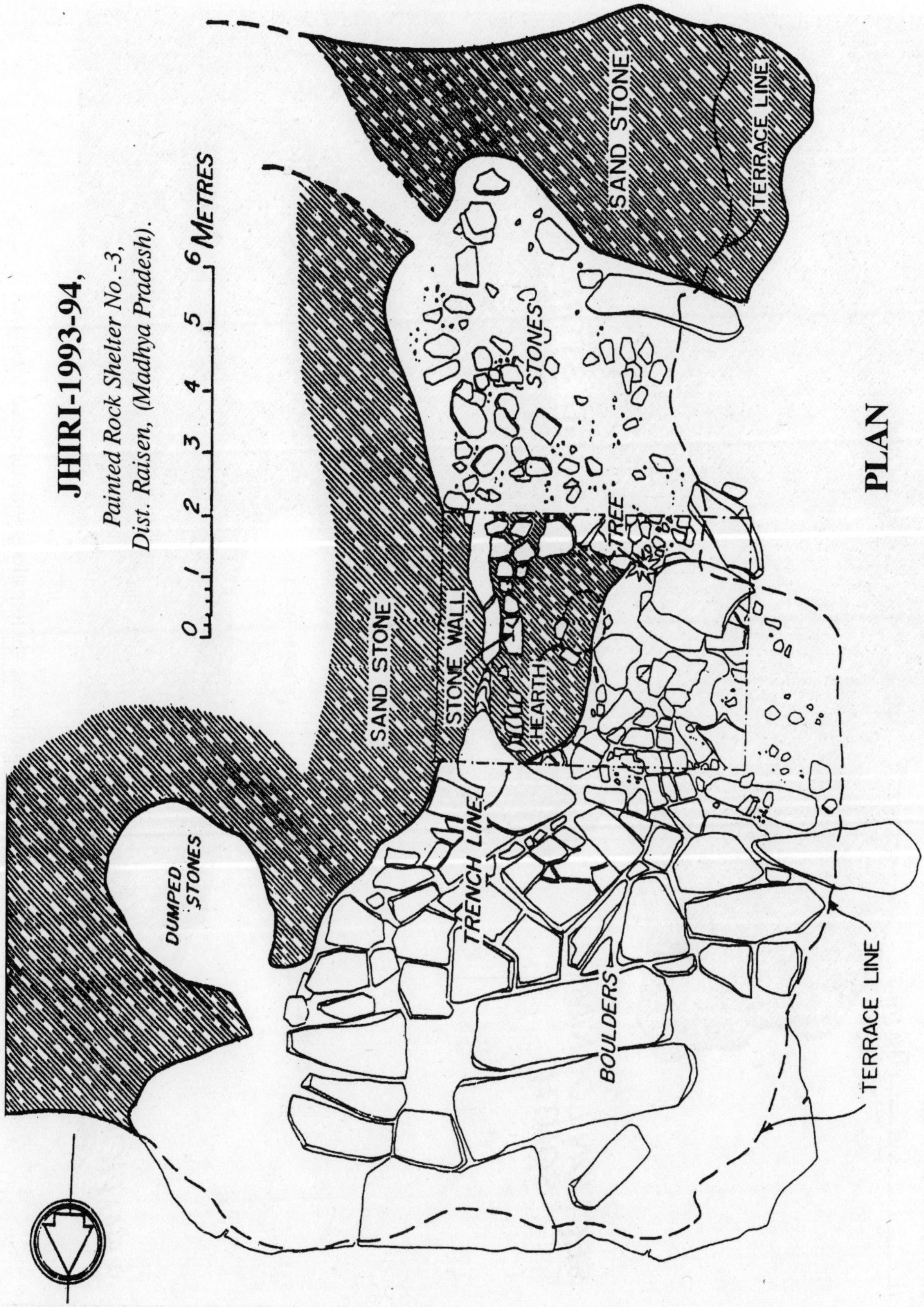

Fig. 3. R.S.No. 3-Plan

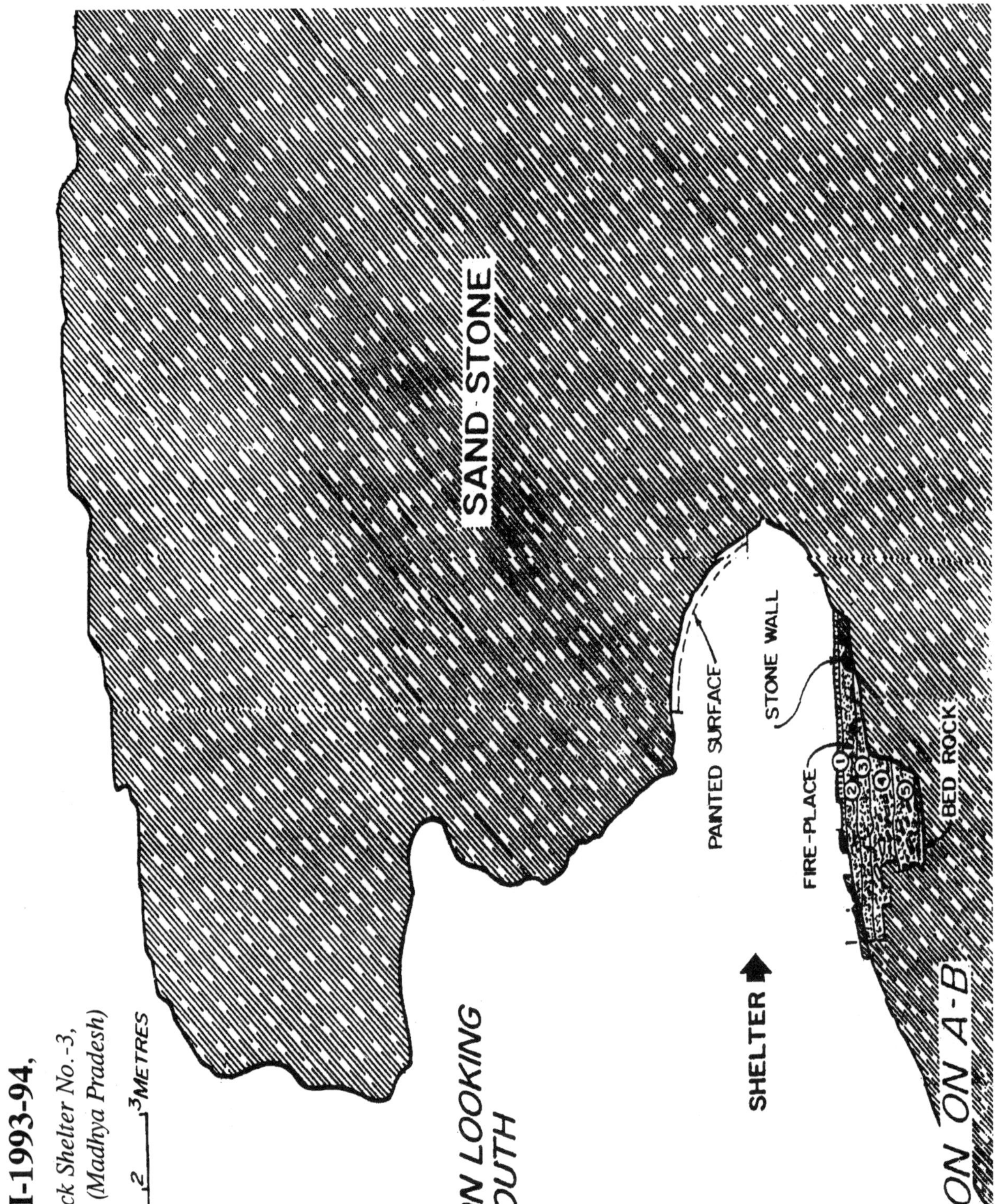

Fig. 4. R.S.No. 3- Section of the shelter alongwith the excavated area

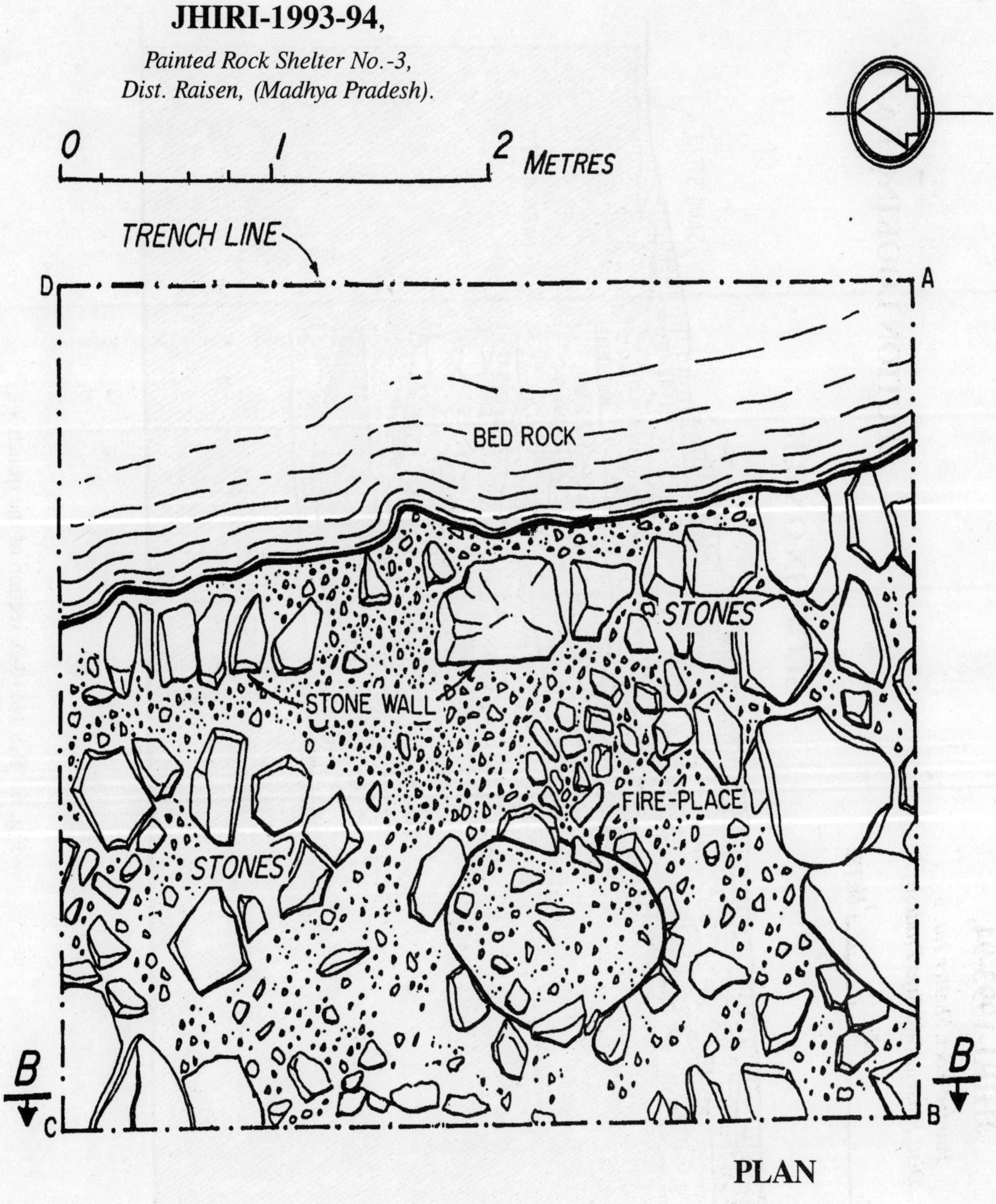

Fig. 5. R.S.No. 3-A plan of the trench

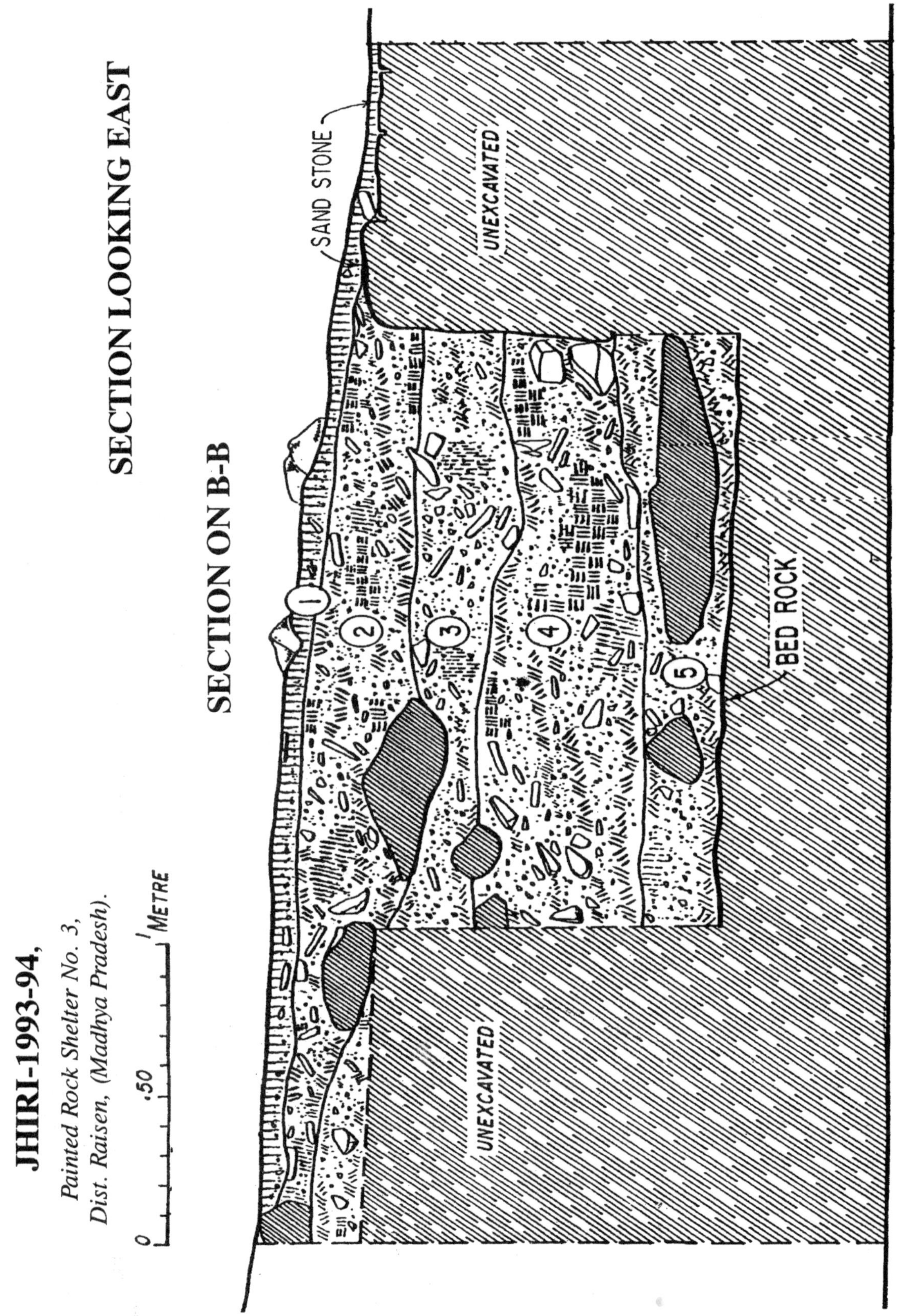

Fig. 6. R.S.No. 3-A section of the trench

A 4x3m trench oriented north-south (N-S=4xE-W=3m) was taken almost in the centre of the floor of the shelter though the maximum deposit is on the southern side (Pl. XII) This area was avoided as it lay directly in front of the opening of the 'panther cave'. The shelter opens directly into the west. The roof including the semi circular eastern wall is adored with paintings. The exposed surface of the bed rock which is fine grained quartzite in the bottom followed by sand stone is very smooth and at the ground level it has acquired polished look, obviously due to constant use by the habitants of this rock shelter.

0.11m thick layer one is composed of loose brownish soil mixed with sandy clay and pieces of stones. The layer yielded cores of quartz, fragments of animal bones, few pieces of earthern red ware, an isolated microlith and a piece of white pigment at the depth of 0.03m (B2.65 ×c 1.50 + 0.03m). Layer two which is 0.20 to 0.50m thick revealed a rectangular structure of flat stones and bolders, having northsouth length of 3.47m (eastern wall) and 3.35m (western wall) (PI. XII). Its width varied from 1.80m on the southern side to 1.08m on the northern side. Almost in the centre of the structure lengthwise and more towards the western side widthwise an oval fire pit having diamensions of 0.97m long north-south, 0.60m wide east-west and 0.30m deep, was encountered (PI. XIII, Figs, 3 & 5). This pit cut in layer 2 is sealed by layer 1 and its bottom touches the bed-rock. On the eatern side this pit is walled by the bed rock whereas on the western side a flat stone slab is kept on the edges to line the pit. The pit yielded ash, charcoal, fragments of animal bones, a stone hop-scotch and large number of microliths (Pls. XVI, XVII A) such as lunates, triangles, trapeze, long serrated blades alongwith waste flakes and cores. A piece of red pigment was also recovered from layer 2.

Layer 3 which is composed of light brown, loose, clayey silt with chips of weathered shales is 0.21 to 0.30m thick. The layer yielded microliths alongwith cores and waste flakes.

Layer 4 composed of loose brown clay mixed with pieces of stone is 0.24 m thick. Microliths along with the cores were obtained from this layer. Just below layer 4 layer 5 composed of yellow compact clay with pieces of stone was encountered. This sterile layer is 0.12m thick. It did not yield any antiquity.

The 4x3 trench was extended towards west by 2m widthwise (Pl. XV, Fig. 3). Layer 1 yielded two uninscribed cast copper coins datable to 3rd-4th century B.C. (PI. XVII B) alongwith fragments of potsherds (Fig. 14). Both the coins were recovered from the depth of 0.03m. lying just over the bed rock. Subsequent layers yielded microliths and few fragments of sherds were recovered only from layer 2. Maximum number of microliths were recovered from layer 3 and 4 from 0.72m to 1.20m depth from the space between the bed rocks. Wood charcoal was collected from the pit for C-14 dating.

B. Rock Shelter No. 8 (PI. XVIII to XXII, Figs. 7-10)

In this shelter also, more towards the northern side a 4 (north-south) ×3m. (east-west) trench was laid in such a manner that it passed touching the eastern wall which is painted. The floor of the shelter slopes from south to north. In the southern half bed-rock is exposed in a sloping fashion in such a way that only the northern half of the rock shelter is having flat surface suitable for occupation. Just above this surface the wall and the roof of the shelter contain three panels of paintings in concave depressions. In the rest of the area of the shelter which was not fit for occupation, the walls and roofs also do not contain any paintings.

Layers 1 is composed of loose greyish soil mixed with stone chips and is having laminations showing seasonal depositions. It is 0.18m thick. From this layer pieces of red pigment (C-3.51 × B 2.40-0.05m) and white pigment (C-2.88x2.63-0.05m), tiny fragments of animal bones and nodules of chertic material were recovered. At the depth of 0.19m layer 2 was reached. It is composed of loose brownish silt and clay mixed with small chunks of weathered shale. The layer yielded microliths, quartz nodules, flakes, bone fragments and pieces of sand stone. This layer'is 0.21m in thickness. Soil samples for pollen analysis were collected from this layer. At the depth of 0.39m layer 3 which is composed of loose redish lateritic clay mixed with pieces of weathered shale was encountered. This layer yielded a number of microliths alongwith flakes of quartz nodules. The microliths included burins, fluted cores, blades etc. The layer is nearly 0.54m thick. A fire pit was encountered in this year (Pl. XX, Fig. 9). It is cut in layer 3 and is sealed by layer 2. At the mouth it is 0.24m wide and goes upto the depth of 0.80m. The fire pit is almost in the centre of the rock shelter. The deposit in it consists of ash, charcoal bits and charred fragments of animal bones. Atleast five flat stones were arranged around the pit to be used as sit stones (PI. XX Fig. 9). Outer diameter of stone circle is E-W-2.75m, N-S-3.50m, inner diameter is N-S-2.10m, E-W-1.80m. Diameter of fire pit is 1.10m. The pit also contained a number of stone pieces. It is likely that the sit stones were arranged to be used for sitting around the fire when the kill and catch of the day was being roasted. Wood charcoal was collected for C-14 dating. From layer 3 downwards a large number of boulders appeared in the trench (Pl. XXI). From the space between the boulders quartz nodules, flakes and microliths were recovered. On further digging at few places bed rock started occurring at the depth of 0.95m and it spread in sloping fashion towards west. Just over the bed rock lies layer 4 which is 0.20m thick and which is composed of red sticky clay mixed with minute chips of shale and few boulders. Good number of microliths were recovered from this layer also. Samples of red ochre pigments were collected from the depth pf 1.11m, where they were found in concentration at a particular spot.

C. Rock Shelter No. 10 (Pls. XXIII to XXVI, Fig. 11)

This is the biggest rock shelter at Jhiri both heightwise and floor area wise. Almost the entire wall surface is profusely painted. The paintings are atleast in five layers depicting episodes right from the Mesolithic period to historical period and even later. Entire floor of the shelter is covered with boulders which appear to have been dumped recently to make the surface even (Pl. XXVI). As it is quite spacious with high roof and faces west, the entire shelter remains well lighted throughout the day.

A 5x5m. trench was taken on the floor of the shelter (PI. XXV). The entire deposit was composed of only boulders and no soil. On the western and southern side of the shelter, on the surface stone alignments of dressed stones could be noticed. These appear to be of recent origin. On the roof of the shelter nearly 0.05m to 0.10m wide grooves had been cut probably to divert rain water from reaching the covered area of the shelter (Pl. XXIII). While removing the boulders few microliths, alongwith quartz nodules and flakes were recovered. The bed rock was encountered at the depth of 0.80m. The surface of bed rock is smooth and it has developed a wide crack just at the junction of the eastern wall and the floor (Pl. XXV). On the western edge of the shelter where the bed rock ends a big quartzitic bolder was found. This was used as a grinding stone as an oval shaped cavity has formed, due of constant use, in the centre of the bolder. The cavity is oriented north-south, lengthwise with its broader side towards north (Pl. XXVI). The grooved depression had two edges. Maximum length of outer edge is 0.24m, whereas maximum length of inner edge is 0.18. Maximum width of outer lines in the centre is 0.13m whereas those of inner lines is 0.090m. Maximum depth of the groove at the center is 0.12m.

The smooth surface of the groove as well as the rough surface of the adjoining areas have acquired

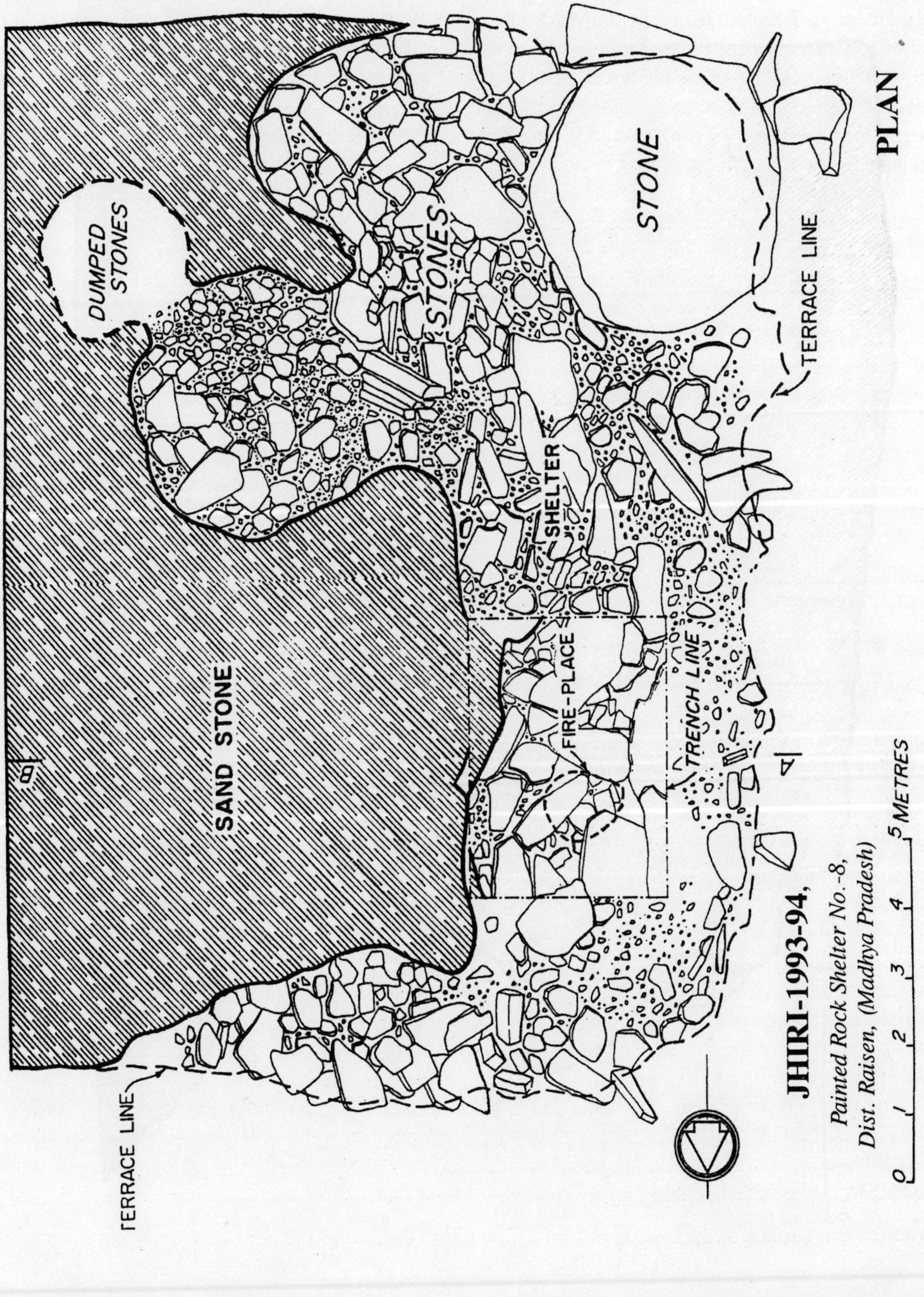

Fig. 7. R.S.No. 8-Plan

SECTION LOOKING SOUTH

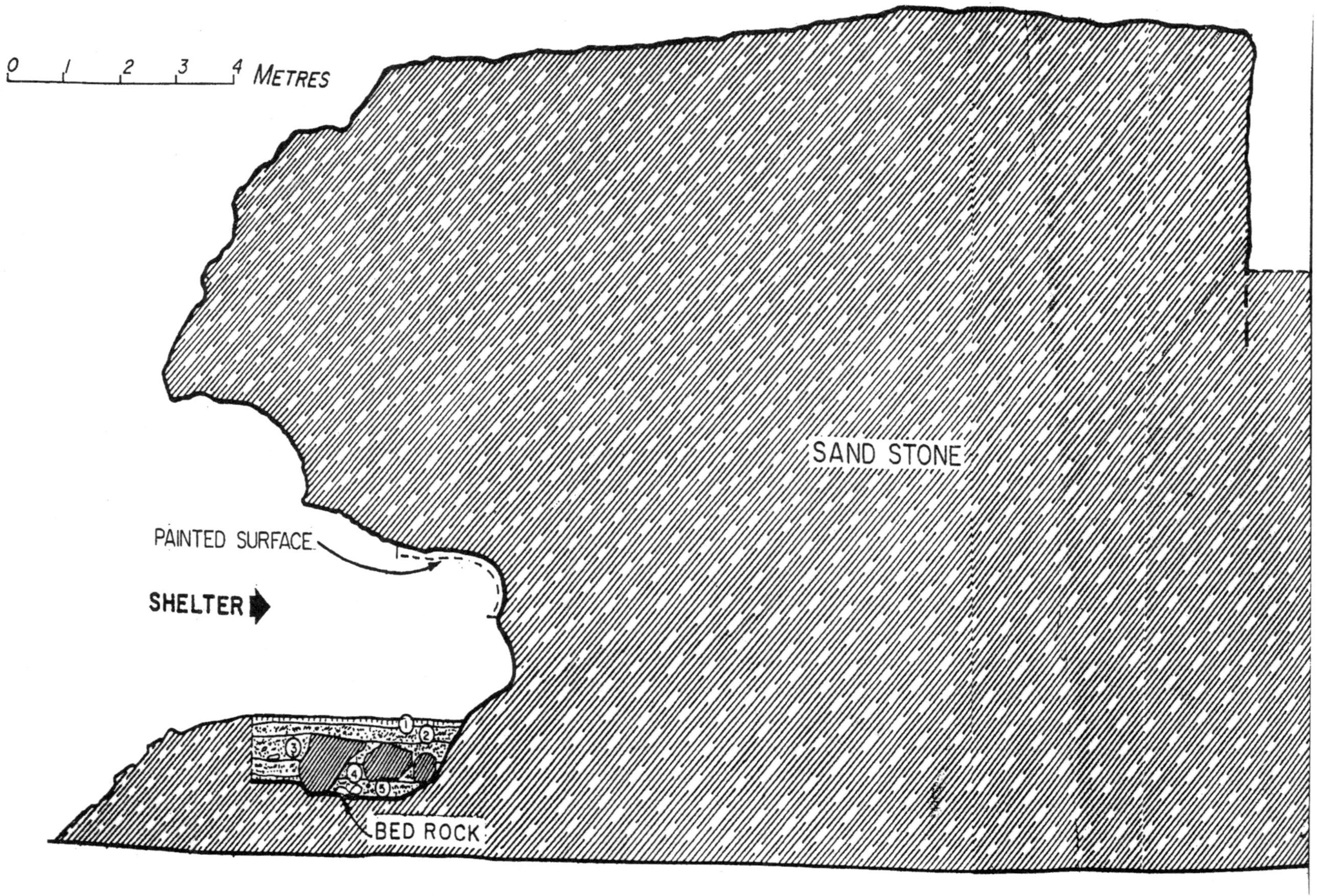

Fig. 8. R.S.No.8-Sectional elevation alongwith the excavated trench

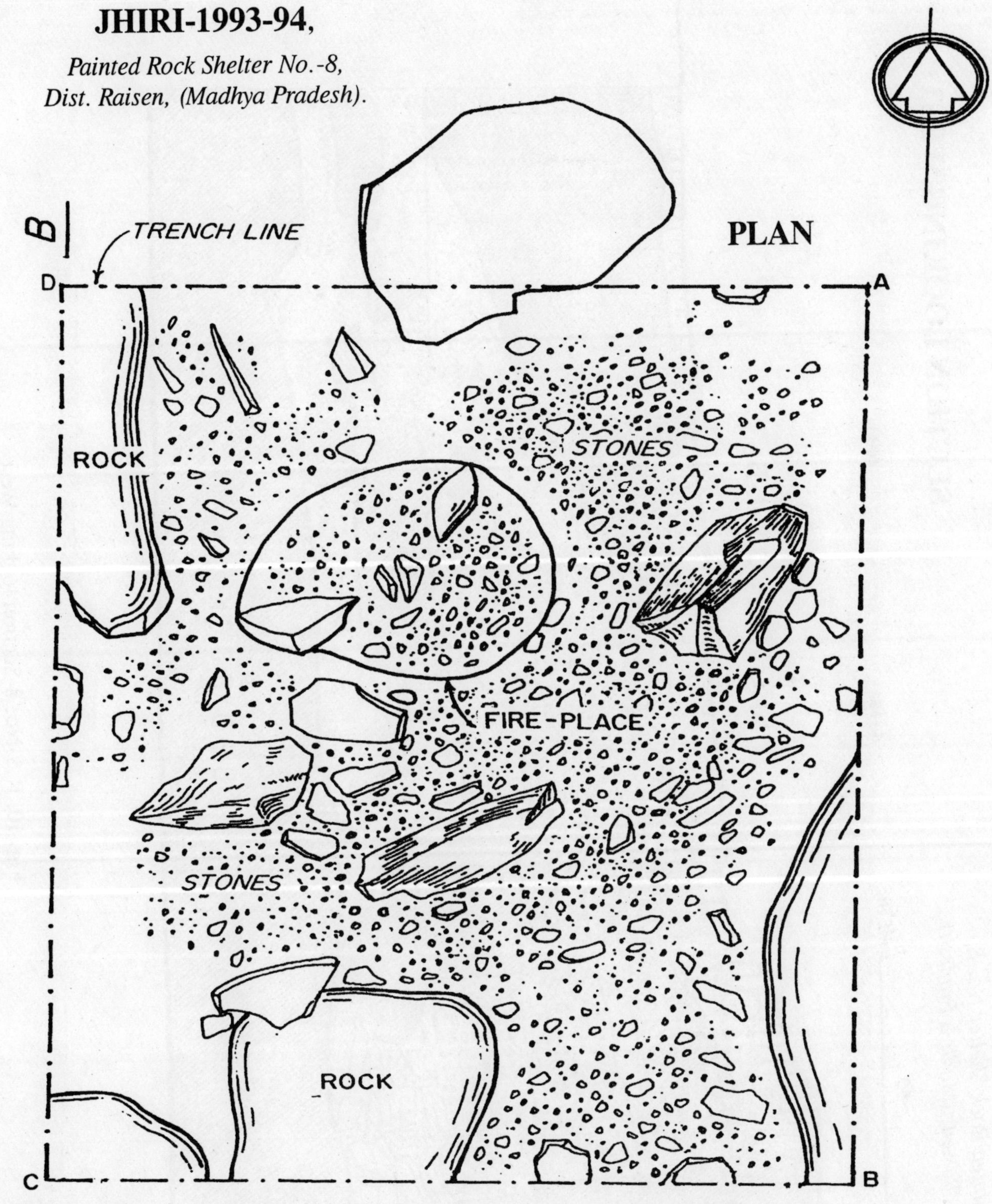

Fig. 9. R.S.No.8- Plan of the trench

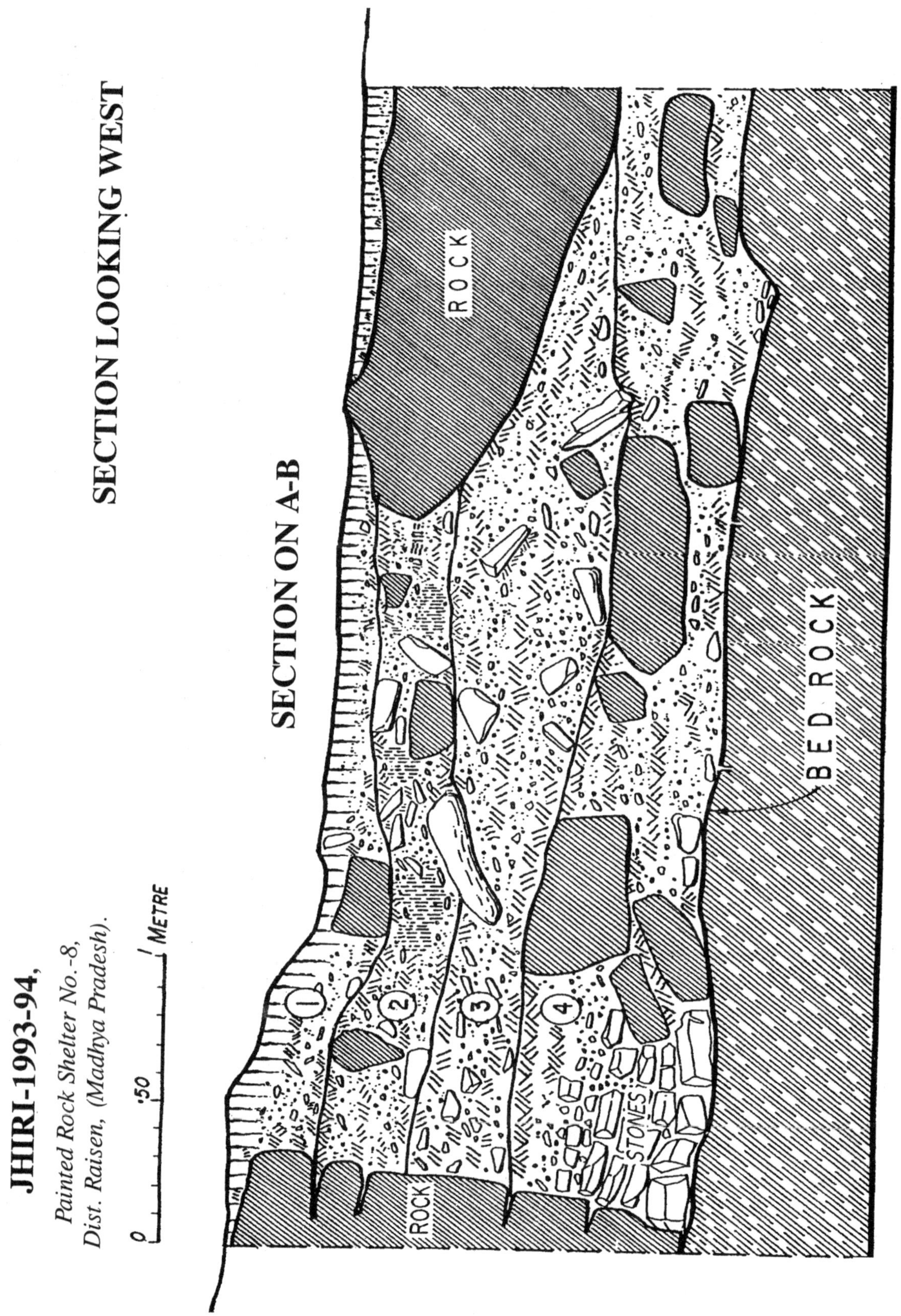

Fig. 10. R.S.No. 8-Section looking West

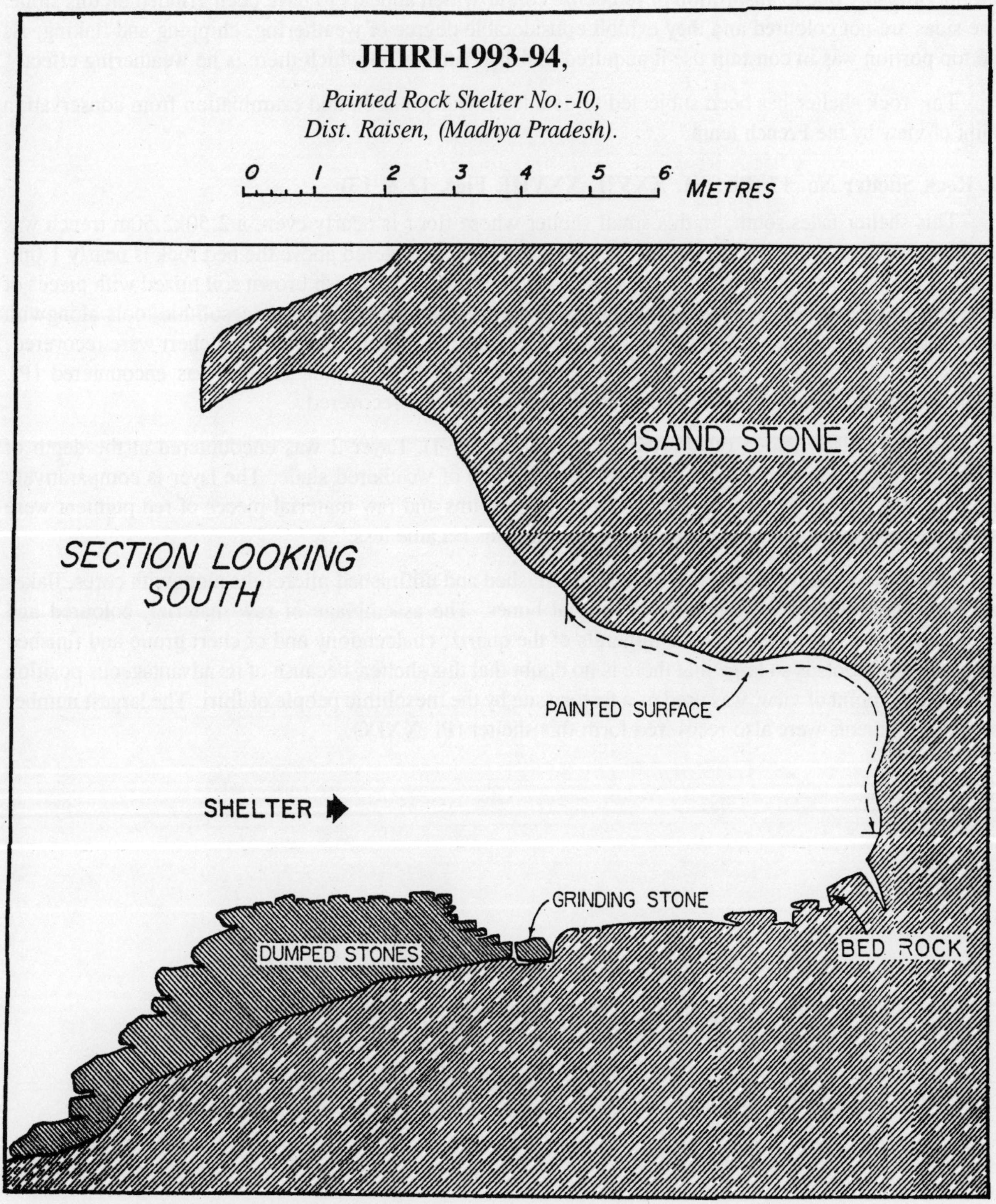

Fig. 11. R.S.No. 10-Sectional elevation

red tint probably due to absorption of red ochre colour which appears to have been grinded on this stone. The sides are not coloured and they exhibit considerable degree of weathering, chipping and flaking. As the top portion was in constant use it acquired polished surface on which there is no weathering effect.

This rock shelter has been subjected to detailed documentation and examination from conservation point of view by the French team.

D. Rock Shelter No. 17 (Pls. VI, XXVII, XXVIII, Figs. 12 & 13)

This shelter faces south. In this small shelter whose floor is nearly even, a 2.50x2.50m trench was taken on the western half of the shelter. The total deposit encountered above the bed rock is nearly 1.0m. The deposit here consists of only two layers. Layer one which is blackish brown soil mixed with pieces of sand stone is 0.28m thick. Right from the surface large number of finished mesolithic tools alongwith waste flakes and nodules of fine grained crystalline quartz in different colours and chert were recovered. On the north-west corner of the trench a pit going upto the depth of 0.29m. was encountered (Pl. XXVIII). From layer one, pieces of colour pigments were also recovered.

The layer also yielded two vertebrae of fish (Pl. XVI). Layer 2 was encountered at the depth of 0.28m. It is composed of reddish soil mixed with chips of weathered shale. The layer is comparatively compact than layer 1. From this layer alongwith microliths and raw material pieces of red pigment were also recovered. After 0.83m the frequency of microliths became less.

The entire trench yielded large number of finished and unfinished microliths alongwith cores, flakes and waste falkes and few fragments of animal bones. The assemblage of raw material, coloured and colourless crptocrystalline siliceous minerals of the quartz, chalcendony and of chert group and finished and unfinished tools is so large that there is no doubt that this shelter, because of its advantageous position from lighting point of view, was used as a factory site by the mesolithic people of Jhiri. The largest number of colour pigments were also recovered form this shelter (Pl. XXIX).

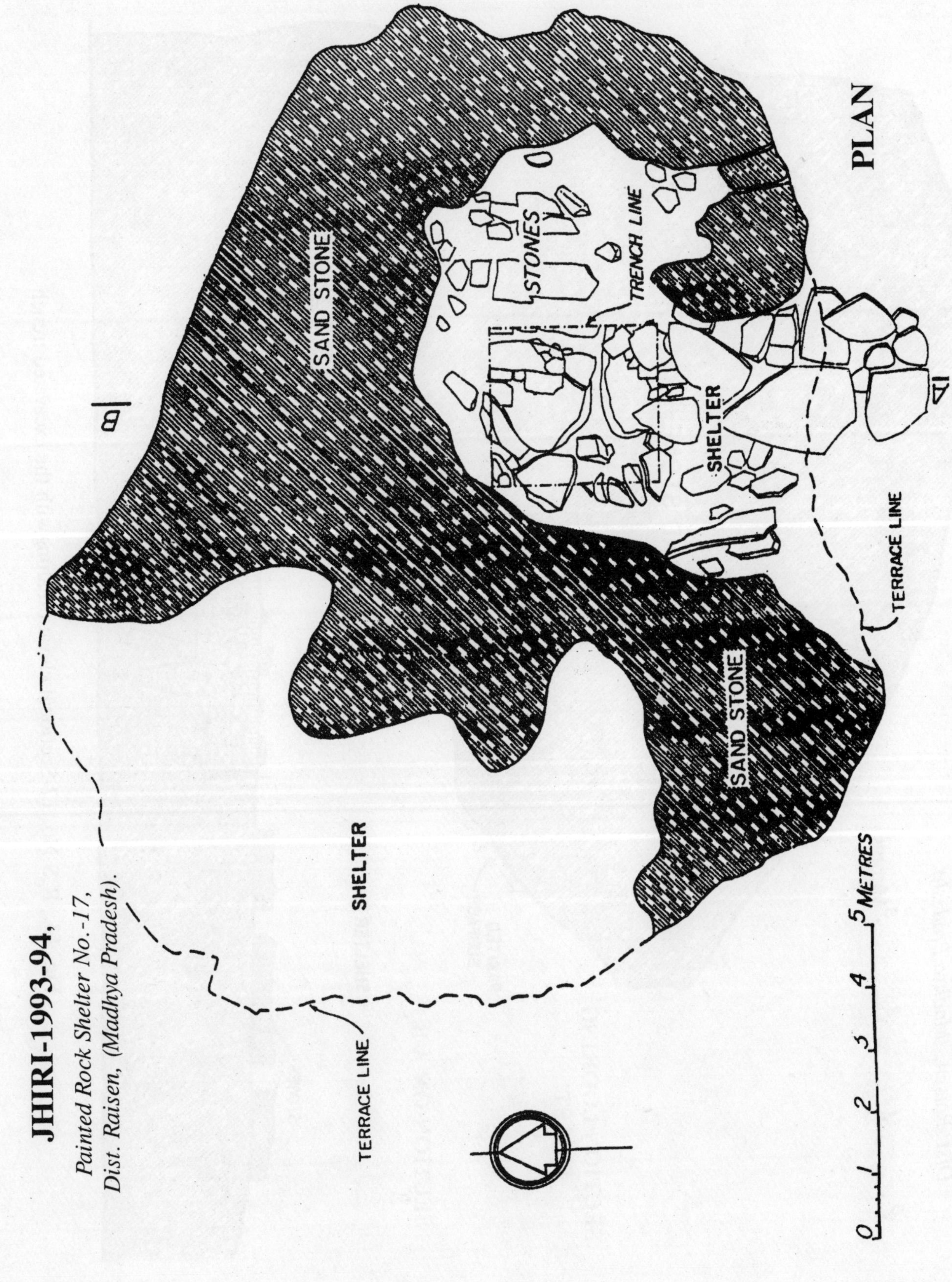

Fig. 12. R.S. No. 17-Plan

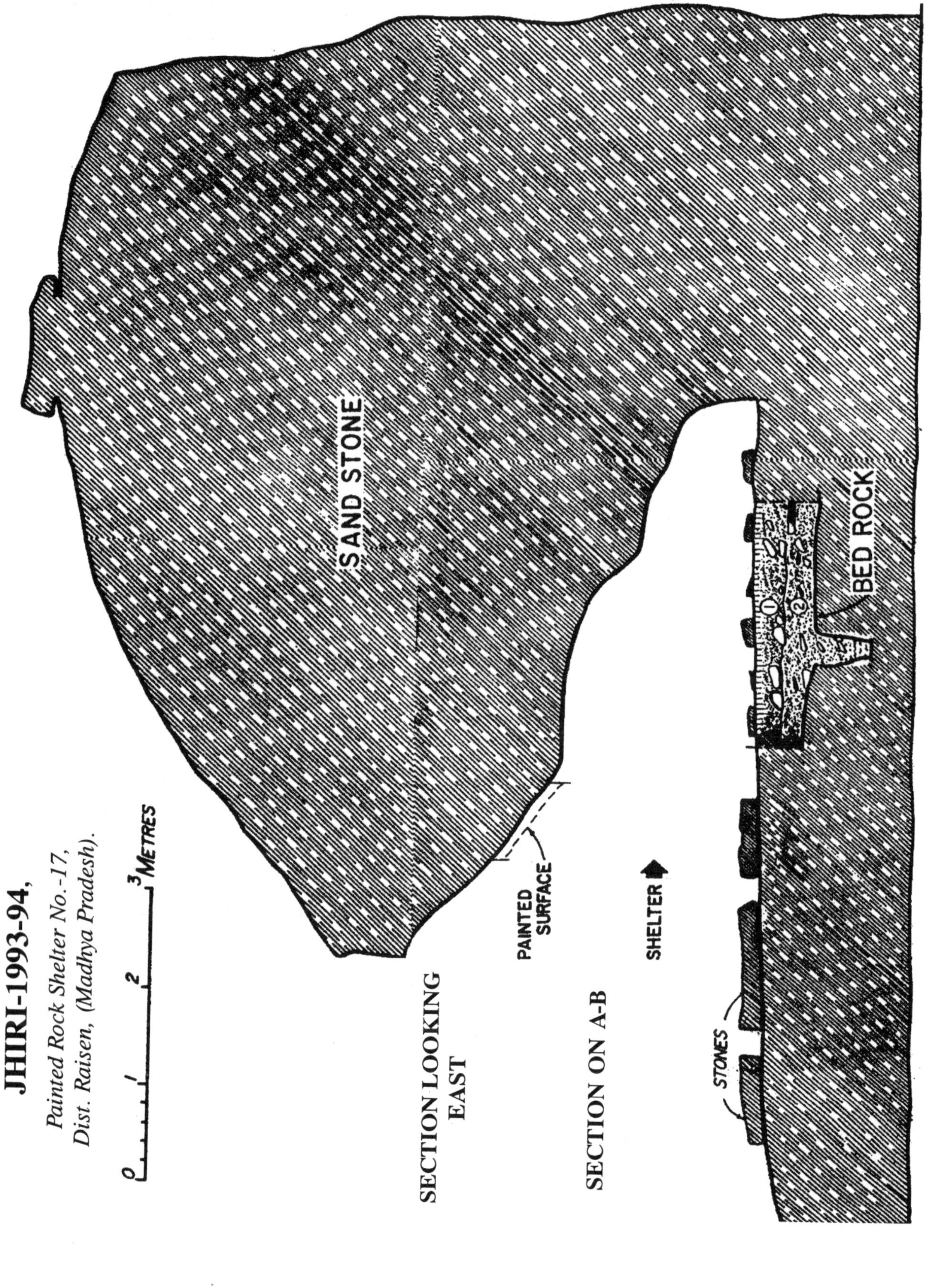

Fig. 13. R.S.No. 17-Sectional elevation alongwith the excavated trench

6

Finds

LATE STONE AGE (MESOLITHIC) TOOLS

(i) Raw Material

The microliths are made on a variety of coloured and colourless cryp-to-crystalling siliceous minerals of the quartz, chalcedony and chert groups. The minerals are mostly derived from the outcerops of Vindhyan rocks. These materials occur in Jhiri area in the form of nodules, littered in the slopes of the hill. Crystalline quartz and milky quartz have been predominantly used for manufacture of tools.

(ii) The Microlithic Industry

As from the excavated trenches a large number of microliths and nodules have been recovered they are being dealt here on the basis of typology. The points and blades, together form the bulk of the microlithic implements. The primary distinction in the case of points is whether the tool is made on a nodule, a flake or a blade. Almost all the points are worked unifacially. Secondary trimming of points on flakes and blades is generally carried out in one direction. A few of the crescents and crescentric points have been backed by bifacial trimming on the same edge producing a mild ridge due to the intersection of the scars.

In the case of blades the basic types are simple blades and retouched blades.

(iii) Typology and Description of Illustrated Specimens

A. POINTS

R.S. NO. 3

1. Quartz — Blade flake is retouched on one edge. Layer 2, 2.3×0.9×0.3 cm.. 15-25 cm. (Pl. XXX-1)

2. Milky quartz — Point on blade backed on the curved side and having short drawn out end suitable as a tang. Layer 2, 30-35 cm., 1.7×0.6×0.2 cm. (Pl. XXX-2).

3. Agate — Made on long narrow blade and sharp projecting point, steeply trimmed on both margins. Cross section triangular. Layer 2,2.4x 0.6×0.2 cm., 35cm. (Pl. XXX-11)

4. Agate	Obliquely blunted pen-knife point. Steeply retouched in two directions. Layer 2, 1.3× 0.4× 0.2 cm., 40.45 cm. (Pl. XXX-18)
5. Quartz	A blade of very symmetrical form, steeply trimmed on one edge and fine nibbling on the other half. Layer 2, 1.4× 0.6× 0.2 cm., 35.40 cm. (Pl. XXX-19)
6. Milky quartz	Point on irregular flake blade with a notch on the right, slightly patinated. Layer 2, 1.8×0.7×0.4 cm., 45 cm. (Pl. XXXI-3)
7. Quartz	Simple blade point with no retouch and having a pointed curved tip. Layer 2, 1.5× 0.6×0.2 cm., 45 cm. (Pl. XXXI-8)
8. Milky quartz	Point fully retouched on the left side and partially on the right side. Layer 2, 1.4× 0.5×0.2 cm., 35 cm. (Pl. XXXI-9)
9. Quartz	Point on irregular flake-blade. Thick, partially retouched on the right side. Layer 2, 1.7×0.6×0.4 cm., 40-45 cm. (Pl. XXXI-12)
10. Agate	Point on irregular flake-blade. Short sub-triangular without retouch. Layer 2, 1.8× 0.7×0.2 cm., 35-40 cm. (Pl. XXXI- 13)
11. Quartz	Point on blade, retouched on one side. Layer 2, 1.9×0.6×0.2 cm., 35-40 cm. (Pl. XXXI- 15)
12. Milky quartz	Point on a long narrow blade. Retouched fully on both margins. Sharp, projecting steeply trimmed point. Layer 2, 1.9×0.4×0.2 cm., 30-35 cm. (Pl. XXXI-16)
13. Quartz	Obliquely blunted pen-knife point, made on a triangular flake, retouched on the left side. Layer 2, 1.6×0.7×0.3 cm., 30-35 cm. (Pl. XXXI-17)
14. Agate	Point on irregular, thin, flake-blade, retouched on the right side and partly on the left side. Layer 2, 1.8×0.7×0.2 cm., 30-35 cm. (Pl. XXXI-18)
15. Agate	Point on thin irregular flake blade. Partly retouched on the left side. Layer 2, 1.8× 0.9×0.2 cm., 30-35 cm. (Pl. XXXI-20)
16. Quartz	Point on thick blade, retouched on the right side, tip broken. Layer 2, 2.1×0.8×0.3 cm., 35-40 cm. (Pl. XXXI-21)
17. Quartz	Slightly patinated, sub-triangular, flake unifacially worked. The sides indented due to deep scars. Faint medial ridge and borer like point. Layer 2, 1.8x1.0x0.3 cm., 40-45 cm. (Pl. XXXI-23)
18. Banded agate	Slightly patinated. Point on a long blade, retouched on both the edges. Layer 2, 2.4×0.6×0.2 cm., 35-40 cm. (Pl. XXXI-25)
19. Agate	Similar to No. 18. Point on a long blade, retouched on both the margins. Layer 2, 2.1×0.5×0.2, 35-40 cm. (Pl. XXXI-26)
20. Milky quartz	Asymmetrical point on flake-blade having cortex on the dorsal side. Layer 2, 2.8× 1.0×0.4 cm., 30-35 cm. (Pl. XXXI-33)

21. Quartz — Point on a medium sized blade, retouched on both the edges except towards base, Layer 3, 1.8×0.5×0.2 cm., 55 cm. (Pl. XXXII-11)

22. Quartz — Point on a long blade, retouched fully on one edge and partially on the other. Layer 3, 1.6×0.4×0.8 cm., 62 cm. (Pl. XXXII-12)

23. Milky quartz — Point on crescentric blade having sharp point had use marks on the sharpened unretouched edge. Layer 3, 2.4×0.7×0.4 cm., 72 cm. (Pl. XXXII-13)

24. Quartz — Point retouched fully on both margins. Made on a narrow blade and sharp projecting point. Layer 3, 2.0×0.5×0.2 cm., 62. (Pl. XXXII-14)

25. Quartz — Point made on a narrow blade and projecting point, steeply trimmed along both the margins. Layer 3, 2.0×0.5×0.2, 62 cm. (Pl. XXXII-15)

26. Quartz — Point made on long narrow crescentric blade with symmetrical outline and having a mid-rib on the dorsal surface. Layer 3, 1.8×0.6×02 cm., 55 cm. (Pl. XXXII-16)

27. Quartz — Point made on a long narrow blade and sharp projecting point, steeply trimmed along both the margins. Layer 4, 2.2×0.5×0.2 cm, 72 cm. (Pl. XXXII-17)

28. Quartz — Point on a long narrow blade, retouched fully on both the margins except near the base. Layer 3, 2.3×0.6×0.2, 55 cm. (Pl. XXXII-19)

29. Quartz — Point on a broad thin blade, steeply retouched on the right edge while left side is retouched in a limited portion. Use marks are visible. Layer 3, 1.9×0.7×0.2 cm 72 cms. (Pl. XXXII-21)

30. Milky quartz — Point on a flake blade, no retouch but pointed tip. Layer 3,2.0×0.8×0.4 cm. 55 cm. (Pl. XXXII-24)

R.S. NO. 8

1. Milky quartz — Point-a core of rhombic outline retouched on the right side and pointed at both the ends. Layer 3, 2.0×1.4×0.7 cm., 68 cm. (Pl. XXXIII-19)

R.S. NO. 17

1. Quartz — Point on blade. A short sub-triangular blade retouched on one edge and ending in a sharp point. Layer 1, 2.2×0.7×0.3 cm., 26 cm. (Pl. XX-XIV-3)

2. Quartz — A simple point on a flake blade, retouched along the entire margin and having a well drawn out point. Layer 1, 2.3×0.9×0.3 cm., 26 cm. (Pl.XXXIV-4)

3. Quartz — A simple point on an irregular flake blade with a notch on the right side. Layer 1, 2.5×0.9×0.4 cm., 26 cm. (Pl. XXXIV-5)

4. Quartz — A thin flake with medial ridge. At the base there is a short tang. Layer 1, 1.9×0.9×0.3 cm., 26 cm. (Pl. XXXIV-10)

5. Quartz — A short sub-triangular blade retouched on one edge and having a sharp point. Layer 1, 1.7×0.7×0.2 cm., 2 cm., (Pl. XXIV -13)

6. Quartz — Point on a crescentric blade, more like a lunate having pointed ends. Layer 1, 1.6× 0.5x0.3 cm., 26cm. (Pl. XXXIV-14)

7. Milky quartz — Point on a crescentric blade with both ends having sharp points. Layer 1, 1.9×0.6× 0.2 cm., 26 cm. (Pl. XXXIV-16)

8. Quartz — A broad blade with oblique retouch on right side. Point on blade. Layer 1, 2.0× 1.0×0.2 cm., 26 cm. (Pl. XXXIV-18)

9. Quartz — Hollow based point on a concave blade having slight trimming. Layer 1, 1.5×0.7× 0.2 cm., 26 cm. (Pl. XXXIV-22)

10. Quartz — A medium-sized pen-knife blade with projecting point and having steepe retouch on the oblique edge. Layer 1, 1.9×0.8×0.3 cm., 26 cm. (Pl. XXXIV-23)

11. Quartz — Point on a crescentric blade. Layer 1, 1.7×0.8×0.3 cm., 26 cm. (Pl. XXXIV-24)

12. Quartz — Point on an irregular thin flake-blade, retouched on the right side. Layer 1, 1.7 xO.7×0.2 cm., 26 cm. (Pl. XXXIV-28)

13. Quartz — A sharp sub-triangular blade, retouched on one edge and having sharp point. Layer 1, 1.7×0.6×0.2 cm., 26 cm., (Pl. XXXIV-29)

14. Quartz — A broad blade with oblique retouch on the right side and having broad base. Layer 1, 2.2×0.7×0.2 cm., 26 cm. (Pl. XXXIV-30)

15 Milky quartz — Point on a thick almond-shaped flake, cortex present in the lower part on the dorsal side, retouched on the right edge. Layer 1, 3.0×1.8×0.7 cm., 26cm., (Pl. XXXIV-31)

16. Milky quartz — Point on a sub-triangular flake having a medial ridge, retouched on the right side, point broken., Layer 1, 2.5×1.3×0.4 cm., 26 cm. (Pl. XXXIV-32)

17. Agate — Patinated, sub-triangular, flake retouched on left edge and also having a notch. Layer 1, 3.9×1.6×0.4 cm., 26 cm. (Pl. XXXIV-36)

18. Quartz — Hollow based point on blade, roughly symmetrical, retouched on both the edges, having a concave base. Layer 2, 1.9×1.0×0.4m 28-40 cm. (Pl. XXXV-2)

19. Quartz — A short sub-triangular blade retouched on one edge and having sharp point and concave underside. Layer 2, 18×0.6×0.2 cm., 28-40 cm. (Pl. XXXV-6)

20. Quartz — Point on an asymmetrical crescentric blade. Concave side retouched. Mid- rib on dorsal side. Layer 2, 1.8×0.5×0.3 cm., 28-40 cm. (Pl. XXXV-11)

21. Quartz — A thin long blade, point steeply retouched on the right margin, cross-section triangular formed by medial ridge on the dorsal side. Layer 2, 2.8×0.5×0.2 cm., 28-40 cm., (Pl. XXXV-12)

22. Green jesper — A thick long blade, with very sharp point, straight left margin retouched. Layer 2, 1.6×0.6×0.4 cm., 28-40 cm., (PI. XXXV-13)

23. Milky quartz	Point on crescentric blade. Pointed end shows use marks, right concave margin has a notch in the centre. Layer 2, 2.9×0.8×0.3 cm., 28-40 cm. (Pl. XXXV-14)
24. Quartzite	Point on crescentric blade. Dorsal side has the patinated cortex over the mid-rib. Layer 2, 3, 2×0.7×0.5 cm., 28-40 cm. (Pl. XXXV-15)
25. Milky quartz	A broad blade of symmetrical form, steeply trimmed on one edge and having an incipient tang at the base. Layer 2, 3.3×0.7×0.2 cm., 28-40 cm. (Pl. XXXV-16)
26. Quartz	Point on crescentric blade. A large symmetrical crescent having prominent pointed ends. Layer 2, 2.7×0.8×0.3 cm., 28-40 cm., (Pl. XXXV-17)
27. Quartzite	Point on sub-triangular blade, retouched on one edge and having sharp point. Layer 2, 3.2×1.3×0.5 cm., 28-40 cm., (Pl. XXXV-33)
29. Milky quartz	Point on crescentric blade, steeply retouched in two directions like Helwan retouch, Layer 2, 1.6×0.6×0.2 cm., 41-55 cm., (Pl. XXXVI-2)
30. Quartz	Obliquely blunted pen-knife point, made on flake and having steep retouch on oblique edge. Layer 2, 1.6×0.4×0. 2 cm, 41-55 cm., (Pl. XXXVI-3)
31. Quartz	Point on irregular flake-blade with a pointed tip and no retouch. Layer 2, 1.6×0.6×0.2 cm., 41-55 cm., (Pl. XXXVI-5)
32. Quartz	A short sub-triangular blade retouched on one edge, the point is broken. Layer 2, 1.7×0.5×0.2 cm., 41-55 cm., (Pl. XXXVI-6)
33. Quartz	A broad pen-knife blade with projecting point, obliquely retouched on the left side. Layer 2, 2.1×0.6×0.2 cm., 41-55 cm., (Pl. XXXVI-7)
34. Quartz	Point on crescentric blade, steeply retouched in two directions like Helwan retouch. Layer 2, 1.9×0.7×0.3 cm., 41-55 cm., (Pl. XXXVI-10)
35. Milky quartz	Point on blade, fully retouched on the right side and partly on the left. Carries use marks and is having a short tang at the base. Layer 2, 1.7×0.5×0.3 cm., 41-55 cm., (Pl. XXXVI-11)
36. Quartz	Point on crescentric blade with a notch on the left and right edge patinated. Layer 2, 2.1×1.7×0.3 cm., 41-55 cm., (Pl. XXXVI-12)
37. Quartz	Point on a thin blade, point broken. Layer 2, 1.9×0.7×0.2 cm., 41-55 cm., (Pl. XXXVI-14)
38. Quartz	Point on a broad sub-triangular blade with oblique retouch on the left side, having oblique base, a notch at the upper left edge. Layer 2, 2.0×0.7×0.4 cm., 41-55 cm., (Pl. XXXVI-15)
39. Quartz	Point on a slender blade having steep retouch on the convex edge. Layer 2, 2.0×0.6×0.3 cm., 41-55 cm., (Pl. XXXVI-16)
40. Quartz	Point on a crescentric blade, backed on the curved side and having a short, drawn

	out end which might have served as a tang. Layer 2,2.4x0.8x0.3 cm., 41-55 cm. (Pl. XXXVI-17)
41. Quartz	Point on crescentric blade, retouched on the right upper half only. Layer 2, 2.5×0.8×0.3 cm., 41-55 cm., (Pl. XXXVI-18)
42. Quartz	Thick triangular flake, slightly retouched at the tip. Layer 2, 2.4×1.5×0.4 cm., 41-55 cm., (Pl. XXXVI-19)
43. Quartz	Almond shaped flake with medial ridge on the front, no retouch. Layer 2, 2.3×1.2×0.3 cm., 41-55 cm., (Pl. XXXVI-20)
44. Quartz	Similar as 43, slightly patinated at the left lower margin. Layer 2, 2.0×1.7×0.4 cm., 41-55 cm., (Pl. XXXVI-21)
45. Quartz	Point on a thin asymmetrical flake, awl like point. Layer 2, 2.1×1.4×0.2 cm., 41-55 cm., (Pl. XXXVI-22)
46. Milky quartz	Almond shaped, retouched only on the left upper end. Left side is thick while right is sharp. Left thick side shows patinated cortex. Layer 2, 2.2×1.7×0.5 cm., 41-55 cm., (Pl. XXXVI-23)
47. Quartz	Similar to 46, but both the edges sharp and a notch on the lower right margin indicates that attempt was made to shape an incipient tang. Layer 2, 1.9×1.0×0.4 cm., 41-55 cm., (Pl. XXXVI-24)
48. Agate	Point on a long blade, fully retouched on the left side and only in the upper half on the right. Layer 2, 2.9×0.9×0.2 cm., 41-55 cm., (Pl. XXXVI-25)
49. Quartz	Sub-triangular flake, unifacially worked, left side fully retouched. Layer 2, 2.4×1.0×0.5 cm., 41-55 cm., (Pl. XXXV1-26)
50. Quartzite	Point on parallel sided long blade having broad base, retouched on right side. Layer 2, 2.0×0.8×0.4 cm., 41-55 cm., (Pl. XXXVI-29)
51. Milky quartz	Point on a thick long blade, point steeply retouched on the right margin. Layer 2, 3.3×1.1×0.5 cm., 41-55 cm., (Pl. XXXVI-32)
52. Quartz	Point on irregular flake-blade, retouched on both the edges. Layer 2, 2.7×0.8×0.4 cm., 41-55 cm. (Pl. XXXVI-34)
53. Chalcedony	A simple point on a thin flake blade with no retouch, a small notch at the tip. Layer 2, 1.6×0.6×0.2 cm., 50-70 cm., (Pl. XXXVII-9)
54. Quartz	A simple point, smaller in size, on a parallel-sided blade with a notch on the right lower end. Layer 2, 1.9×0.6×0.3 cm., 50-70 cm., (Pl. XXXVII-10)
55. Quartzite	A simple flake point with no retouch. Layer 2, 2.0×1.0×0.3 cm., 50-70 cm., (Pl. XXXVII-24)
56. Quartz	A pen-knife type blade having a notch at the base forming an incipient tang. Layer 2, 2.0×0.7×0.2 cm., 50-70 cm., (Pl. XXXVII-26)

57. Quartz — Point on an irregular flake-blade with retouch only in the cavity of the concave edge. Layer 2, 2.3×1.0×0.2 cm., 50-70 cm., (Pl. XXXVII-34)

58. Quartz — A beautiful example of a tanged point on a thin flake with medial ridge on the front. By taking out falkes on both the margins of the base a long tang has been achieved which could easily be fixed in the arrow shaft. Layer 2, 3.0×1.3×0.3 cm., 50-70 cm., (Pl. XXXVII-36)

B. Borers and Awls

Borers and awls are useful for piercing holes in wood, bone and hide. Distinction between the two types is made on the basis of the size and sharpness of the working points.

R.S.NO. 3

1. Chalcedony — Awl on a broad blade, the awl point is symmetrical. Retouched on the right near the tip. Layer 2, 1.6×0.7×0.4 cm., 30-35 cm. (Pl. XXXI-2)

2 Agate — Awl on a broad blade, the awl point is symmetrical, two shoulders perhaps obtained by burin- like faceting. Layer 2, 1.9×0.9×0.3 cm., 35-40 cm (Pl. XXXI-19)

3 Milky quartz — Borer. A tabular rod-like nodule is steeply but finely chipped all along the margin and towards the tapering point. Slightly patinated at the point. Layer 2, 3.3×1.0× 0.4 cm., 35-40 cm. (Pl. XXXI - 35)

4 Chalcedony — Awl. On a thin broad blade, retouched on the right side. Layer 4, 1.4×0.6×0.2 cm., 75 cms., (Pl. XXXII-20)

R.S. NO. 17

1. Quartz — Awl on a short blade, dorsal side showing mid-rib. The awl point is symmetrical, retouching on the right edge. Layer 1, 1.3×0.7×0.2 cm., 26 cm., (PI. XXXIV-21)

2. Pale Yellow Chalcedony — Awl Made on a blade. The awl point is achieved by a deep scar on both the sides near the tip. The scars are almost like notches. Retouch on the right extends all along the edge. Layer 2, 2.1×0.9×0.4 cm., 28-40 cm., (Pl. XXXV-3)

3. Quartz — On a broad blade, the awl point is symmetrical, retouching is on the right edge. Layer 2, 1.4×0.6×0.3 cm., 50-70 cm., (Pl. XXXVII-8)

C. Triangles

There are two sub-types-

(i) isoceles triangles having more or less two equal adjacent sides, and

(ii) scalene triangles where all three sides are unequal in length. The sizes of the triangles differ and all are finely trimmed on any two adjacent sides.

R.S. NO. 3

1. Agate — Scalene triangle, larger in size. Layer 2, 1.6×0.6×0.3 cm., 25-30 cm (Pl. XXX-12)

2 Quartz	Large in size, tip broken. Layer 2,1.9×0.9×0.2 cm., 15-20 cm. (Pl. XXX-9)
3 Quartz	Isosceles triangle of small size. Layer 3, 1.0×0.4×0.2 cm., 62 cm., (Pl. XXXII-22)
4. Quartz	Scalene triangle, slightly larger in size. Layer 3, 1.2×0.4×0.3, 62 cm., (Pl. XXXII-23)

R.S. NO. 17

1. Quartz	Scalene triangle, larger in size, layer 1, 2.4×0.8×0.2 cm., 26 cm., (Pl. XXXIV-19)
2 Red Jesper	Scalene triangle. Layer 1, 1.9×0.7×0.2 cm., 26 cm., (Pl. XXXIV-25)
3. Quartz	Isosceles triangle with a minute notch at the pointed upper end. Layer 1, 1.8×0.6× 0.2 cm., 26 cm., (Pl. XXXIV-26)
4. Milky quartz	Scalene triangle of a smaller size with a retouch on the right edge and oblique base. Layer 2, 1.7×0.6×0.3 cm., 28-40 cm., (Pl. XXXV-9)
5. Smoky quartz	Scalene triangle. Layer 2, 1.5×0.6×0.2 cm., 41-55 cm., (Pl. XXXVI-1)
6. Quartz	Scalene triangle. Layer 2, 1.5×0.6×0.2 cm., 41-55 cm., (Pl. XXXVI-4)
7. Quartz	Scalene triangle with very sharp points. Layer 2, 1.5×0.4×0.3 cm., 41- 55 cm., (Pl. XXXVI-8)
8. Quartzite	Isosceles triangle, small in size. Layer 2, 1.7×0.5×0.4 cm., 41-55 cm., (Pl. XXXVI-9)
9. Quartz	Scalene triangle on a thin flake blade. Layer 2, 1.6×0.8×0.2 cm., 50-70 cm., (Pl. XXXVII-2)

D. Tranchets

R.S. NO. 3

1 Quartz	Made on a thin blade fragments, little worked on one side. Layer 2, 1.3×1.0×0.34 cm., 15-20 cm., (Pl. XXX-3)
2 Quartz	A sub-rectangular flake-blade having a chisel like sharp edge. Slightly retouched on one of the edges. Layer 2, 20×1.7×0.9 cm., 15-20 cm. (Pl. XXX-21)
3 Milky quartz	A triangular, thick broad flake, with a mid-rib and sharp point Both the edges of the triangle retouched towards top half. Might have been used as an arrow-head. Layer 2, 2.8×1.9×0.7 cm., 20-25 cm. (Pl. XXX-22)
4 Milky quartz	A sub-triangular flake-blade may have been utilized as a harpoon, Layer 4, 1.2× 1.0×0.4 cm., 75 cm., (Pl. XXXII-26)

R.S. NO. 8

1 Quartz	Tranchet : A sub-rectangular flake blade, retouched on the right edge Layer 3, 1.4×0.6×0.3 cm., 68 cm., (Pl. XXXIII-11)

2. Quartz	Tranchet. On a sub-rectangular flake blade, might have been utilized as a transverse arrow-head, retouched on the right side. Layer 3, 1.5×0.7×0.4 cm., 68 cm., (Pl. XXXIII-12)
3. Green jesper	Tranchet. Resembles a trapeze but has typical blade scar which is the characteristic feature of a tranchet. Layer 3, 1.8×1.3×04 cm., 68 cms., (Pl. XXXIII-14)
4. Milky quartz	Tranchet made on a fragment from a thick blade. Only the thin left working edge is trimmed. Layer 3, 2.1×1.6×0.9 cm., 68 cms., (Pl. XXXIII-16)

R.S. NO. 17

1. Chalcedony	Tranchet, made on a thick blade fragment, little worked on the left side. Layer 2, 1.8×1.3×0.4 cm., 28-40 cm., (Pl. XXXV-4)
2. Quartz	A sub-rectangular flake which may have been used as a transverse arrow head. Layer 2. 1.5×0.8×0.3 cm., 50-70 cms., (Pl. XXXVII-3)
3. Milky quartz	Made on a thick blade fragment with little retouch on the left margin. Layer 2, 1.9× 1.0×0.4 cm., 50-70 cm., (Pl. XXXVII-19)
4. Agate	A sub-rectangular flake which may have been used as a transverse arrowhead as there is a notch in the centre of the base. Layer 2, 2.1×0.9×0.3 cm., 50-70 cm., (Pl. XXXVII-27)

E. Trapeze

R.S. NO. 3

1. Milky quartz	A fine example of trapeze with three sides worked. Layer 2, 2.3×1.2×0.5 cm., 25-30 cm. (Pl. XXXI- 30)

R.S. NO. 8

1. Agate	Trapeze of crude type with three sides worked. At the base a straight, flat platform has been formed due to deep flaking. Layers 3, 2.3×1.8×1.7 cm., 68 cms., (Pl. XXXIII-7)
2. Milky quartz	Trapeze, a tiny specimen with three sides worked. Layer 3, 1.5×1.1x0.5 cm., 68 cm., (Pl. XXXVIII-15)

R.S. NO. 17

1. Red jesper	A crude form of trapeze almost a rectangle, left side worked. Layer 1, 1.9×0.9× 0.3 cm., 67 cm., (Pl. XXXIV-11)

F. Scrapers

The scrapers are made on cores or nodules, flakes and blades. The core scrapers are generally of larger size. A number of fluted blade cores have been steeply retouched to serve as scrapers. The core scrapers are made on pebbles, and split- pebbles.

R. S. NO. 3

1. Milky quartz	A core scraper, minutely touched at the top to produce a thin scraper-edge. Left side has been worked. Layer 2, 2.2×1.3×1.3 cm., 35-40 cm. (Pl. XXX-5)
2. Quartz	Scraper. A thick flake is steeply trimmed on the two sides towards the pointed end. Right side is concave. Layer 2, 2.4×0.8×0.4 cm., 30-35 cm. (Pl. XXX-16)
3. Quartz	Scraper. A thin blade has been retouched on the convave side. Layer 2, 2.1×0.8×0.2 cm., 25-30 cm. (Pl. XXXI-1)
4. Quartz	Side-scraper shaped out of thick blade. Left concave side used as a scraper. Layer 2, 3.5×1.5×0.6 cm., 25-30 cm. (Pl. XXXI-36)
5. Milky quartz	Side-scraper. A sub-triangular flake with fan shaped straight edged top. Right side has been used as scraper. Layer 2, 2.9×1.6×0.9 cm., 25-30 cm. (Pl. XXXI-37)
6. Quartz	Core scraper on a triangular core. On the dorsal side cortex is present. Right side and a part of upper end of left side is used as scraper. Slightly notched. Layer 2, 2.4×1.5×1.1 cm., 15-20 cm. (Pl. XXXI-38)
7. Quartz	A nodular thick flake is steeply but finely trimmed on the two sides towards the pointed end. Left side is concave. Layer 2, 2.9×1.3×0.5 cm., 25-30 cm. (Pl. XXXI-40)

R.S. NO. 8

1. Quartzite	retouched side scraper. A tabular fragment is steeply retouched on the long side, and the other, parallel, side has a deep notch. Layer 2, 4.0×2.0×0.9 cm., 34 cm., (Pl. XXXIII-21)

R.S. NO. 17

1. Red Jesper	Blade, retouched on left side to produce a thin scraper-edge. Layer 1, 2.3×1.0×0.2 cm., 26 cm., (Pl. XXXIV-12)
2. Quartz	End scraper on blade, minutely retouched on the top and on right edge to produce thin scraper edges. Layer 1, 2.0×1.2×0.4 cm., 26 cm., (Pl. XXXIV-33)
3. Chalcedony	A large flake has been removed from the right side of a cylindrical core producing deep scar bed so that a short convex scraper edge is formed. Layer 1, 2.3×1.2×1.0 cm., 26 cm., (Pl. XXXIV-35).
4. Quartz	A long blade, right side retouched to be used as a side scraper. Layer 2, 3.6×0.8×0.2 cm., 28-40 cm., (Pl. XXXV-19).
5. Milky quartz	A long blade with ventral side concave, bottom blunted, right margin used as a side scraper. Layer 2, 3.3×1.1×0.4 cm., 28-40 cm., (Pl. XXXV-30)
6 Quartzite	Long blade, thick on left edge and sharp on right due to retouching. Right edge used as side scraper. Layer 2, 3.8×1.2×0.4 cm., 28-40 cm., (Pl. XXXV-31)

7. Agate — Long blade, left margin sharp to be used as side scraper. Slight retouching on right side. Layer 2, 4.0×1.2×0.4 cm., 28-40 cm., (Pl. XXXV-35)

8. Quartz — A long, broad blade with both the ends pointed. Left upper half concave and sharp. Both the margins finely retouched to be used as side scraper. Layer 2, 2.9×1.4×1.0×0.2 cm., 41-55 cm., (Pl. XXXVI-13)

9. Milky quartz — Similar to No. 8, with a thick straight base. Left concave upper half used as a hollow scraper. Layer 2, 3.2×1.4×0.5 cm., 41-55 cm., (Pl. XXXVI-31)

10. Milky quartz — A thick blade, whose both margins have been retouched to be used as side scraper. Layer 2, 2.1×1.0×0.4 cm., 50-70 cm., (Pl. XXXVII-20)

11. Chalcedony — A long curved blade, the concave margin has been used as a notched side scraper. Layer 2, 2.5×0.6×0.3 cm., 50-70 cms., (Pl. XXXVII-23)

12. Quartz — A thick flake-blade, left margin of which has been retouched throughout to work as a side scraper. Layer 2, 2.2×1.2×0.4 cm., 50-70 cms., (Pl. XX-XVII-28)

13. Quartz — An almond shaped thin flake with left margin patinated while right sharp used as scraper. Layer 2, 2.2×1.2×0.4 cm., 50-70 cms., (Pl. XX-XVII-30)

G. Burins

Burins form an important tool type in the microlithic industry. This tool is characteristic of the Upper Paleolithic but is equally common in the Mesolithic industries. They are shaped out of nodules, flakes and blades. There are few micro-burins typical representatives of the Mesolithic.

R.S. NO. 3

1 Milky quartz — On a thin blade, the edge formed by the intersection of the two oblique of scars on each side at the bulbous-end the blade. A very sharp burin edge has been obtained. Layer 2, 1.6×0.9×0.3 cm., 25-30 cm., (PI. XXX-14)

2 Quartz — Burin on a small thin small flake. Layer 2, 1.4×0.6×0.2 cm., 20-30 cm., (Pl. XXX-19)

3. Agate — On a small sub-triangular flake. The working end is obtained by removing one oblique spall against a deep scar of the flake taken from the front. Layer 2, 1.1×0.7 cm., 20-30 cm. (Pl. XXXI-5)

R.S. NO. 8

1 Quartz — Burin on a small thick sub-triangular flake. The working end is obtained by removing one oblique spall against a deep scar of the flake. Taken from the front. Layer 2, 2.2×1.5×0.7 cm., 42 cm. (PI. XXXIII-23)

2. Milky Quartz — Burin, on a small thick sub-triangular flake. The working end is obtained by removing one oblique spall against a deep scar of the flake taken from the front. Layer 2, 2.2×1.9×0.5 cm., 40 cm. (Pl. XXXIII-24)

R.S. NO. 17

1 Quartz	On a small, thin triangular flake. The burin edge is produced by removal of two oblique spalls opposed to another set of similar spalls. Layer 1, 1.4×1.0×0.2 cm., 26 cms., (XXXIV-27)
2 Agate	Burin on a small, thick, sub-triangular flake. The working end is obtained by removing one oblique spall against a deep scar of the flake on the left side near the tip. Layer 2, 1.6×1.7×0.3 cm., 28-40 cms., (Pl. XXXV-1)
3 Yellow Chalcedony	Burin made on a sub-triangular nodule. The burin edge is produced by removal of two oblique spalls opposed to another set of similar spalls. Layer 2, 2.2×1.7×1.3 cm., 28-40 cms., (Pl. XXXV-32)
4. Quartz	On a small, thin sub-triangular flake. The burin edge is produced by the removal of an oblique spall from the right side tip, while the thick right side retains the cortex. Left side has been retouched to give a sharp margin. Layer 2, 1.4×0.9×0.4 cm., 50-70 cms., (PI. XXXVII-4)
5. Quartz	Made on a triangular flake. The working end is formed by taking one oblique spall against a deep scar of the flake taken from the front. Layer 2, 1.3×1.2×0.4 cm., 50-70 cms., (PI. XXXVII-5)
6. Quartz	On a small, thin, sub-triangular flake. The burin edge is produced by the removal of two oblique spalls opposed to another set of similar spalls. Layer 2, 1.6×1.1×0.3 cm., 50-70 cms., (PI. XXXVII-6)

H. Blades

In the microlithic industry the majority of tools are worked on blades. The blades themselves are utilized for variety of purposes. There are fine examples of parallel sided blades in the collection. There are also blades with crested-ridge which generally come from chalcolithic levels. As such blades occurred at Jhiri alongwith copper and pottery, generally Red Ware, it indicates the presence of a chalcolithic level.

R.S. NO. 3

1. Quartz	An asymmetrical blade, blunted on one straight edge, thick on left edge and sharp on the right showing use marks. Layer 2, 1.7×0.8×0.6 cm., 30-35 cms., (P. XXX-4)
2. Quartz	A serrated blade, parallel sided having deep and close flaking on the right edge producing serrated edge. Layer 2, 2.7×0.8×0.3 cm., 25-30 cms., (PI. XXX-6)
3. Quartz	Parallel sided, serrated blade having deep and close flaking on both the edges. Layer 2, 2.3×0.7×0.3 cm., 30-35 cms., (PI. XXX-7)
4. Quartz	Simple, untouched blade, parallel sided, snapped at one edge. Layer 2, 2.0×0.9×01.2 cm., 30-35 cms., (PI. XXX-8)
5. Quartz	A flake blade, notched on the right edge. Long, broken at the tip. Layer 2, 2.4×0.5×0.2 cm., 25-30 cms., (PI. XXX-10)

6. Agate	Crescentric blade. A fine example of a symmetrical lunate. The upper surface has a short mid-rib. Underside is plain. Steeply blunted on the curved edge by two directional flaking. Layer 2, 2.2×0.6×0.4 cm., 30-35 cms., (PI. XXX-13)
7. Quartz	Serrated blade, parallel-sided. Left curved edge is serrated and shows use marks. Layer 2, 1.9×0.6×0.3 cm., 25-30 cm. (PI. XXX-15)
8 Green jesper	A flake blade notched on the left edge. No retouch on the notched portion or elsewhere. Layer 2, 1.4×0.6×0.2, 25-30 cm. (PI. XXX-17)
9 Quartz	A nearly parallel-sided blade, retouched on right edge and displays use marks. Layer 2, 1.8×0.7×0.2 cm., 25-30 cm. (PI. XXX-20)
10 Green jesper	A small flake blade, notched at the left bottom edge. Layer 2, 1.1.×0.4×0.2 cm., 25-30 cm., (PI. XXXI-4)
11 Milky quartz	Parallel sided blade, blunted on one edge. Both the edges have been retouched. Layer 2, 1.3×0.9×0.2 cm., 30-40 cm. (PI. XXXI-6)
12 Quartz	Simple, parallel sided, unretouched blade, snapped at both ends. Layer 2, 1.4×0.5×0.2 cm., 25-30 cm. (PI. XXXI-7)
13 Quartz	A flake blade, parallel sided, notched at one end. Layer 2, 1.3×0.6×0.2 cm., 20-25 cm., (Pl. XXXI-10)
14 Agate	Simple, parallel sided, un-retouched blade, layer 2, 1.1×0.5×0.2 cm., 20-25 cm. (Pl. XXXI-11)
15 Quartz	A short, parallel sided blade having deep and close flaking on the left edge producing the serrated edge. Layer 2, 1.6×0.7×0.3 cm., 25-30 cm., (Pl. XXXI-14)
16 Milky quartz	A flake blade notched on the left edge. Layer 2, 1.9×1.0×0.2 cm., 25-30 cm., (Pl. XXXI-22)
17. Agate	A thick, parallel-sided unretouched blade. Layer 2, 2.1×0.8×0.5 cm., 30-35 cm. (Pl. XXXI-24)
18 Agate	Parallel-sided blade, snapped at both ends. Left side is serrated Layer 2, 2.0×0.6×0.3 cm., 25-30 cm., (Pl. XXXI-27)
19 Quartz	Parallel-sided, un-retouched blade. Layer 2, 2.0×0.6×0.3 cm., 30-35 cm. (Pl. XXXI-28)
20. Chert	Parallel-sided, thick on the right edge which is blunted by retouching. The sharper edge shows use mark. Layer 2, 2.0×0.6×0.4 cm., 30-35 cm. (Pl. XXXI-29)
21. Quartz	Blade with crested ridge. Large parallel-sided. Layer 2, 3.2×1.1.×0.5 cm., 30-33 cm. (Pl. XXXI-31)
22. Agate	An asymmetrical flake-blade, having deep and close retouch on the left edge producing a short serrated edge. Layer 2, 2.7×1.2×0.2 cm., 30-35 cm., (Pl. XXXI-32)

23. Milky quartz	Parallel-sided, blunted blade with right edge sharp. Layer 2, 2.1×0.9×0.4 cm., 25-30 cm., Pl. XXXI-34)
24. Quartz	A parallel sided blade, thick on left edge which is blunted by retouching. The sharper edge shows use marks. Layer 3, 2.1×0.7×0.4 cm., 50 cms., (Pl. XXXII-1)
25. Quartz	Serrated blade on asymmetrical flake blade having deep and close flaking on the left edge producing a short serrated edge. Layer 3, 2.2×1.1.×0.4 cm., 52 cm., (Pl. XXXII-2)
26. Quartz	Notched blade. A short parallel sided blade with two notches near the base on the left side and one notch in the centre of the base. Layer 2, 1.9×0.5×0.3 cm., 55 cm. (Pl. XXXII-3)
27. Quartz	Serrated blade. Parallel sided blade having deep and close retouching on the right margin, producing serrated edge. Layer 3, 1.9×0.5×0.2 cm., 62 cm., (Pl. XXXII-4)
28. Quartz	An asymmetrical blade having deep and close flaking on the left producing a serrated edge. Layer 3, 1.7×0.9×0.2 cm., 62 cm., (XXXII-5)
29. Quartz	Similar to No. 5. Flaking is on the right side producing a short serrated edge. Layer 3, 1.5×0.6×0.2 cm., (0.55 cm., (Pl. XXXII-6)
30. Quartz	A short but broad blade having deep and close flaking on the right producing a short serrated edge. Layer 3, 1.2×0.7×0.2 cm., 72 cm., (Pl. XXXII-7)
31. Quartz	A small parallel-sided blade, thick on the right edge which is blunted by retouching. The other sharper edge shows use marks. Layer 3, 1.4×0.5×0.2 cm., 55 cm., (Pl. XXXII-8)
32. Quartz	A short but broad parallel sided blade having deep and close flaking on the right edge producing a short serrated edge. Layer 3, 1.0×0.6×0.2 cm., 55 cm., (Pl. XXXII-9)
33 Quartz	Simple unretouched blade, parallel sided. Layer 3, 1.2×0.6×0.2 cm., 55 cm., (PI. XXXII-10)
34. Quartz	Crescentric blade. A fine example of a lunate. The surface has a mid-rib and underside is plain. Layer 3, 2.2×0.6×0.2 cm., 62 cm., (PI. XII-18)
35 Quartz	An asymmetrical flake blade having deep and close flaking on the right edge producing a short serrated edge. Layer 3, 2.1.×0.7×0.3 cm., 55 cm., (PI. XXXII-28)
36. Green jesper	Simple, parallel-sided unretouched blade, Layer 4, 1.3×0.5×0.2 cm., 75 cm., (PI. XXXII-29)

R.S. NO. 8

1. Quartz	A thick, broad, parallel-sided blade. Right edge and tip are retouched. Layer 3, 2.4×1.7×0.7 cm., 54 cm. (PI. XXXIII-1)

2 Quartz	A parallel sided blade retouched on the left edge. Layer 3, 2.2×1.2×0.4 cm., 54 cm. (PI. XXXIII-2)
3 Quartz	An asymmetrical flake blade having deep and close flaking on the left edge producing a short serrated edge. Layer 3, 1.9×0.6×0.4 cm., 54 cm. (PI. XXXIII-3)
4. Milky quartz	A short but broad parallel sided blade, left edge and tips have been retouched. Layer 3, 1.6×1.0×0.3 cm., 54 cm. (PI. XXXIII-4)
5. Quartz	A large crescent of symmetrical outline with cortex present on dorsal side. Layer 3, 2.4×1.0×0.5 cm., 54 cm. (PI. XXXIII-5)
6. Banded agate	A large parallel sided blade, thick on the left edge and sharp on the right. Layer 3, 3.2×1.6×0.6 cm., 68 cm (PI. XXXIII-6)
7 Quartz	A thick un-retouched blade. Layer 3, 1.9×1.1×0.5 cm., 68 cm. (PI. XXXIII-8)
8 Milky quartz	A long blade, blunted on one edge. Pen-knife blade. Layer 3, 1.9×0.6×0.3 cm., 68 cm. (PI. XXXIII-9)
9 Agate	A small pen-knife blade. Layer 3, 1.5×0.6×0.3 cm., 68 cm (PI. XX=XIII-10)
10. Milky quartz	An unclassified blade with right edge sharp. Layer 3, 2.1×0.9×0.4 cm., 68 cm. (PI. XXXIII-13)
11. Milky quartz	A parallel sided, un-retouched blade. Layer 3. 2.5×0.9×0.5 cm., 68 cm., (PL XXXIII-20)
12. Agate	An asymmetrical flake blade having deep and close flaking, sharp on the right edge. Layer 1, 2.1×1.0×0.5 cm., 10 cm. (PL XXXIII-25)

R.S. NO. 17

1 Quartz	Serrated blade on an asymmetrical flake blade having deep and close flaking on the left edge producing a short serrated edge. Layer 1, 2.8×1.1×0.2 cm., 26cm. (PL XXXIV-1)
2 Quartz	Serrated blade similar to No. 1, Layer 1, 2.4×0.7×0.2 cm., 26 cm., (Pl. XXXIV-2)
3 Quartz	Blade blunted on an straight edge. A large parallel sided blade thick on the right edge which is blunted by retouching. The other sharper edge shows use marks. Layer 1, 2.8×0.9×0.4 cm., 26 cm. (Pl. XXXIV-6)
4. Quartz	A parallel-sided, un-retouched blade snapped at one end. Layer 1, 1.8×0.8×0.2 cm., 26 cm., (Pl. XXXIV-7)
5. Milky quartz	Simple, parallel sided, unretouched blade snapped at one end. Layer 1, 2.0×0.7×0.2 cm., 26 cm. (PL XXXIV-8)
6 Milky quartz	A parallel sided blade, thick on the left edge and sharper with retouching on the right edge. Layer 1, 1.7×0.7×0.2 cm., 26 cm. (PL XXXIV-9)

7. Quartz	Crescent blade. A fine example of a symmetrical lunate, the upper surface has a mid rib and underside is plain. Layer 1, 1.6×0.6×0.3 cm., 26 cm. (PL XXXLV-15)
8 Milky quartz	Crescentric blade. A fine example of a symmetrical lunate similar to No. 7. Layer 1, 1.7×0.6×0.3 cm., 26 cm. (Pl. XXXIV-19)
9 Quartz	Notched blade. An unretouched flake blade notched on the upper end of left edge. Layer 1, 1.8×0.7×0.2 cm., 26 cm. (Pl. XXXIV-20)
10. Milky quartz	Blade. A short but parallel-sided blade blunted on straight edge. Layer 1, 1.9×1.3× 0.4 cm., 26 cm. (Pl. XXXIV-34)
11. Chalcedony	A pen-knife blade, snapped at the base, both the margins sharp and show use marks. Layer 2, 1.6×0.6×0.2 cm., 28-40 cms., (PI. XXXV-5)
12. Quartz	A crescent of asymmetrical outline, having curved edge, flaring at the end. Layer 2, 1.4×0.6×0.3 cm., 28-40 cm., (PI. XXXV-7)
13. Quartz	Crescentric blade of asymmetrical outline. Right sharp edge and point worked. Layer 2, 1.6×0.8×0.2 cm., 28-40 cms., (PI. XXXV-8)
14. Quartz	Crescentric blade with right margin having retouch throughout. Mid rib prominent. Layer 2, 1.7×0.6×0.2 cm., 28-40 cm., (XXXV-10)
15. Milky quartz	A short but broad parallel-sided blade with a notch upper right hand corner. Layer 2, 2.5×0.9×0.3 cm., 28-40 cm., (XXX-18)
16. Milky quartz	A long parallel-sided, unretouched blade, snapped at both ends. Layer 2, 3.2×0.9× 0.3, 28-40 cm., (PI. XXXV-20)
17. Milky quartz	A symmetrical flake blade having deep and close flaking on the right edge producing a short serrated edge. Layer 2, 2.4×0.6×0.2 cm., 28-40 cm., (PI. XXXV-21)
18. Quartzite	A short parallel-sided blade thick on the right but sharp on the left edge. Layer 2, 2.0×0.5×0.2 cm., 28-40 cm., (PI. XXXV-22)
19. Dark Brown Chalcedony	A small, parallel-sided blade, retouched on both the sides. Layer 2, 3.7×0.7×0.8 ×0.2 cm., 28-40 cm., (PI. XXXV-23)
20. Milky quartz	A long, parallel-sided blade, retouched on both the sides. Layer 2, 3.7×0.7×0.2 cm., 28-40 cm., (PI. XXXV-24)
21. Quartz	A parallel-sided blade blunted on one straight edge and left edge sharp. Layer 2, 2.7×0.8×0.2 cm., 28-40 cm., (PI. XXXV-25)
22. Quartz	Parallel-sided, thin blade, with both the edges sharp and having a deep notch on the bottom right edge. Layer 2, 2.6×0.9×0.2 cm., 28-40 cms., (PI. XXV-26)
23. Green jesper	A parallel-sided, unretouched blade. Layer 2, 2.3×1.2×0.4 cm., 28-40 cms., (PI. XXXV-28)
24. Milky quartz	A thick, parallel-sided blade, thick on the right edge and sharp on the left. Layer 2, 2.7×1.1×0.4 cm., 28-40 cms., (PI. XXXV-29)

25. Quartz	Pen knife blade, blunted on one edge and the other edge is sharp. Layer 2, 1.8×0.7×0.2 cm., 41-55 cms., (PI. XXXVI-27)
26. Quartz	Parallel-sided, simple, unretouched blade, having a notch near the left upper margin. Layer 2, 1.9×0.5×0.2 cm., 41-55 cms., (PI. XXXVI-28)
27. Quartzite	Long blade, blunted on one straight edge, thick on right edge, the other edge which is sharp shows use marks. Layer 2, 2.9×0.7×0.9 cm., 41-55 cms., (PI. XXXVI-30)
28. Quartz	A long, thick and broad blade, broken at the tip. Left curved margin retouched and sharp. Used as a pen-knife blade. Layer 2, 3.1×1.0×0.8 cm., 41-55 cms., (Pl. XXXVI-35)
29. Smoky quartz	A parallel-sided blade, sharp on both the margins. Layer 2, 1.6×0.6×0.2 cm., 50-70 cms., (PI. XXXVII-1)
30. Quartz	A small parallel-sided blade, blunted on one small edge. Layer 2, 1.6×0.6×0.3 cm., 50-70 cms., (PI. XXXVII-11)
31. Quartz	A small parallel-sided blade, blunted on one small edge. Layer 2, 1.6×0.6×0.3 cm., 50-70 cms., (PI. XXXVII-14)
32. Quartz	Pen knife blade. Layer 2, 1.6×0.6×0.2 cm., 50-70 cms., (PI. XXXVII-12)
33. Banded Agate	A medium sized, thin parallel-sided blade. Layer 2, 2.4×0.5×0.2 cm., 50-70 cms., (PI. XXXVII-13)
34. Agate	A small parallel-sided blade with both margins retouched. Layer 2, 2.0×0.5×0.3 cm., 50-70 cm., (PI. XXXVII-14)
35. Green jesper	A sub-rectangular blade, with both the margins sharp. Layer 2, 1.9×0.6×0.2 cm., 50-70 cm., (PI. XXXVII-15)
36. Quartz	Blade with a crested ridge on the front and plain under surface. Layer 2, 2.4×0.7×0.3 cm., 50-70 cm., (PI. XXXVII-16)
37. Quartz	A parallel sided, un-retouched blade having a small notch at the base. Layer 2, 2.1×0.7×0.2 cm., 50-70 cms., (PI. XXXVII-17)
38. Grey and brown Chert	A simple un-retouched parallel sided blade, snapped at one end. Layer 2, 2.5×0.9×0.2 cm., 50-70 cms., (PI. XXXVII-18)
39. Quartz	A simple, parallel-sided blade. Layer 2, 1.8×0.6×0.3, 50-70 cms., (PI. XXXVII-21)
40. Quartz	A tanged blade, parallel-sided, with medial ridge on the front. Trimmed at the right margin and the base where there is a short tang. Actually a tanged point, which is broken. Layer 2, 2.4×0.6×0.2 cm., 50-70 cms., (Pl. XXXVII-22)
41. Quartz	Parallel-sided, un-retouched blade, snapped at one end. Layer 2, 2.1×0.7×0.3 cm., 50-70 cms., (PI. XXXVII-25)

42 Quartzite	A crescentric blade (lunate). Layer 2, 1.7×0.6×0.3 cm., 50-70 cm., (Pl. XXXVII-29)
43. Milky quartz	A large parallel-sided blade, thick on the left which is blunted by retouching. The sharper edge shows use marks. Layer 2, 2.4×1.1×0.4 cm., 50-70 cms., (Pl. XXXVII-31)
44. Quartz	Simple, un-retouched blade with a patch of cortex at the bottom which is snapped. Layer 2, 2.1×1.0×0.4 cm., 50-70 cms., (PI. XXXVII-32)
45. Quartz	A flake blade with irregular sides, lower end snapped. Layer 2, 2.4×1.0×0.3 cm., 50-70 cm., (PI. XXXVII-33)
46. Agate	Simple, un-retouched blade with bottom snapped. Layer 2, 2.4×1.0×0.3 cm., 50-70 cms., (PI. XXXVII-35)

I. Cores and Core Tools

From different levels of different trenches good number of cores have been obtained. Majority of them come from the factory site in R.S. No. 17. Some cores having sharp edges were used as tools also.

R.S. NO. 3

1. Milky quartz	Discoid core. Scars indicate removal of flakes of small dismensions from both the surfaces. Those removed from the dorsal surface were small flakes whereas from ventral surface long blades were removed. Layer 2, 2.6×2.7×1.4 cm., 25-30 cm. (PI. XXX-23)
2. Quartz	A cylindrical core with blade scars all around. Layer 2, 2.9×1.3×0.5 cm., 15-20 cm. (PI. XXXI-40)
3. Quartz	Cylindrical core having blade scars all around. Layer 3, 2.4×1.5×1.0 cm., 72 cms., (PI. XXXII-25)
4 Quartz	Cylindrical core with slender body with blade scars all around. Layer 3, 2.0×1.3×1.0 cm., 55 cm., (PI. XXXII-27)
5 Milky quartz	Cylindrical core, with blade scars all around. Layer 3, 2.2×1.1×1.0 cm., 62 cm., (PI. XXXII-30)

R.S. NO. 8

1 Quartz	Cylindrical core, almost completely flaked on all sides. Layer 3, 2.3×1.8×1.7 cm., 68 cms. (PI. XXXIII-17)
2 Milky quartz	Sub-rectangular in form showing scars of blades taken from the striking platform. On the underside there is a deep scar of a flake removed from the core. Layer 3, 1.7×1.4×0.9 cm., 68 cm. (Pl. XXXIII-18)
3 Quartz	Conical fluted core, the base is made flat by flaking. Scars of blades are present. Layer, 2, 2.3×1.9×1.6 cm., 42 cm. (Pl. XXXIII-22)

R.S. NO. 17

1 Quartz — A symmetrical specimen worked on a pebble. The front carries blade scars while the underside is covered with pebble cortex and a shoulder at the base. Layer 2, 2.3×1.7×1.6 cm., 28-40 cms., (PI. XXXV-34)

2 Quartz — A discoidal core. Scars all around indicate removal of flakes of small dimensions. Layer 2, 2.8×2.3×1.3 cm., 41-55 cms., (Pl. XXXVI-33)

II. Hopscotches (PI. XVII A)

All the four hopscotches made on coarse grained sandstone were recovered from layer one, two from R.S. 3 and two from R.S. 8.

1. Medium sized, shaped out of coarse grained sand stone, reddish in colour. From pit 1 sealed by layer 1 of rock shelter 3. Diameter 0.04 m., thickness-0.05 m., (PI. XVII A-l)
2. Small in size, shaped out of very rough sand stone, highly patinated, reddish in colour. From layer 1 of rock shelter 3, Diameter 0.31 m., thickness 0.07 m. (PI. XVII A-2)
3. From layer 1 of R.S. No. 8. Shaped out of coarse grained sand stone, reddish in colour., Diameter 0.72 m., thickness 0.18 m. (PI. XVII A-3)
4. From layer 1 of R.S. No. 8. Shaped out of course grained sand stone, brown in colour. Diameter 0.53 m., thickness 0.18 m. (PI. XVII A-4)

III. Copper Objects

(a) Coins

Two uninscribed cast copper coins were recovered from layer 1 of R.S. No. 3. On the basis of animal, tree and other symbols they are datable to 3rd-4th century B.C. Similar coins have been reported from many sites in central India.

1. A square uninscribed cast copper coin showing a *Stumbha* and an elephant motif on observe and ….. on the reverse. Dimension 0.14 m×0.13 m×0.02 m. It was recovered from 0.03 m. depth. (PI. XVII B-l)
2. A roughly circular uninscribed cast copper coin showing *tri-ratna* symbol on the obverse and …. on the reverse. Recovered from 0.03 m. depth. Dimensions 0.20 m., thickness 0.04 m. (PI. XVII B-2)

(b) Ring

Nearly half of a circular finger ring, solid, circular in section. Outer diameter 0.24 m., thickness 0.02 m.

IV. Colour Pigments (XXIX)

(a) White

(i) R.S. No. 3, layer 1, depth 0.03 m.

(ii) R.S. No. 8, layer 1, depth 0.05m.

(iii) R.S. No. 17, layer 1, depth 0.14 m.

(b) Red

(i) Brick-red	R.S. No. 03, layer 2, depth 0.18 m.
(ii) Red-ochre	R.S. No. 17, layer 1, depth 0.18 m. R.S. No. 17, layer 2, depth 0.93 m.
(iii) Chocolate red	R.S. No. 17, layer 1, depth 0.18 m. R.S. No. 17, layer 2, depth 0.64 m. R.S. No. 17, layer 2, depth 0.93 m.

V. Bone Fragments (Pl. XVI)

Fragments of both animal and human bones were recovered from R.S. No. 3, 8 and 17. From R S. No. 3 fragments of shafts of human long bones were recovered from layer 2 at the depth of 0.38 m. Fragment of a human clavicle was recovered from layer 1 of this shelter at the depth of 0.06m. A human molar was recovered from layer 2 of R.S. No. 17 at the depth of 0.29 m. The cusps are totally worn out indicating advanced age of the person. Fragments of shafts of long bones belonging to animals were found from layer 1 and 2 of R.S. No. 3, 8 and 17. One piece was badly charred. Those recovered from R.S. No. 8 were from the fire pit. Few of the fragments of animal bones were used as tools, mostly as scrapers to scrap the fat and piercers to remove flesh from bone. One of the fragments from R.S. No. 3, layer 2 shows teeth marks and gnawing marks. From R.S. No. 17, layer 1 two vertebrae of fish were recovered. One belongs to a very small variety of fish whereas the other to a medium sized fish indicating that during the mesolithic period fish from the nearby shallow water resources also formed a part of diet.

VI. Binding Material (Pl. III)

The highest percentage of plants next to teak wood at Jhiri are those of *dhaora* (*Angeissus latifolia*) a fibrous plant with long and slender fruits. From the green fruit, branches and trunk of this tree a white, thick, milky latex oozes out when a cut is made. When dries, it acts as a firm adherent. It is also a good solvent for various pigments. After field experiments it was found that this milky latex might have been used as a solvent and adherent for pigments by early men who painted on the walls of the rock-shelters. The samples of this latex has been collected for laboratory analysis. If the chemical composition of this sample on analysis tallies with that of the pigment collected from the painted surface, our finding will get confirmed.

VII. Pottery (Fig. 14)

The entire pottery assemblage was recovered from R.S. No. 3. Those recovered from R.S. No. 8 are only tiny fragments and no shapes. Except few sherds of thick red ware from layer 2 of R.S. No. 3, all other sherds were recovered from layer 1 of this shelter. All the sherds are in red ware except few which are in rough gritty ware.

1. A large-sized lid cum-bowl with a vertically thickened rim and ledged shoulder. Of medium fabric, it is treated with a thin reddish slip on both the sides. Interior of the rim is decorated with horizontal parallel lines of ridges and furrows. From layer 1, depth 8.0 cm.

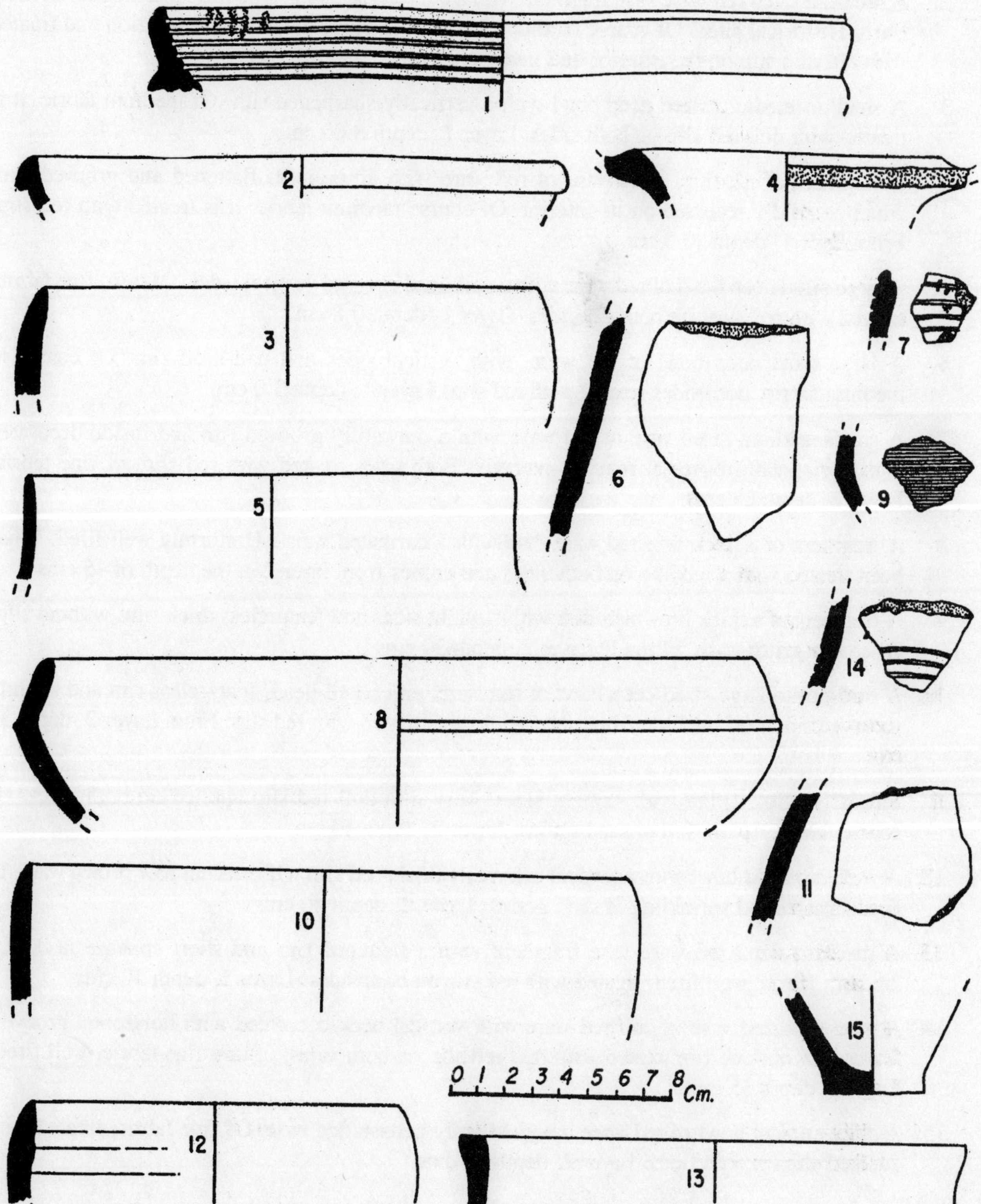

Fig. 14. Pottery

2. A medium sized red ware vase fragment with a curved rim. This type has its analogues in most Early Historical sites. Of coarse medium fabric, it is burnt black in core-section and treated with red thin slip on the exterior and interior. Layer 1, depth 8.0 cm.
3. A small to medium sized deep bowl with a vertically sharpened rim. Of medium fabric, it is treated with dull red slip on both sides. Layer 1, depth 8.00 cm.
4. A fragment of medium sized vase of red ware with an everted, flattened and grooved rim, which is mildly recessed on its interior. Of course medium fabric. It is treated with red slip. From layer 1, depth 10.0 cm.
5. A large sized deep bowl of red ware with a nail-head rim and vertical sides. Of thin, fine fabric, treated with red slips on both the sides. Layer 1, depth 0.8 cm.
6. A large sized deep bowl of red ware, with vertical sides and nail-head rim. Of coarse to medium fabric, both sides treated with red slip. Layer 1, depth 3.0 cm.
7. A small medium sized vase of red ware with a outwardly grooved rim and inside decorated with horizontal grooves at regular intervals. Both sides treated with red slip, of fine fabric. Layer 2, depth 25 cms.
8. A fragment of a thick fine red ware dish with a carinated waist. Uniformly well fired, it has been treated with a red slip on both sides and comes from layer 2 at the depth of 15 cms.
9. A fragment of a thick brownish dish with straight sides and featureless thick rim, without slip. Of coarse gritty ware, ill fired. Layer 2, depth 30 cms.
10. A medium to large sized deep bowl of red ware with a nail-head, featureless rim and slightly incurved sides. Of medium fabric, both sides are treated with red slip. From Layer 2, depth 35 cms.
11. Similar to No. 10 but with straight sides. Very thin dull red slip applied on both sides. Of coarse fabric, matrix full of sand grains. Layer 2, depth 40 cm.
12. A wide mouthed bowl with a vertical externally thickened rim. Of medium pale brown ware, ill fired, matrix had sprinkling of sand grains. Layer 2, depth 40 cms
13. A medium sized red ware vase fragment with a flattened rim and short concave neck. Of medium fabric, well fired, treated with red slip on both sides. Layer 2, depth 40 cms.
14. A medium sized vase in dull red ware with vertical neck decorated with horizontal grooves, featureless oblique rim treated with dull red slip on both sides, of thin fine fabric, well fired. Layer 2, depth 35 cm.
15. A thick conical bowl of red ware with a slightly pedastalled base. Of fine fabric, treated with dull red slip on both sides. Layer 2, depth 40 cms.

7

CHRONOLOGY

The aim of excavation at Jhiri was to examine the habitational deposits of Early Man, search out for datable material like charcoal, charred bones, pigments etc. in stratified deposits and try to correlate the deposits with different layers of paintings so that the paintings could be dated. In almost all the sites in India, the tradition or rock paintings which originated in distant prehistoric past continued till the late historical times. The controversy regarding dating of various layers of paintings still persits as there is great distrust amongst the scholars about 'stylistic chronologies'. With the excavations at Jhiri, the physico-chemical analysis of wall pigments method, has now reached India as samples of colour pigments were collected from various levels of the habitational deposits and the painted surface for such analysis. When the results of chemical analysis of these pigments will be compared with the results of wall pigments, it would be possible to arrive at some scientific conclusions. Apart from colour pigments charcoal samples have also been collected and sent for C-14 dating.

As the method of scientific excavation is accepted as the most reliable for the purpose of dating, the sequence obtained at Jhiri are very valuable. The basal deposit contains non-geometric microliths without any pottery. This level is followed by geometric microliths, alongwith charred animal bones but without pottery From above the predominantly microlithic bearing levels slipped red ware alongwith a copper ring were recovered. The pottery belongs to the Chalcolithic period. The top most level yielded few sherds belonging to historical period and two uninscribed copper coins definitely datable to 3rd-4th century B.C. The occurance of datable coins clearly shows that these rock shelters, at least some of them, were under use during the later half of the first millennium B.C The depiction of caparisoned horses, row of well dressed soldiers holding swords and shields and other scenes indicate that though these shelters were not under occupation after 3rd-4th century B.C. but the later people definitely frequented them and left the evidence in the forms of paintings. As per the historical accounts available some of these shelters were occupied by the local chieftains who had left their mark in the form of grooves on the roof of rock shelter no. 10, which were created to divert the rain water from dripping down in the sheltered area.

The above chronological sequence shows that the deposits of Jhiri rock shelters had a continuous sequence right from Mesolithic period to historical times. The sequence of paintings on the walls even on 'stylistic grounds' show atleast five super impositions belonging to different periods On the basis of available evidence of sequences it could be stated that the occupants and frequnters to these rock shelters apart from leaving the evidences in the form of archaeological remains, also left the marks of their artistic abilities on the walls and roofs of these shelters. There is no doubt that these shelters were under occupation for the longest span by mesolithic folks who practised hunting-gathering economy and were yet to learn agricultural operations and pastoralism. Naturally bulk of the paintings belong to this period depicting mostly hunting scenes, moods of the animals and occasionally scenes from family life. A scene in R.S. No. 10 shows a masked man carrying a bow and three arrows. The arrows have been made by hafting atleast five microliths on each on a thin wooden stick (PI. XXXVIII).

The C-14 dates for microlithic deposits from Lekhama are 3560+ 105 (3600+110) B.P. The C-14 dates for the early microlithic deposit of Adamgarh is 7240+125 (7450+130) B.P. After the laboratory. analysis of charcoal samples and colour pigments from the excavations and the walls are known we would be able to to fix the absolute dates of the deposits at Jhiri and hopefully will be able to date the paintings.

8

DISCUSSION

The entire Vindhyan range and its off-shoots are dotted with innumerable natural rock-shelters. At Jhiri, the basal deposit contains Mesolithic industries, both non-geometrical and geomaterical. The geometrical tools parallel the tools found at Adamgarh and Bhimbetka The lower and middle levels are characterised by total absence of pottery whereas in the upper levels sherds of thick redware and few of rough gritty ware occur. Other material in mesolithic levels consist of stone hopscotches, fragments of animal bones, colour pigments and a grinder. The hopscotches are shaped out of course grained sand stone. To the south of Narmada are the well known rock shelters of the Mahadeo Hills, the most important of which are around Pachmarhi which are also very rich in microlithic industries. Hunter G.R.[1] excavated a few rock shelters at Pachmarhi. His report was published in 1935-36. V.S. Wakankar[2] conducted trial excavations in the rock shelters at Modi in Mandsore district of M.P. in the year 1959. The earliest occupants of these shelters probably belonged to Middle Stone Age The deposits above it yielded few scrapers, points, burins, retouched flakes, fluted cores, few triangles and one trapeze. Little above, more parallel sided blades and triangles and few lunates and trapezes were found. A stone anvil was also recovered alongwith a heap of haematite granules near which was lying a stone having a painted circle on it. The pigment of the haematite found in the deposit and of the painting above on the rock was the same. Middle levels yielded a fire place but no charcoal. Upper levels were associated with pottery, unslipped red were belonging to 10th to 13th century A.D. No bones were recovered from the excavation.

R.V. Joshi[3] excavated in and outside the rock-shelters at Adamgarh in Hoshangabad district of M.P. in 1962. He got a succession of deposits beginning from Early Stone Age (Acheulian) to Middle Stone Age and than to Late Stone Age. The microliths were geometric and associated with plain red ware. There was no non-pottery-bearing horizon or non-geometric horizon. The microliths were found embedded in the black clay which rested over the red lateritic deposit. The Early and Middle Stone Age tools were mostly recovered from outside the shelters. The black clay does not show any soil profile indicative of its *in situ* formation. The deposition appear to be due to wind action. Joshi thinks that may be throughout the period of microlithic habitation and perhaps even during the later periods wind activity was more intense and spread over a longer duration each year then at present. The most important features of the Adamgarh microlithic industry are:—

(i) Presence of the so-called geometric elements like triangles and trapezes;

(ii) Presence of pottery;

(iii) Frequent occurance of haematite nodules more or less in all the levels;

(iv) Occurance of animal bones and charcoal fragments practically throughout the deposits;

(v) Presence of ring stones in the upper level;

(vi) Presence of glass, iron objects and beads in the shallow deposits;

(vii) Limited occurance of Chalcolithic-type pottery and crested ridge flakes.

Near the surface Chalcolithic, Neolithic and Iron Age deposits were also encountered.

A large group of rock shelters similar to those at Jhiri occur on the northern bank of the Narmada at Bhimbetka (22° 30'N; 77° 37'E). Seven of these were excavated by V.N. Misra[4] and Wakankar. Here the basal deposit contains the Acheulian industries showing very advanced forms. Acheulian industries are succeeded by very rich Middle Paleolithic industries. At the top occurs the Mesolithic industry which is geometric in nature and parallels the tools found at Adamgarh. Other materials in mesolithic level consist of hammers, querns, rubbers and few perforated discs, all made largely on basalt. In the top most layer tiny sherds of plain red and grey wares occur in small numbers

At Kharwai the shelters excavated yielded microliths alongwith pottery. The courseness of the pottery indicates that the people belonged to the historical period who knew the use of iron. The rock shelters at Baniberi near Pachmarhi in Narsinghpur district of M.P. yielded microliths from top to bottom. As Shahadkarar the top most layer yielded pottery which belonged to the Gupta period and early medieval period. The middle levels alongwith few cores, flakes and finished microlithic tools yielded pottery belonging to Chalcolithic period. The lowest levels yielded microliths mainly consisting of unretouched blades, blunted blades and scrapers.

All these and many other rock shelter localities are famous for painting. The location of all these shelters and their mesolithic tool kit are very similar with Jhiri shelters. The location of the microlithic sites in these rock shelters in the Vindhya-Satpura region seems to have been governed by the occurance of such natural sheltered spots, perennial supply of spring water nearby and abundance of wild animals around.

At Jhiri the microlithic industry is based primarily on blades, although the flake and core components are not rare. The largest number of points, awls and crescents are made on blades. The flakes have been utilized mainly for scrapers and points, while the fluted blade cores have been used as scrapers. The average size of microliths at Jhiri varies from 28x14x5 to 16x5x2 mm.

The triangles and crescents could have been used as barbs for arrows or as component parts of a composite tool like the sickle or for making harpoons. The occurance of crescents is certainly an important aspect. Since its manufacture from a parallel sided blade involves the elaborate process of shaping and retouching, its presence shows some measure of technological knowledge. It serves both as a cutting tool and as a hunting implement depending on the form of mounting. The scrapers constitute about 5% of the total collection. There was dominant use of cores for making scrapers. Most of the core-scrapers are made on fluted cores. Awls and borers are generally used for boring bones to extract bone marrow. There presence in good number shows that the Mesolithic people at Jhiri after eating the flesh, used to extract bone-marrow by boring holes with bones in the extremities of bones, particularly the long bones. Scrapers were used for scraping flesh and fat from the animal. The occurance of large number of points indicates hunting economy. The blades found in largest numbers were used as cutting tools either singly or in composite form. These tools were used for both dismembering various parts of the animal and for removing flesh and then slicing them into small pieces.

The most striking features of the Jhiri microlithic assemblage are :—

(i) presence of non-geometric, non pottery horizon at the bottom;

(ii) presence of geometric elements like triangles and trapezes alongwith tiny fragment of charred animal bones;

(iii) frequent occurance of colour pigments more or less in all levels;

(iv) occurance of animal bones throughout the deposit;

(v) occurance of few bone tools shaped out of generally shafts;

(vi) occurance of charcoal fragments in the upper levels;

(vii) presence of stone hop-scotches of various sizes.

From the top levels pottery, generally slipped coarse red ware, belonging to historical period were recovered alongwith few microliths and two uninscribed cast copper coins datable to 3rd-4th century B.C. The succession of deposits at Jhiri clearly indicate that these rock shelters were either inhabited or frequented by man right from the Mesolithic times to very recent periods. This evidence is supported by the succession of paintings on the walls and roofs of these shelters, where atleast five super-impositions in different colours could be counted.

Tradition never dies. It changes alongwith the times. Even this day one of the rock-shelters at Jhiri is regularly visited on Makar-sankranti day and on other auspicious occasions, by the people from the nearly villages, who come and light fire inside the shelter. They believe that these shelters in the remote past gave shelter to their forefathers. The tribal populations around Jhiri is dominated by Gonds and Korkus. The walls of their wattle and daub huts are beautifully decorated with paintings in variety of colours, amongst which red, yellow and green dominate; depicting scenes from religious beliefs, day-to-day life and hunting-grazing etc. The medium of depiction has shifted from rock surfaces to the walls of huts. Detailed ethnological studies of these tribal traditions may help us in establishing the link between the past and the present.

FOOTNOTES

1. Hunter, G.R. Excavations at Pachmarhi, Nagpur University Journal, Nagpur, 1936.
2. Wakankar, V.S. *Prehistoric rock paintings of the Chambal Valley.* Paper delivered at the All India History Congress, 1959.
3. Joshi R.V. *Stone Age cultures of Central India,* Pune, 1978.
4. Misra, V.N. 'Prehistoric culture sequence of Bhimbetka' in *Prehistoric Man and his art in Central India,* Pune, 1970.

APPENDICES

APPENDIX 1

PALINOLOGICAL REPORT OF FIVE SAMPLES RECEIVED FROM INDIRA GANDHI NATIONAL CENTRE FOR THE ARTS, JANPATH, NEW DELHI

(i)	Nature of the sediments	:	Sandy/silty clay
(ii)	Colour of the sediment	:	Light brown-Brown
(iii)	Organic contents	:	Negligible
(iv)	Inorganic contents	:	Medium to small sized sand and silt
(v)	Sample weight taken for analysis	:	500 gms
(vi)	Pollen Preservation	:	Good
(vii)	Pollen Frequency	:	Sample no. 1 is rich both quantitatively and qualitatively as well. Whereas, sample nos. 2, 3, 4 and 5 are moderate in pollen content.
(viii)	Chemical processing		
	(a) KOH	:	Samples were first treated with 10% aqueous solutions and boiled for 5 minutes to deflocculate the matrix and to dissolve the extraneous material. Thereafter, several washings with distilled water were given and sieved.
	(b) HF	:	Fifteen days treatment was given in order to dissolve Silica.
	(c) HCl	:	To dissolve cutines/ suberines, etc.
	(d) Acetolysis	:	Mixture of acetic anhydride and conc. H_2SO_4 in the ratio of 9:1 was given for removing humic acid and colouration of pollen/ spore in golden brown.
	(e) Glycerine	:	To preserve macerals in 50% glycerine aqueous solution with a few drops of phenol.

(f) Polyvinyl Alcohol : To make the permanent slides.

(g) Pollen counts : 150-200 grains per samples.

(h) Photography : All important taxa have been photographed for documentation.

POLLEN ANALYTICAL RESULTS
(FIG. -15)

Sample No. 1: Is dominated by *Madhuca Indica* (Mahua) and co-dominated by *Azadirachta, Lagerstroemia*. Other tree taxa recorded in low frequency are *Terminalia, Symplocos* and Lannaea *grandis*.

The non-arboreal vegetation is dominated by grasses followed by *Caryophyllaceae, Strobilanthes, Chenopodiaceae, Celosia, Impatiends, Lamiaceae, Justicia, Cyperaceae* and ferns. The most significant feature of the sample is the presence of *Cerealia* pollen grains to the tune of 3.5% of the total assemblage.

Sample No. 2: It records slightly low frequency *of Madhuca Indica* whereas *Azadirachta* has improved in its values as compared to the preceding sample.

Amongst the non-arboreals *Chenopodiaceae, Strobilanthes, Asteraceae, Celosia* and grasses have improved considerably but, *Caryohyllaceae* has reduced.

Sample No. 3: In this sample the values for *Madhuca indica* regained and other arboreal constituents like *Terminalia, Azadirachta, Salmalia, Buchanania, Oleaceae, Moraceae, Rosaceae* remains subdued.

The ground vegetation remained dominated by grasses, *Caryophyllaceae, Celosia, Ranunculaceae, Cyperaceae* and ferns. The farming activities seems to be activated as evidenced by higher values of *Cerealia* pollen.

Sample No. 4: *Madhuca Indica* has reduced substantially whereas, *Azadirachta* has improved. The other tree taxa present in low values are *Anogeissus, Oleaceae,* etc.

The non-arboreal vegetation is marked ever high values of *Celosia* and *Asteraceae* whereas, grasses remained more or less same as in sample No. 3 although *Cerealia* pollen has reduced. Ferns also recorded enhanced values.

Sample No. 5: *Madhuca indica and Azadirachta* increased to attain 24% and 14%, respectively. The other tree taxa recorded are *Lagerstroemia* and *Oleaceae*

The ground vegetation has reduced remarkably recording low values of *Strobilanthes, Caryophyllaceae, Celosia, Ranunculaceae* and *Chenopodiaceae.* The grasses-and ferns also reduced relatively.

INTERPRETATION

The pollen studies of sample Nos. 1-3 has revealed that Tropical moist climatic condition prevailed upon.

The study of Sample No. 4 has envisaged the reduction in the precipitation under the tropical climatic regimes which encouraged the proliferation of *Celosis* and *Asteraceae.*

The study of Sample No. 5 denotes the increase in the precipitation providing a clue of Tropical moist environment where-in *Madhuca indica* and *Azadirachta indica* colonised forming a forest.

EXPLANATION OF PLATES

(Plate-XXXIX)

1. *Madhuca indica* (Mahua)
2. *Azadirachta indica*
3. *Lagerstroemia parviflora*
4. *Acacia* sp.
5. *Strobilanthes* sp.
6. *Lannaea grandis*
7. *Justicia simplex*
8. *Cyperaceae*
9. *Ranunculaceae*
10. *Monolete* fern spore
11. *Trilete* fern spore
12. *Poaceae*
13. *Buchanania lanzan*
14. *Caryophyllaceae*

15-16. *Asteraceae*

17. *Impatients* sp.

18-19. *Terminalia* sp.

20-21. *Celosia* sp.

22. *Trilete* fern spore

1-6. Fungal spores

7. *Concentricystis rubinus*

8-15. Fungal spores

16. Unidentified

17. Fungal spore

18. *Curvularia* sp.

19-22. Fungal spores

23. *Fungal hypha*

24-26. Fungal spores

27. *Finns* sp.

28. *Poaceae*

29. Unidentified pollen

30-31. Fungal spores

APPENDIX-2

PRELIMINARY STUDY OF ROCK ART IN JHIRI, NEAR BHOPAL, MADHYA PRADESH, INDIA.

MISSION REPORT OF THE FRENCH TEAM LED BY MICHEL LORBLANCHET FROM DECEMBER 7TH TO 20TH 1993.

The joint research in the decorated caves of Jhiri, situated 40 kms south of Bhopal, was carried out by the Indian and French teams, led by Dr. A.K. Sharma, Y Mathpal, and Michel Lorblanchet (Directeur de Recherches au CNRS). Our thanks are due to the Indira Gandhi National Centre for the Arts (New Delhi), and the Cultural Service of the French Embassy in particular the centre for Human Sciences (New Delhi), for making this collaboration possible and so enjoyable.

This international and multi-disciplinary research project is only in its initial stages. A first field mission was carried out by the French team between December 7th and 20th 1993 while the Indian team also started on its research.

The French team was composed of three groups, each with its own speciality:

- a group to record the paintings (M Lorblanchet, J Lorblanchet, D Molez)
- a topographer, G Bariviera, to establish the map of the shelter and the contour map of the decorated wall. Thanks to The alliance Francaise in Bhopal which gave support in the field, G. Bariviera was assisted by a young indian student, Rahul Vaidya
- experts in the conservation of paintings, Mr. J Brunet and P Vidal, from the Laboratoire des Monuments Historiques in Champs-sur-Marne.

First Recordings of the Paintings

With only two weeks at our disposal, the Fresh team had to be content with the following operations:

(a) To begin recording section A3 of shelter No. 10, corresponding to the most richly decorated one of this central shelter where the largest collection of rock art in the Jhiri cliff is to be found (Fig 22)

(b) To take the first samples of pigment from the rock paintings for physical analysis (Figs. 28, 29)

(c) To make supplementary recordings to a bird in section B2 and an ox in section B3 of shelter No. 10 and a small group of figures in shelter No. 9 (Figs. 28, 30).

(d) To draw up an overall map of shelters 10 and 11 (Fig. 16)

(e) To begin drawing up the contour map of the decorated wall of shelter No. 1 0 using a laser theodolite (Fig 19, 20).

(f) To study the state of conservation of the paintings in all the decorated shelters of the Jhiri cliffs (work carried out by Mrs Vidal and Brunet, report enclosed)

In addition to this, we were able, thanks to Dr. A.K. Sharma, to visit villages near the Jhiri cliffs where the houses contain mural paintings. A comparative study with the local rock art will soon be undertaken in collaboration with Indian ethnologists.

Recording of the paintings of section A3 in shelter No10 (Fig. 21)

Method used:

An initial recording was made of a zone 4, 5m long by 1, 50m high, comprising about fifty figures. The following procedure was followed in recording;

(1) Photographs were taken of the paintings in black and white and in colour. For the black and white photos, different filters were used to highlight certain hues and thus make visible figures that were almost obliterated. The films were developed each evening and enlargements made in a makeshift drarkroom in the bathroom of our hotel in Bhopal.

(2) Tracing over photographs was done in the shelters, in front of the originals with constant reference to the paintings. This method avoids contact with the painted rock surface which could otherwise be damaged. Enlargement of the photographs can be made either life size or half size, as required.

Moreover, using photographs taken with filters which accentuate the contrasts makes it easier to read and draw the figures.

Most of the paintings being at a height of between 1, 50m and 2, 20m, it was necessary to build scaffolding in order to examine them at ease.

(3) An initial colour recording, life size, was made on the site. It was presented at New Delhi in the IGNCA on 22nd December 1993. (After completing it, this life size recording could be used for exhibitions).

The drawing was then reduced and copied out neatly in an easy to handle format making further additions and corrections simpler for the work still to be carried out on site.

First information brought by the recordings:

(1) The recording of the figures has enabled the motifs to be deciphered and counted. 51 figures have thus been noted for A3 (Fig. 21). They have been numbered from left to right. There are 19 horsemen, 10 soldiers, 9 miscellaneous human figures, 8 animal figures (horses, a stag No. 1, and a bird No.39), one object, probably a standard (No.26) and 4 indeterminable objects. Other elements, obliterated or hidden beneath the recorded motifs will most probably come to light in the course of the study.

The largest figures are found at the top of the panel; the horses Nos.10 and 29 measure 75cm and 68 cm respectively, whereas at the bottom of the frieze the figures measure an average of 20 to 30 cm.

Above pannel A3 the paintings on he vault, several meters above the ground, are even bigger, some measuring over 1m.

(2) Precise observations on the style of the figurations were noted down;

The drawings fall into the category of "intellectual realism" where the artist depicts what he knows of the subject, rather than "visual realism", a reproduction of what he can see. The drawings are extremely stereotyped, with a repetition of the same graphic conventions. The horses all stand on hindlegs, the front legs slightly bent without touching the ground, a convention representing movement and aggresivity.

There is a constant use of merging planes; the horse's legs are never drawn one over the other but side by side, the same goes for the ears. Whereas the horse's head is drawn in profile, the two eyes are represented full on. The rider's legs are often missing, but when they are represented, they are shown in profile, although the body is drawn full face, arms held out in a conventional position.

The proportions of the animals are constant; hind-quarters bigger than fore-quarters. As a rule, the horses seem to have been drawn over and over again, especially at the base of the frieze, giving the silhouettes a stiff, clumsy, almost geometrical aspect (Nos. 14, 16, 21, 22). Repeating the outline seems to have progressively diminished its realism; for many of the horses in the lower zone three humps representing the ears and the tuft of hair surmount a head which has become too small (Nos 13, 14, 16,. 22). These horses have been copied time after time, not all the motifs are original figures representing a precise reality.

Transparency is another graphic device used on this pannel. The horses' anatomy remains visible despite the caps and harnesses which sometimes cover them.

The unity of this group however, does not hide the fact that there are two different styles of horses.

One style, at the top of the pannel, is represented by a series of large, elegant horses filled in with white. Their bodies are well proportioned and graceful. (Nos.8, 9, 10, 11, 13, 14 27, 29, 43, 41).

The other style, at the bottom of the frieze, a small number of heavier, thicker horses, with a big body, short legs and thick neck (Nos. 18, 23, 30, 31). These are the oldest as they lie beneath the big white horses.

(3) Recording work also revealed that, over a length of 4.5 m, the composition of the frieze consists of two groups of horsemen, moving towards each other. The hourses, half-reared up, carry heavy harnesses; they are often armoured and have richly decorated blankets over them, the saddle forms a curve on either side of the rider. One of the horses on the right (Nos.41) even has a kind of canopy under which two people are sheltered.

The decorations inside the horses are so rich that they could represent body paintings (Nos.9, 10, 13, 27 etc.).

The whole seems to represent a battle scene in which two armies are confronted An imaginary line divides the pannel in two halves, on either side of which the horses and their riders face opposite directions (Figs. 23, 24,). This vertical line separates horses 10, 11 and 19 from horses 29, 27 and 18. In the lower part of the pannel, where the figures are smaller and more numerous, the dividing line is less obvious. Here the two sides are partially overlapping, showing that the battle is being engaged i.e.; horses 21 and 22 overlap, although heading in opposite directions.

The two armies present seem to possess similar equipment, there are armoured horses on either side. Many of th riders and foot soldiers wear helmets. On the left hand side, however, the riders are mainly armed with spears whereas on the right they carry swords and sometimes shields (Nos.27). The helmets or headdresses are of several types which we will discuss further on. Some of the head ornaments are difficult to classify, i.e., rider No.31 with his long dangling ears. Some of the objects drawn could be standards (Nos. 7, 26, 41).

In the two groups the foot soldiers follow the riders, Nos. 15 on the left and Nos. 32, 34, and 45 on the right. They are armed with bows and swords and sometimes carry two or three arrows in their hand (Nos.3 and 45). The riders, however,-never carry bows, but spears and swords.

Two archers at the top left-hand corner pose a problem. They are painted in an orange-brown pigment quite different from the other warriors and occupy a marginal position on the pannel. They are moving towards the left, so would thus seem to belong to the right-hand side armed group, even if they are separated from it. They closely resemble the foot soldiers Nos.32 and 34 on the right, they are in the same attitude, of the same morphology, carry the same weapons and most significantly wear the same helmet, a sort of hat with an upturned brim worn slightly on the right of the head. Such similarities enable us to establish a link between these figures.

At the top of the pannel on the left, another foot soldier carrying a shield and sword in his belt (No. 5) is moving left and may also belong to the army on the right although drawn in an orange colour quite different from that used for the men on the right.

(4) The recordings led to the start of a typological study of the weapons and costumes depicted which remains to be developed.

There are two different kinds of sword (Fig 26);

- straight swords generally with triangular blades (Nos.27, 30, 45). Some of the blades seem to be oval, bigger at the top. (No. 21).
- curved swords (No. 14, 32) resembling a simitar, some of which have notch on the side.

These curved swords and swords with a notched side are known in rock art in the Bhopal area, especially in many of the shelters in Bhimbetka (Y. Mathpal: *Prehistoric rock paintings of Bhimbetka* 1984, p. 209. E. Neumayer: *Lines on stones, the prehistoric Rock Art of India, 1993* p. 211-212 figs 568 and 569) and in Naryaoli and Adamgarh (S. K. Pandey: *Indian Rock Art,* Delhi 1993, p. 210).

The soldiers are holding their swords either in the left or right hands. Some of them carry them at their belt (Nos.3 and 45). Some even seem to have placed them in a sheath on the horse's chest (No. 21).

The spears (Fig 26) have roughly triangular points, sometimes irregular or slightly oval. A sphere can sometimes be seen at the base of the shaft (No. 31).

There are also a great variety of shields (Fig 26): some are round with spoke-like decoration (Nos.5, 27). Others have a curved shape deriving from a rectangle or oval (Nos.15, 32, 41). Round and curved shields like these are known in Rock Art in Bhimbetka

The bows are simple in shape (Fig 26), but on some the sinew seems to be attached to the wood by means of an extra cord (Nos.3 and 36) which concords with the bows so frequently found in the Mahadeo Hills and which Neumayer describes as follows: "The bow is frequently shown detailed enough to understand that the sinew was prepared from a bamboo-splinter, which was fastened to the bow by a flexible string." (Neumayer 1993, p; 228). The arrows are held in clusters of two or three (Nos.3 and 45) they are out of proportion with the archers and have a triangular flanged point (Nos.45) and a notched base with feathers.

- On the right-hand edge of the pannel two soldiers (Nos.36 and 40) have an arc and rounded sticks, probably clubs (figs. (21, 22,) These orange figures in a strange style probably do not belong to the war scene[2]

- In detailing the soldiers' costume it is necessary to mention the shape of the heads (Fig 27). The rounded faces are conventionally divided in two by a vertical line either side of which are placed the eyes (like the horses' heads). Three main shapes of head are identifiable:

- Round spoke filled heads ((Nos. 21, 41, 44)

- Laterally developed heads, evoking a bonnet or headdress (Nos.6, 9, 13, 14). Head No.45 is included in this category because of the ornaments dangling on the side.

- Heads wearing a hat, probably a helmet (Nos. 2, 3, 11, 32, 34)

We also noted that several figures wear a sort of scarf over their shoulder (Nos.3 and 34) perhaps revealing the presence of a quiver and most wear clothing forming an X on the chest.

They wear trousers, not skirts, except for the two soldiers Nos. 36 and 40 who are in any case painted in a different style and colour (orange).

The horses' harnesses (Fig 27), reins coming from the mouth of the animal crossing the back of the head and held in the riders' hands, indicate the use of the bit However, spurs are absent, as is true with all Indian Rock Art. The ornaments of the horses protective blankets, as well as the shape of the saddle, are interesting elements, like the canopy on Horse Nos.41, which will be further investigated.

Of the three instruments (Fig 27) interpreted as standards (Nos. 7, 26, 41) one is undoubtedly carried by a foot soldier, No. 7, whose head is protected by a helmet. Further investigation into the frieze will reveal whether for Nos.26 and 41 they are attached to the horse's neck or carried by foot soldiers barely visible (this second hypothesis seems to be plausible).

However it may be, the type of standard present in Jhiri is identical to those found in the historical period in Bhimbetka.

(5) Recording has furnished a number of indications concerning the superposition of hues.;

- Our initial research has enabled us to establish that there are several pictural phases (figs. 23, 24, 25).

- (a) The battle scene consists of at least two successive stages which correspond to the two styles of horses previously described (big elegant white horses and smaller thicker red or yellow ones).

It may well be that the first battle scene was painted over a whitish base covering older paintings. This now creamy coloured base would seem to persist in the upper part and on the right of the pannel. However, we wish to continue investigation into this point as the accumulation of white figures over one surface can lead to the impression of a "base coat¿. Further recordings and pigment analysis will provide the necessary information.

- (b) Paintings older than the battle scene are visible on the sides of the pannel and between the elements of the war scene (Fig 25).

On the far left is a yellow stag, its antlers decorated with round shapes (No 1), in the lower part a small white animal (No. 12), a badly conserved red human figures (No 51) traces of white figures (No.49), another small white animal (No.25), a white human figure (No. 28) and on the far right, several white figures, one of which looks like a pig or boar (No.35), two white people and a bird (a peacock?) (Nos.33, 37, 39). A number of these white figures predating the riders seem to correspond to the paintings on the vault.

Again on the right, two orange soldiers or hunters (Nos. 40, 36) wear a kind of skirt (spool-shaped body) and carry an arc and what seems to be a club. A small person in a skirt can be seen on the extreme right-hand limit near a small human face.

In the upper part of the pannel, the remains of black marks belong, either to old figures, or to the unfinished drawing of a big horse (No.29) in which case it could be the remains of the rider.

Further recordings will concentrate on distinguishing these motifs underneath the paintings of the historic period.

The recordings have also revealed that the majority of the historic paintings have been renovated and redrawn in a repetitive manner. On many of the horses the two superimposed hues are visible, vermilion and wine-red.

- Horse No.9 was first drawn with wine-red pigment, the interior of the animal being daubed with a yellowish cream coloured pigment. Then the animal was entirely redrawn in vermilion following the outer contour. This procedure is most visible on the reins, neck and head The man too has been redrawn in red. Then two vertical white bars have been drawn across this figure in a thick pasty substance. Lastly flaking has occurred.
- Horse No. 11 has also been redrawn using two different reds; there is a double line to its chest.
- At the top, the large white horse No. 10 has been painted in yellowish brown with the tail and rider, over a surface already oriented in creamy yellow. Then white filling-in has covered over the previous tail. The rider has been surrounded in white then the outline of the horse's back and legs has been redrawn in wine-red and the line of its belly lowered.

Lastly come two vermilion splashes on the belly and chest (star shapes). A vermilion slash has also been made at the base of the tail.

- Horse No. 31 and its rider holding a spear were first painted in brown then redrawn in dark wine-red, which explains the three hind legs.

- Figure No.20 is a foot soldier first painted in brownish wine-red then entirely redrawn in vermilion. A white horse and its rider was then superimposed over it. This detail alone is proof that the frieze has undergone successive transformations.
- Other redrawings are visible on figure No. 14, comprising two slightly overlapping superimposed horses and riders. Here the same motif has been redrawn in almost the same place.
- No. 41 and 42 also reveal two drawings of horses partially superposed, one only with red outline, the other with both outline and white filling. The frequency with which the paintings have been redrawn underlines the importance of physico-chemical analysis of pigments.

Start of the Contour Map of the wall

In order to understand better the way in which the paintings fit into the space, and how they use the rock forms (cavities, protuberances, vault etc.) a general map of the painted wall, the back of the shelter, has been undertaken. Another aim of this contour map is to , reproduce at will any section of the decorated wall. It enables a facsimile (3D replica) to be made of the decorated cave. Thus, this type of map has a dual purpose, scientific and museographic (Fig 19, 20).

Work has started on the map but is not finished.

The apparatus used is a TOPCON laser theodolite. It is very sophisticated piece of equipment with an integrated computer which memorizes the data recorded in the field.

Some 2600 measurements were taken during the two weeks spent in the field. The points measured were situated on a blanket photograph of the decorated wall.

Back in France, the map was drawn up by computer. This must now be checked on site and the measurements must be continued in order to complete the wall map, especially in section B, which remains to be recorded. The points of measurement have to be multiplied in order to obtain a precise drawing of the figures.

In the course of this first mission, pannel D5, main pannel of shelter No. 11, recorded by Dr. Y Mathpal, was mapped using the theodolite.

Analysis of the wall pigments:

To further archaeological research we carried out the first of a series of samples of pigments taken from the figures being studied. To start with as a test, we only took 7 samples (Fig 28, 29)

The amount of material removed for each sample is so small that it leaves no visible trace on the paintings. In this way analyses can, if necessary, be renewed without damage to the paintings. The problems encountered during the recording phase determined where the samples were taken from.

These problems which guide analysis arose for the following points:

(a) The composition of the green pigment of a human figure in shelter No. 9, which could lead to dating. This figure belongs to the "green dancer" type, which Wakankar and most Indian specialists attribute to the paleolithic period. Direct dating of one of these ancient figures would provide precise elements as to the origins of Indian Rock Art (Fig. 28).

(b) The successive renovations of the riders (Fig 29). Analysis will enable confirmation of the use of different pigments when the drawings were successively repainted. Three samples (No. 2, 3 and 4) were taken from horses 9 and 11, in particular from the drawing with different colours (wine red and vermillion). A comparison will also be made between the white filling of horse No.9 and the cream colour surrounding this horse, in order to check whether a cream background was applied before painting the riders (samples No. 5 and 6).

(c) The 7th sample was taken from black traces (No. 50) above the unfinished horse No.29 (Fig 14). Are these traces charcoal which can be dated? or are they are part of figure No.29 (a rider)? or even older?

(d) Lastly Dr. A.K. Sharma has sent us nodules of red ochre colouring which he discovered in the archaeological levels of the Panther shelter during his excavations.

We have sent these samples to be analysed in the same way as the wall pigments.

Analysis of these ochre nodules is of the greatest importance as it can reveal traces of minerals in the hematite which will be used as markers and could thus be retraced in the wall pigments of the same or nearby shelters. In this way pigment analysis could establish a link between the archaeological levels and the paintings, providing yet another means of dating the wall paintings.

The physicist, Mr. Michel Labeau of the Ecole Nationale Superieure de Physique et Institute Polytechnique de Grenoble (France) is in charge of all the analyses carried out with scanning electron microscope (SEM), X-ray microanalysis and X-ray diffraction.

Mr. Labeau has communicated the initial results obtained from samples Nos. 1 to 4. These are only incomplete indications which will be further developed: the other samples and the nodules discovered during Mr. A.K. Sharma's excavations are next to be analysed.

Three essential conclusions arise from Mr. Labeau's initial analyses:

(1) The existence *of organic matter* in the green pigment of the dancer in shelter No.9.

(2) The thick white substance of the bars crossing the riders Nos. 9 and 11 consists essentially of Calcium.

(3) No explanation has yet been found for the different hues (wine-red and vermilion) used to draw and redraw the horses, particularly horse No.9. It could be due to a more diluted form of the same colouring or to a different composition, more analyses are needed.

Although incomplete and provisional, these results are very important:

- they reveal that the green pigment can be radiocarbon dated. The organic phase (containing Carbon) present in the pigment remains to be identified.
- they show that the thick white paint of the final elements (vertical bars) is probably a Calcium Carbonate, i.e. a substance commonly used today in daily Indian life, confirming the recent addition of these traces.

Further analyses, in particular using X-ray diffraction, in order to identify the phases present in the pigments, requires more samples to be taken.

The next mission in Jhiri will thus aim to bring back more samples in the hope of obtaining a direct dating of the first wall paintings in India (green human figures).

The report given by Mr. Michel Labeau:

First Analyses of the pigments of the Jhiri Shelters Near Bhopal, India.

Sample No.l, green figure of shelter No.9:

The appearance of the sample is different from that of the other samples. With the naked eye it looks like green tinted translucent plates. After flattening it with a spatula it has a smooth shining aspect.

At low magnification (X200) the electron (MEB) microscope reveals at laminated structure with plates of a few tenths of millimeters in length. With a high magnification the surface of these plates shows a topography full of bowl shaped hollows of 2-10 microns in diameter. On the surface of these plates a number of grains are dispersed, whose form and dimension remind one of those of the other samples (0.5-5 microns)

The analysis of the whole sample shows the presence of a majority of silicon, of Calcium, Sulphur, Iron and Chromium and a trace of Potassium:

Si:56% Ca:15% Fe:14% S:7% Cr:3% K:5%

The analysis of the plates, the dispersed grains being excluded, reveals no constituent and therefore shows that the plates are formed of light elements (i.e. with low atomic weight) and probably correspond to an organic phase, whereas the dispersed grains probably correspond to mineral phases.

Local analyses have been carried out on several grains scattered on the surface of the plaques and show the presence of:

- phases with Silicium, Potassium and Iron
- phases containing Iron, Chromium and Nickel with a bit of Silicium:

Fe: 69% Cr: 18% Ni: 7% Si:6%

In conclusion, the pigment is made of a phase formed of light elements probably organic and of dispersed grains constituating mineral phases, some containing Iron, Chromium and Nickel, may be giving the green colouring to the pigment.

Sample No.2: *White paint on the hoof of the horse No. 11:*

The image obtained with the (MEB) electron microscope is the same as that of most of the pigment grains and agglomerated grains without particular morphology

The analysis of the whole sample shows that it consists mainly of Calcium with a bit of Silicium, Sulphur and perhaps Chlorine.

Ca:91% S:4% Sl:4% Cl:1%

Sample No.3 *lower strap on the neck of the horse No. 9 :*

The image is as usual: grains and agglomerates of 0.5 to 3 microns. The global analysis shows that Calcium is the majority. Sulphur, Iron, Silicium and traces of Aluminium and perhaps Potassium are also present:

Ca:60% S:26% Fe:7% Si:5% AL:2%

Sample No.4: *forehead of the horse No. 9 :*

Same image as the previous one with a greater range of the sizes of the grains: 0.5 to 10 microns.

The global analysis shows that Calcium is the majority. Sulphur, Iron, Silicium and Aluminium traces are also present.

Local analyses have been carried out on several grains. They reveal:

- the existence of phases containing Silicium and Iron
- and phases containing Calcium and Sulphur which could be Calcite CaCo3, Anhydrite SO4Ca, or Gypsum SO4Ca. 2H20. This remains to be verified and to be correlated to the geological environment.

13th july 1994
Michel Labeau
LMGP Institut National Polytechnique de Grenoble

The wall paintings in the villages neighbouring the decorated shelters in Jhiri.

Dr. A. K. Sharma took us to different villages in the neighbourhood of Jhiri, particularly the Korku tribe, having painted or sculpted the house walls. The ethnographical context of Jhiri rock art is most interesting.

Comparison could be made between the art of the shelters and that of the present day houses: age old traditions may survive in the wall art, bringing light to the interpretations of the latest paintings in the shelters. Some of the figures of the rock art in the sites we studied would seem to be extremely recent.

Amongst the most spectacular wall paintings, those in a house situated only a few hundred meters from shelter No. 10 are particularly noteworthy (Photo 20).

According to the explanation given to Dr. A. K. Sharma by the owner, these red, black and white paintings illustrate the festival of "Greenliness" named RAKHI and HARIYALI. These paintings are drawn each year during the rainy season (August) by young nubile boys, at the time when the crops turn green. Their aim is to celebrate the forces of nature so that the fruit come up to the expectation of the flowers, so that the harvest will be good and the young boys grow up to become full-blown adults. One scene in particular shows a man pierced by a bowman's arrows, lying on the ground: the symbol of the evil spirit vanquished by the village

Shaman: the triumph of good over evil. The image of the peacock on the same pannel is a symbol of prosperity.

These mural paintings are redrawn during the monsoon. One wonders if rock art too was a seasonal activity.

In collaboration with Indian ethnologists we would like to participate in future research in depth into the traditional mural paintings, their recording and the study of their relation with rock art.

Conclusions and content of the next Mission.

The first mission to study the rock art in the Jhiri shelters was very short. The French team only stayed a fortnight on the site, insufficient time to study such a rich collection.

The objectives set for the study were as follows:

(1) To show the continuity in the use of the site and to identify the different periods of the paintings drawn or superimposed on the rock.

(2) To characterize the pigments and date the different phases of the paintings, in particular the green figures belonging to the beginning of rock art in India.

(3) To study the most recent paintings and compare the rock art of the shelters with the present day murals in the neighbouring villages.

(4) To study the state of conservation of the rock art (c.f. enclosed report by Mrs Brunet and Vidal)

The French team's first mission in Jhiri recorded fifty eight figures in the most richly decorated zone of the site. The recordings have brought information concerning the superimposition of the figures, the type of weapons represented, the pigments used and the successive redrawings of the paintings.

Pigment analysis has confirmed the possibility of direct dating on the oldest figures.

The topographical study of the site has been undertaken: not only have maps of shelters Nos. 10, 11 and 12 been drawn, but a contour map of the decorated shelter has also been undertaken. This type of map has a scientific, and museographic importance (for replica making).

The state of conservation has been identified. (Mrs Brunet and Vidal)

The programme for the future field mission is as follows:

(1) To continue the research and recording of the paintings of shelters No. 7 (the panther shelter excavated by Mr. A. K. Sharma), No. 10 and No. 14 in Jhiri.

(2) To collect further samples of pigment for analysis and dating.

(3) To continue the topographical recording of the shelter map and complete the contour map of the decorated walls.

(4) In order to compare the two, to study and record some of the painted panels of the famous shelters on the Kathotia site on the other side of the valley, a few kilometers from Jhiri.

(5) To participate in the study of the relation between local mural art and rock art. We would particularly like to carry out recordings of the murals in order to compare these with rock art (with an additional study of the pigments used in both cases). The meaning of these murals ought to be studied by an Indian ethnologist.

This mission should take place in 1995; The French team would stay at the site for 4 to 5 weeks.

Collaboration with the Indian team is indispensable, in particular with Drs A.K. Sharma and Y. Mathpal, specialists in this field. Dr Sharma should continue his excavations in Jhiri and Kathotia in order to date occupation of the shelters being studied. Dr Mathpal should continue his participation in the recording of the paintings in Jhiri and Kathotia: his method of recording being particularly interesting (a possibility of comparing methodologies). His knowledge of Indian rock art is most useful.

We would like to express our warmest thanks to Dr Kapila Vatsyan and Dr. Saraswati of the IGNCA (New Delhi), to Mr I 'Attache Culturel de L 'Ambassade de France in New Delhi, to Dr O. Guillaume, Director of the CSH New Delhi, to Mr le Directeur de l'Alliance Francaise in Bhopal, to Mr Riffault (SLOM-ESSlLOR-Paris) to Mrs B Sainte Marie and Ph. Polibarbe in Toulose, for the invaluable help they have brought to the work of the French team.

Michel Lorblanchet
Directeur de Recherches au CNRS
(UMR 9933-Bordeaux)
Roc des Monges
46200-Saint Sozy-France. (Tel 65 32 28 45)

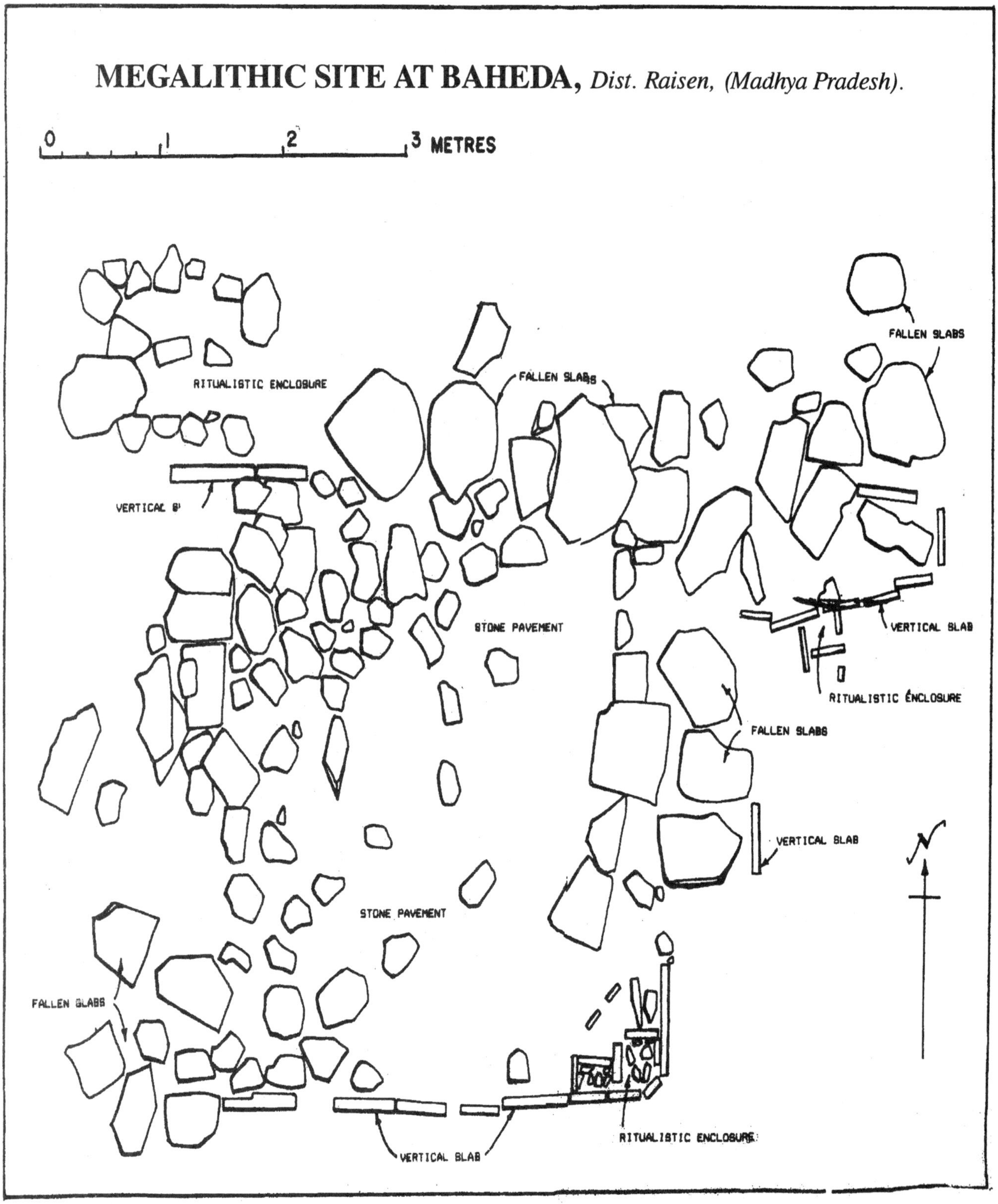

Fig. 15. Baheda-Megalithic site.

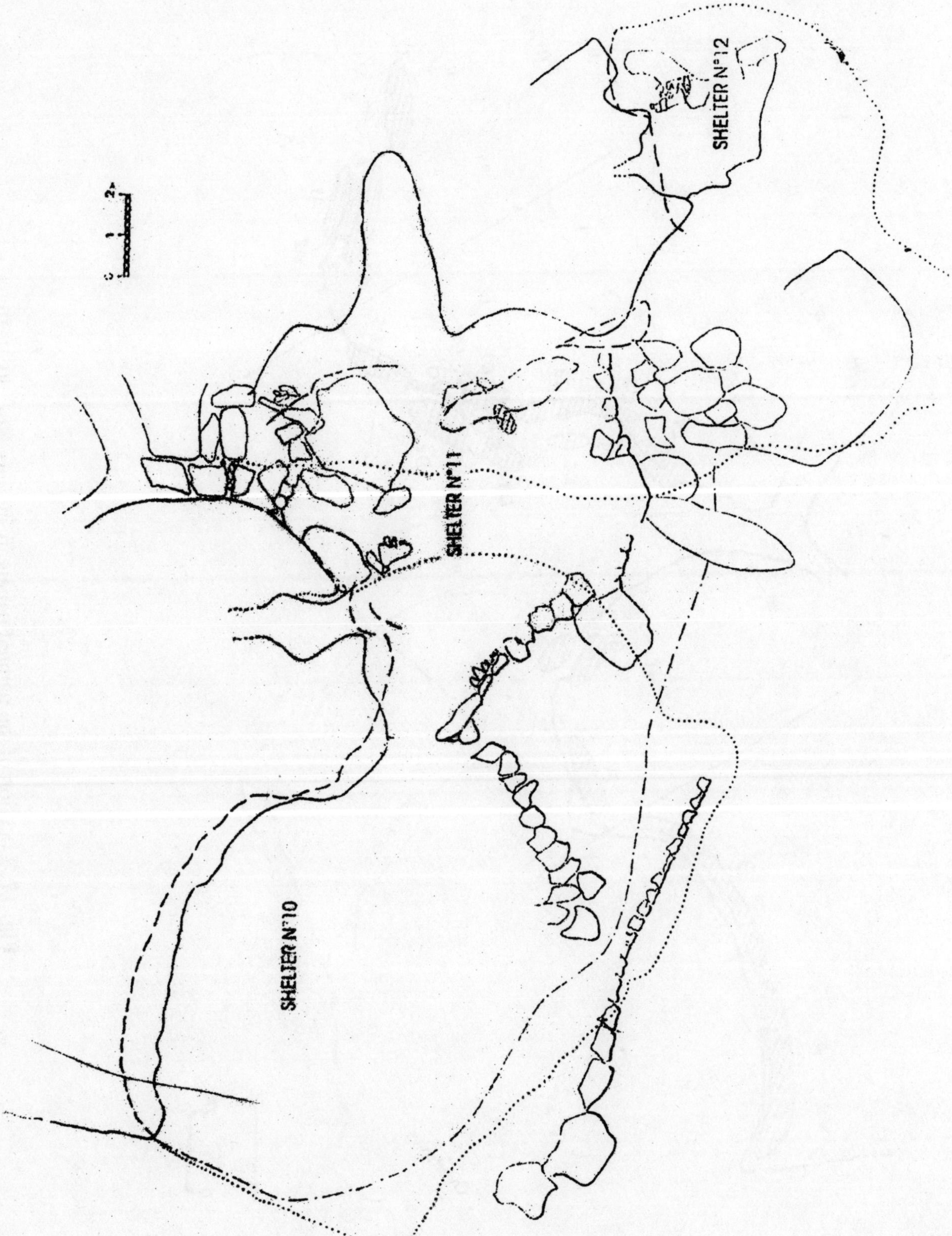

Fig. 16. Map of painted rock-shelters Nos. 10, 11, 12.

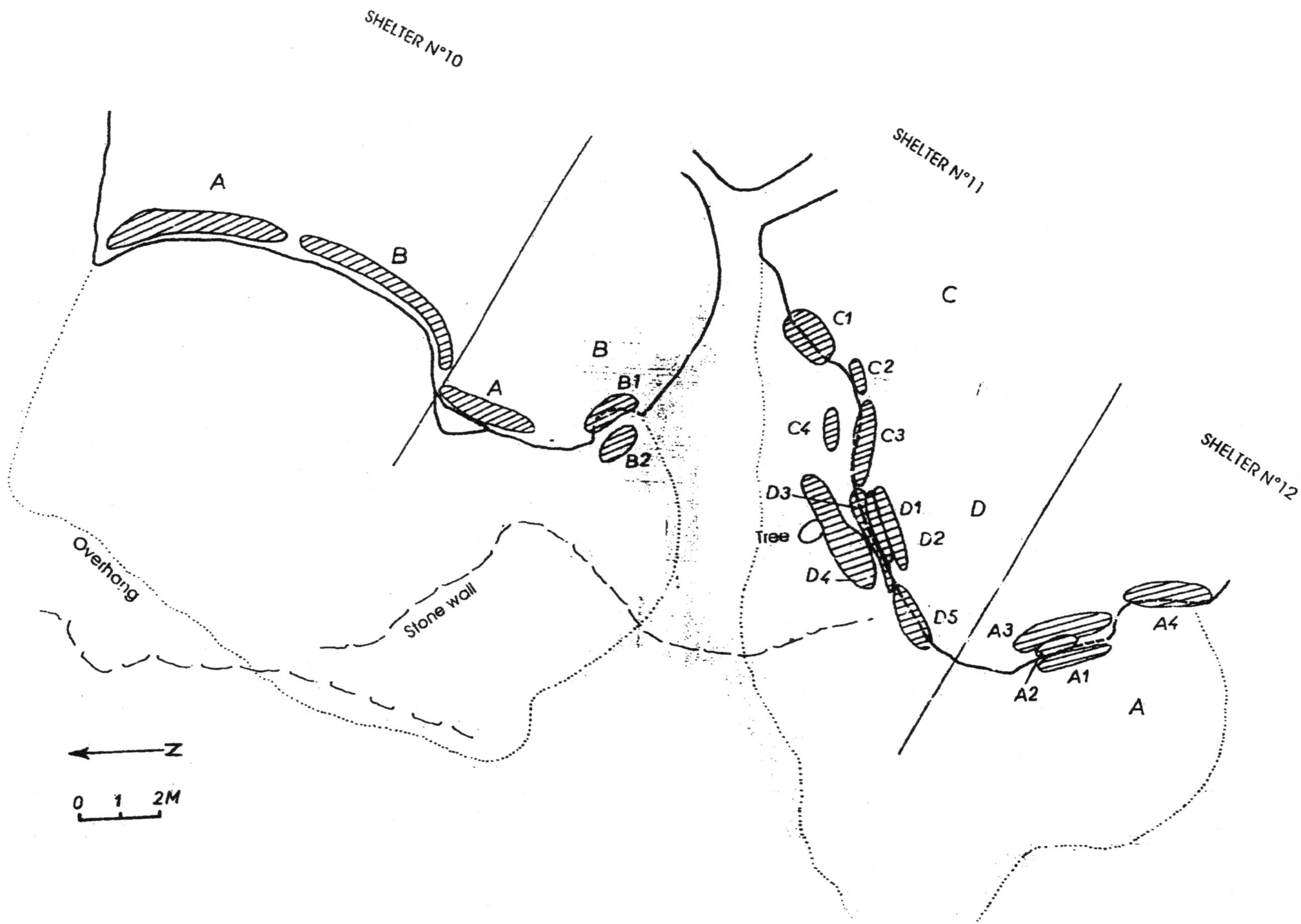

Fig. 17. Location of the painted panels in shelters Nos. 10, 11, 12.

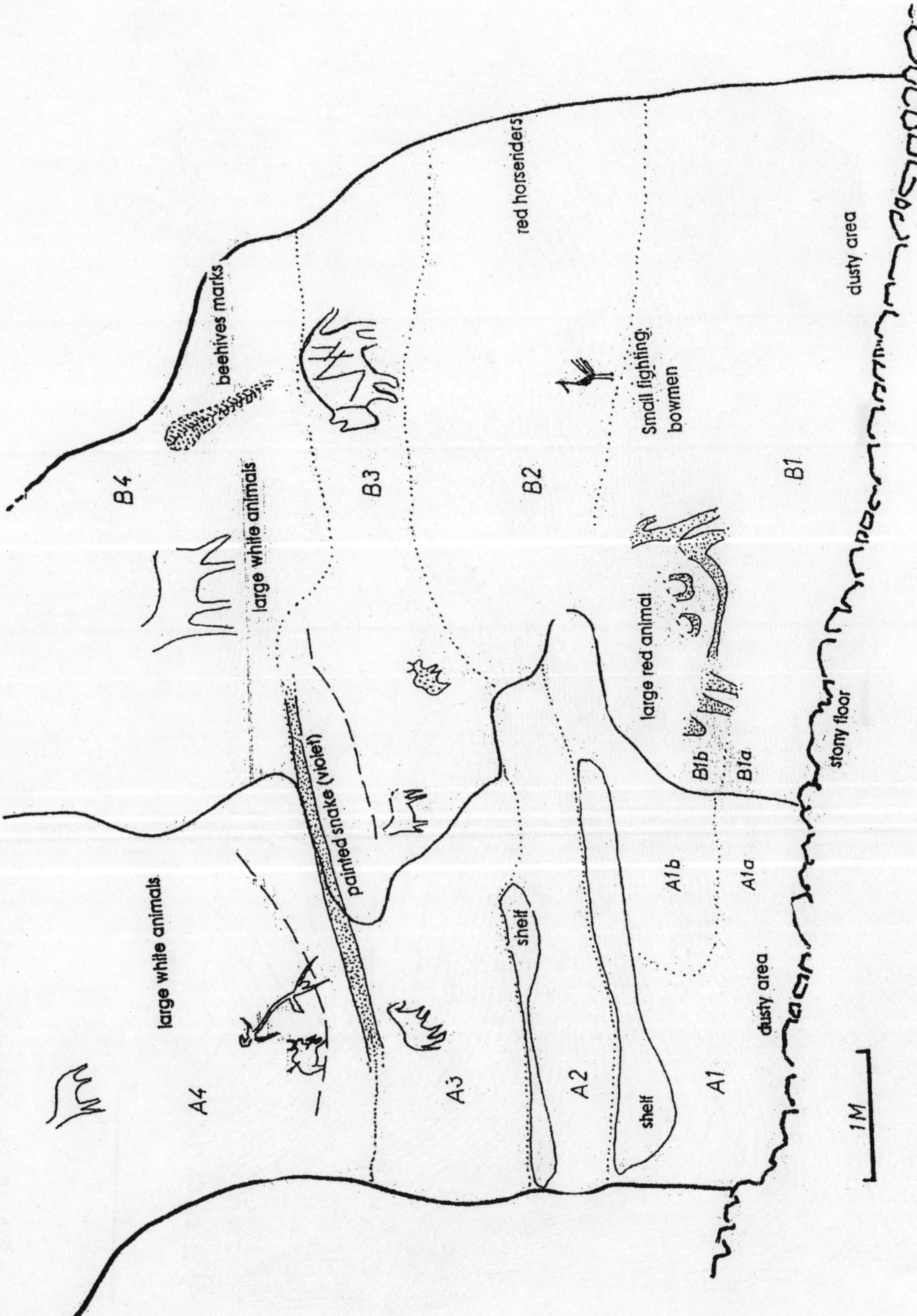

Fig. 18. Zoning of the paintings in shelters No. 10.

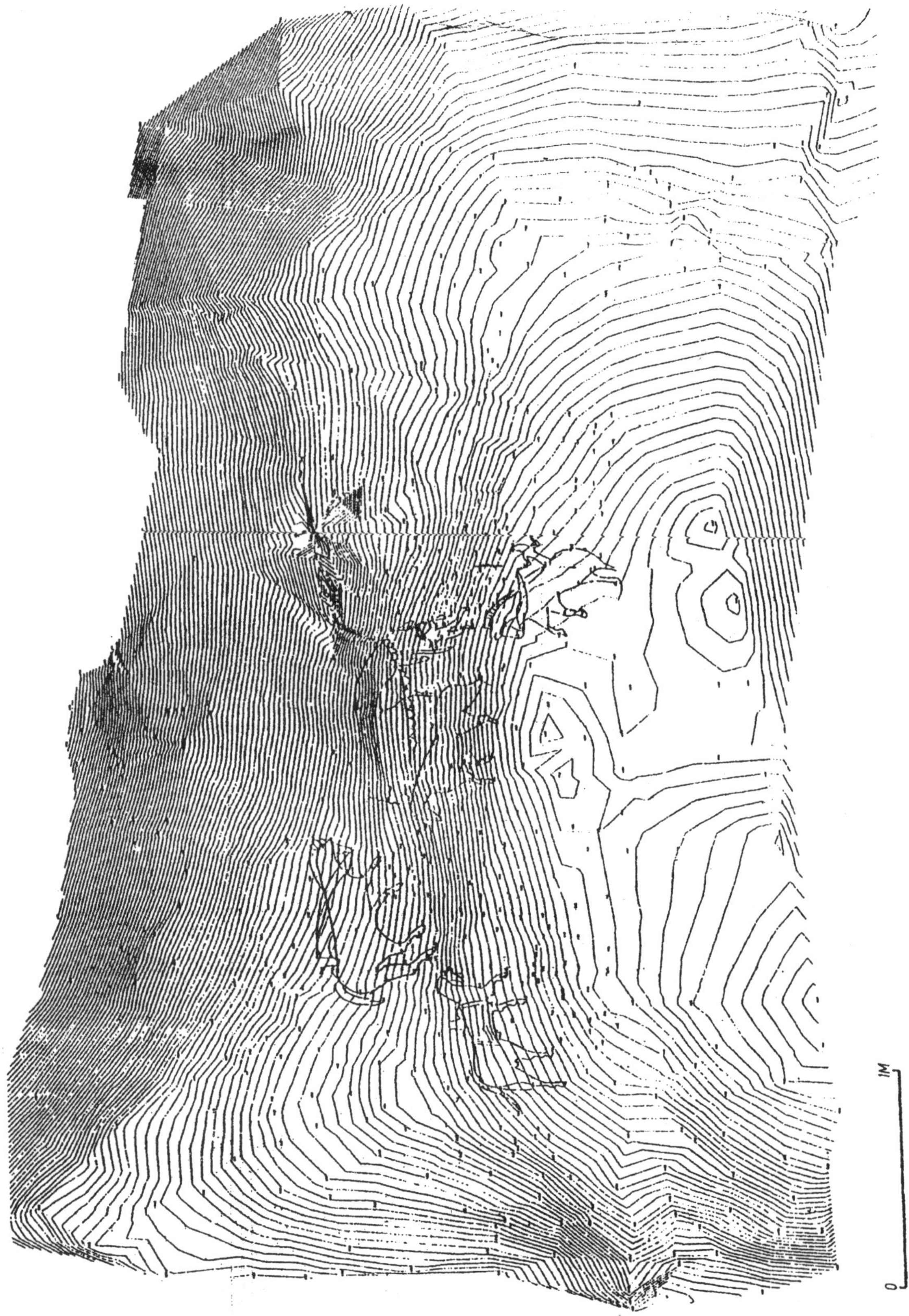

Fig. 19. Rock-shelter No. 10-Contour map of the painted wall with the locaiton of a few figures of panel A3.

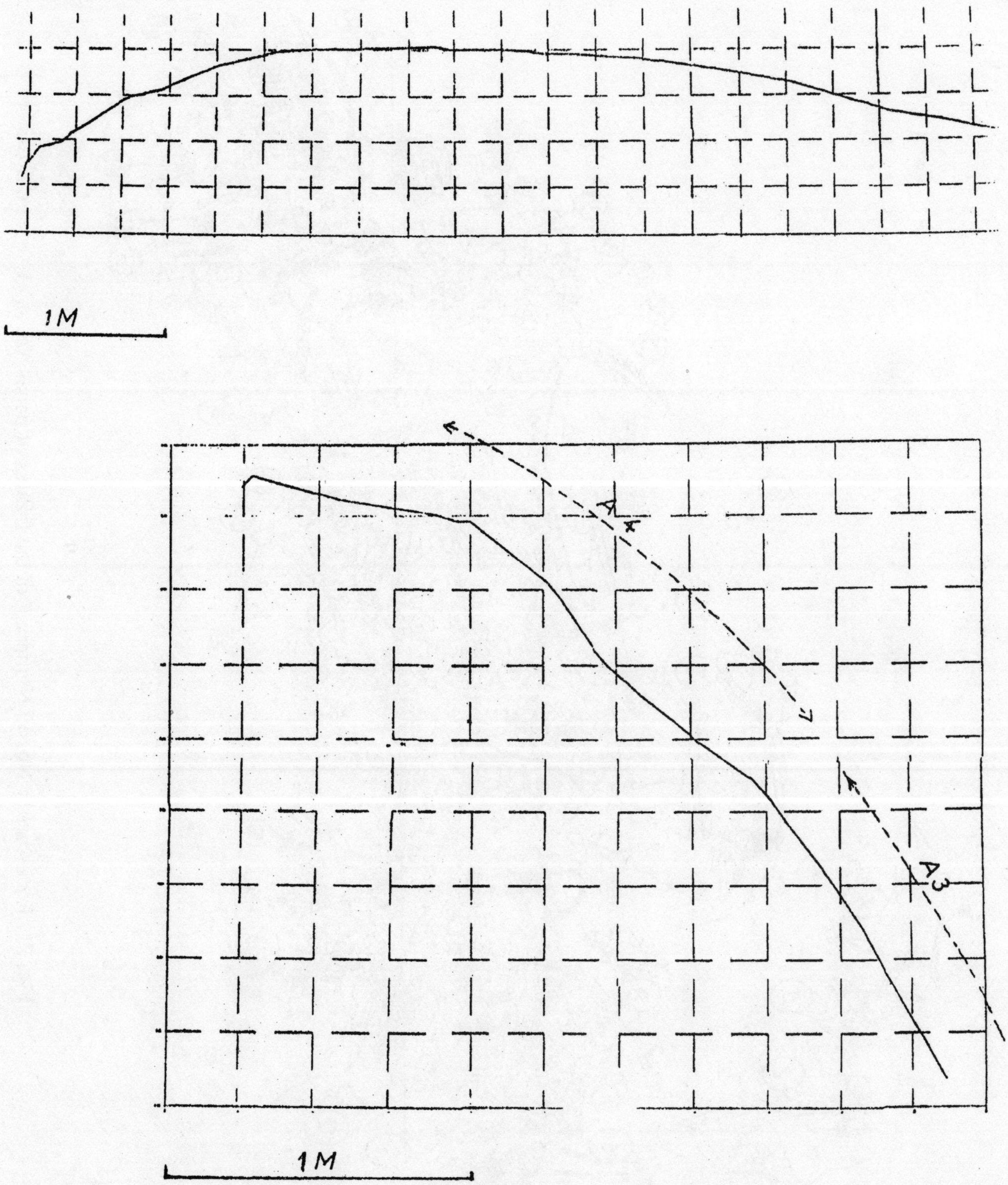

Fig. 20. Rock-shelter No. 10-Horizontal and vertical sections of painted surface passing by the point No. 81.

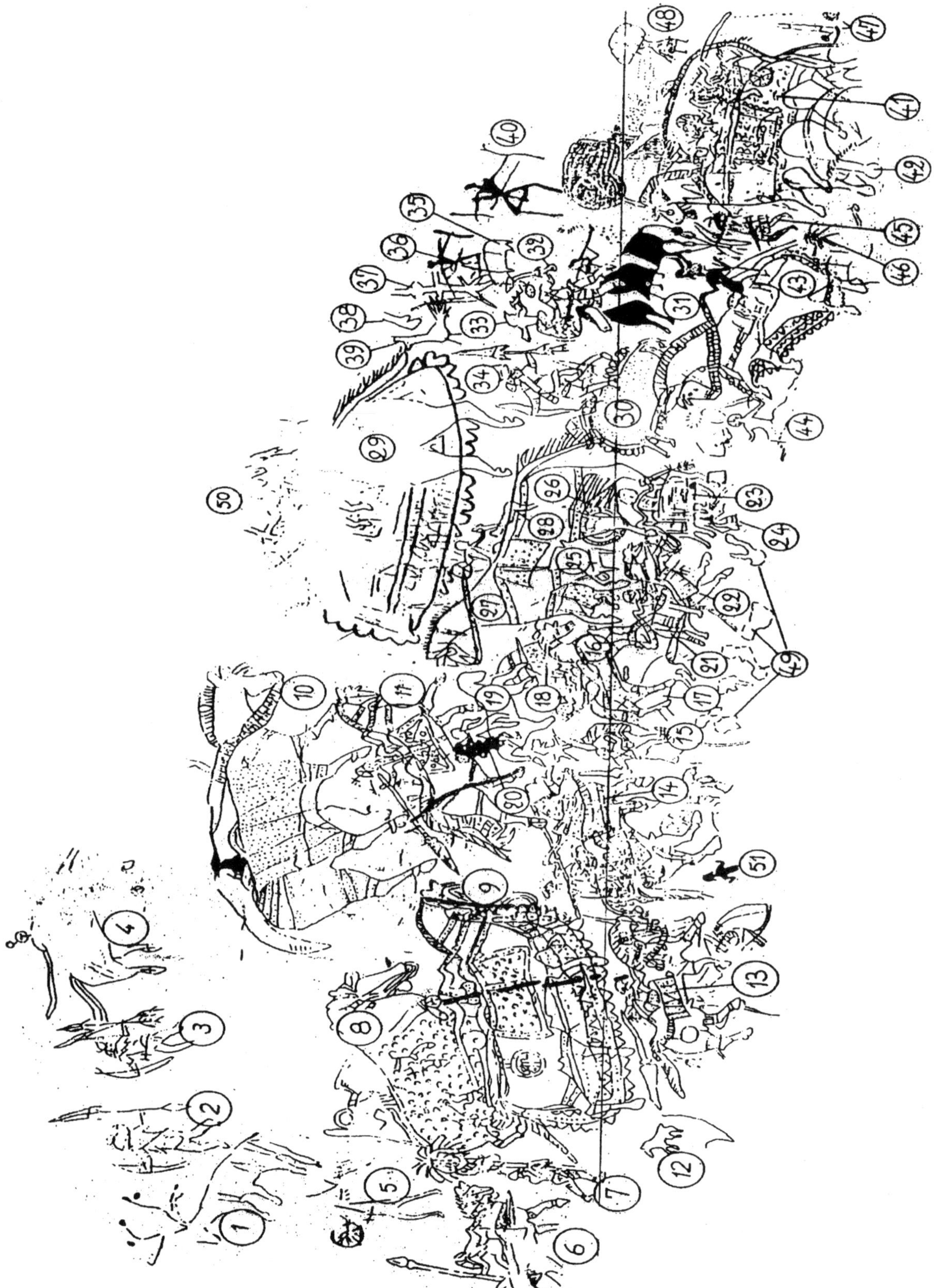

Fig. 21. Rock-shelter No. 10 Numering of the figures of panel No. A. 3.

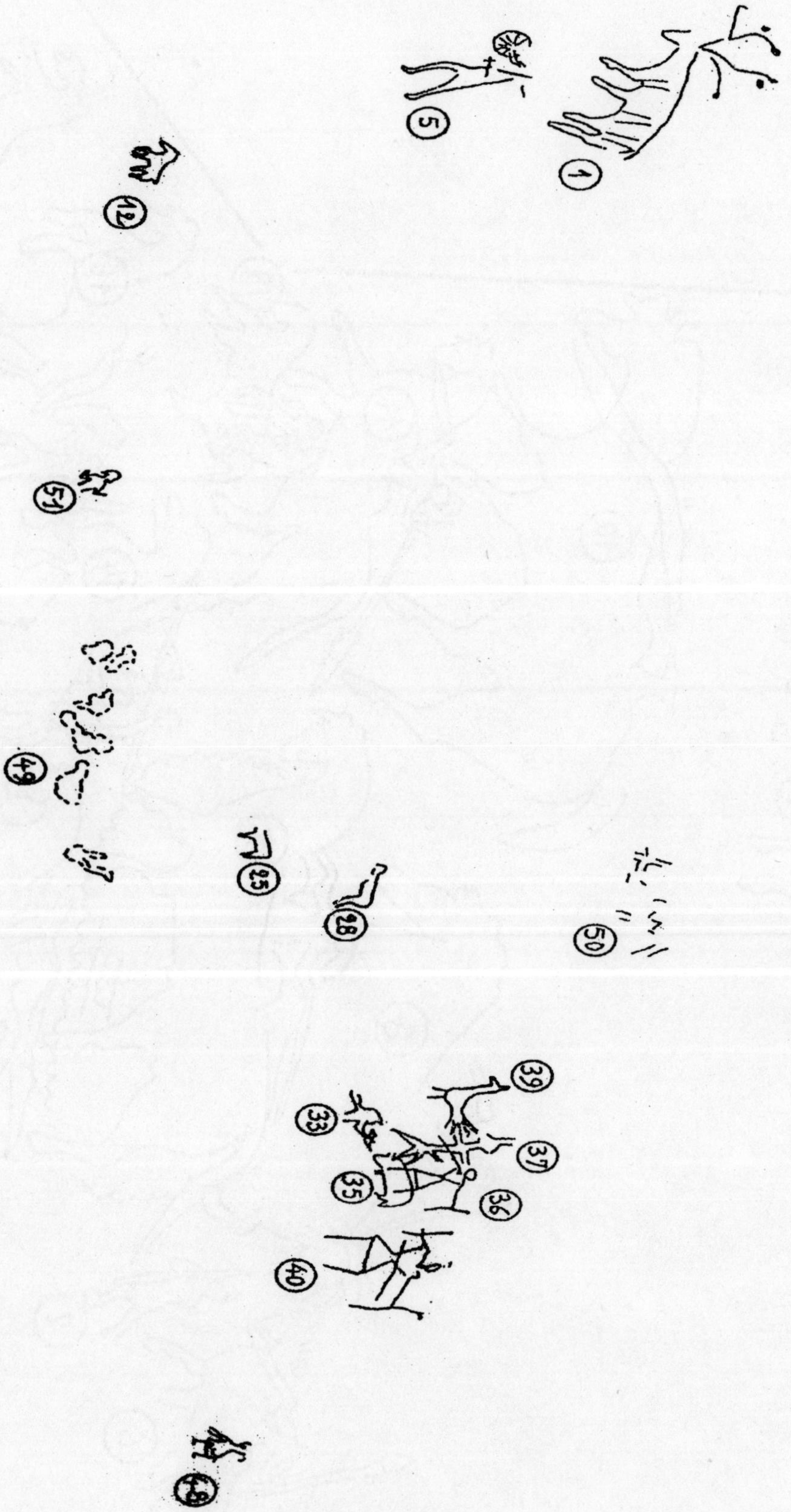

Fig. 22. Rock-shelter No. 10 Numering of the figures of panel No. A.3.

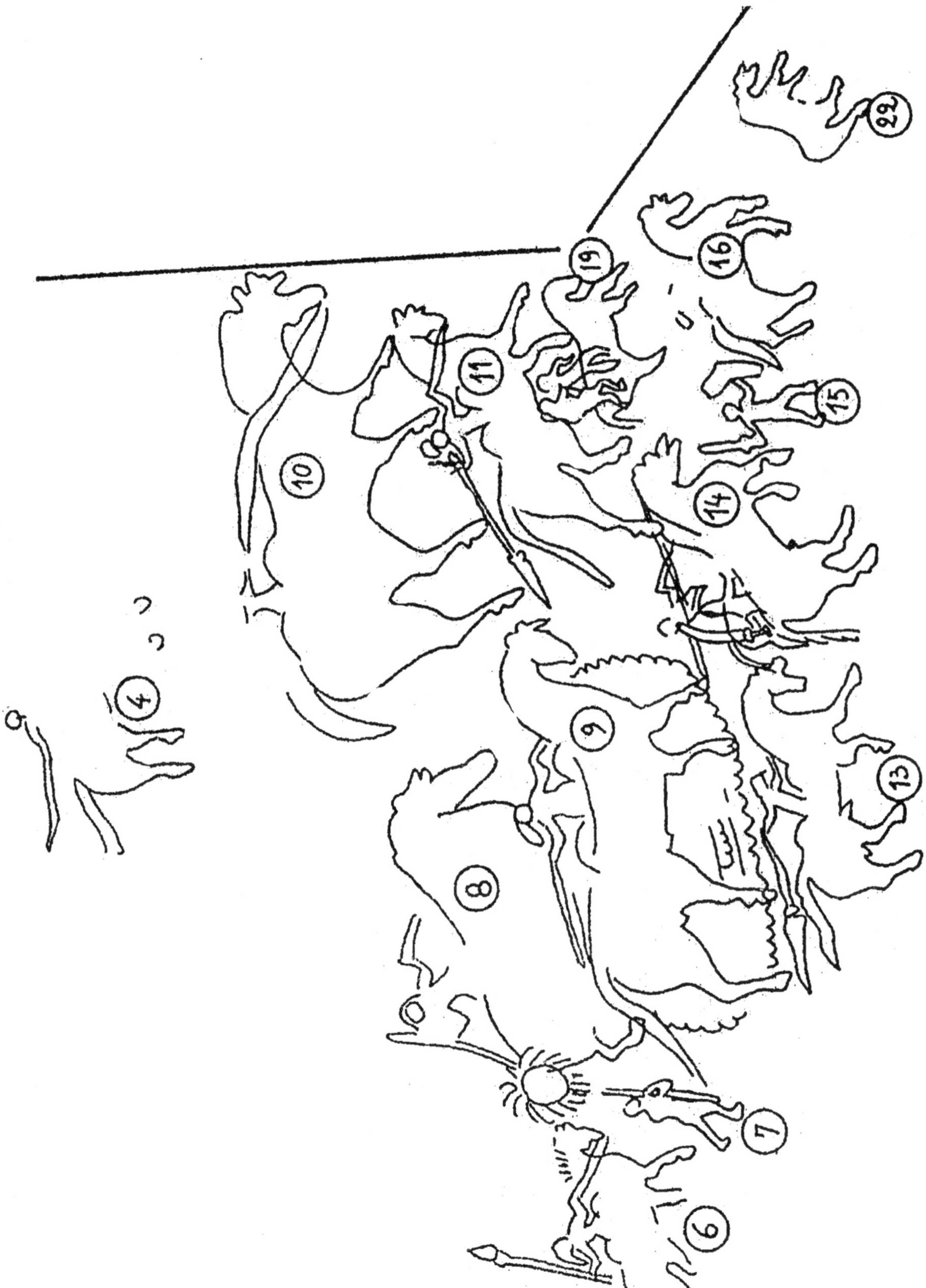

Fig. 23. Rock-shelter No. 10 Composition of panel A-3, the left group of the battle scene.

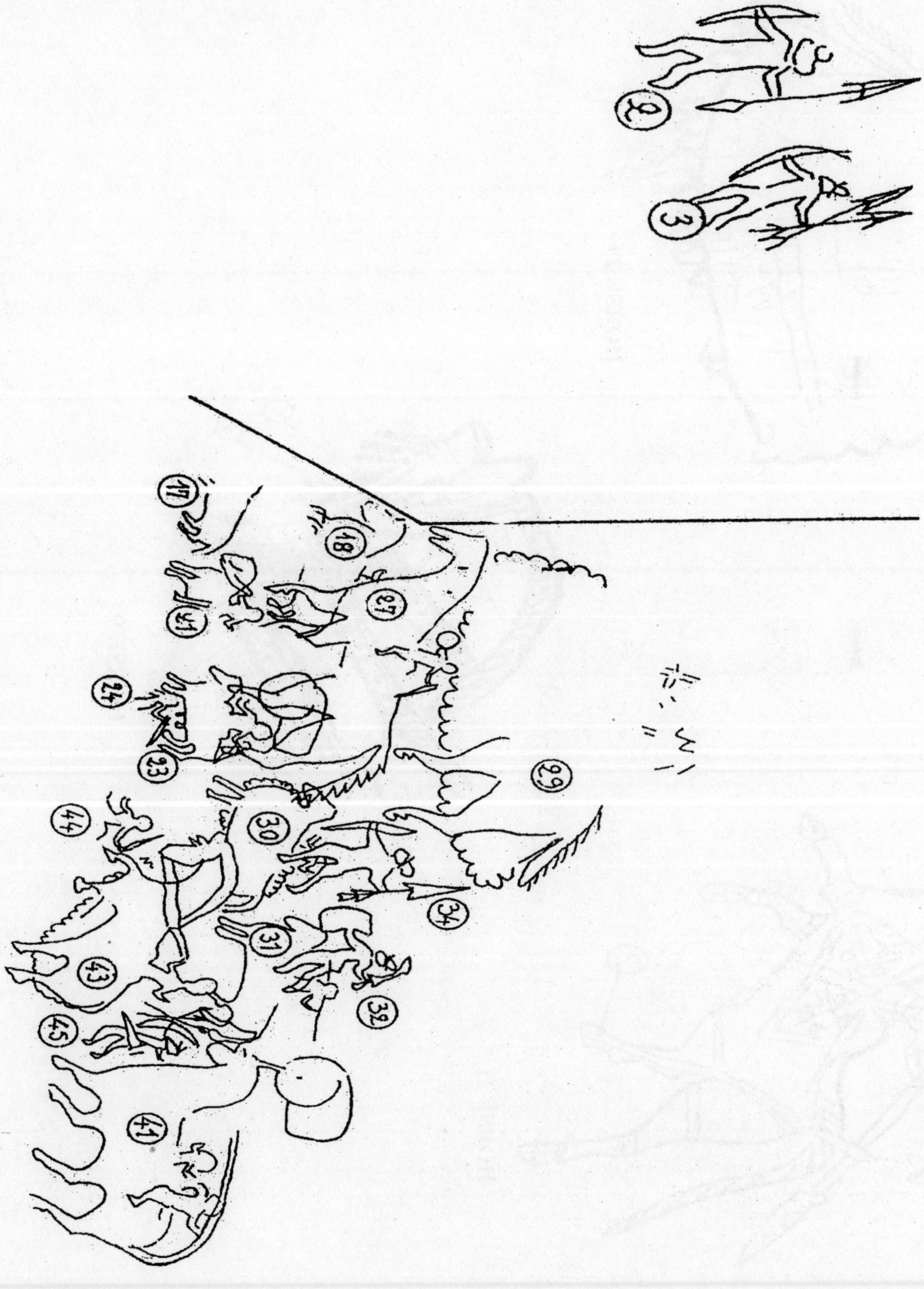

Fig. 24. Rock-shelter No. 10-composition of panel A. 3, the right group of the battle scene.

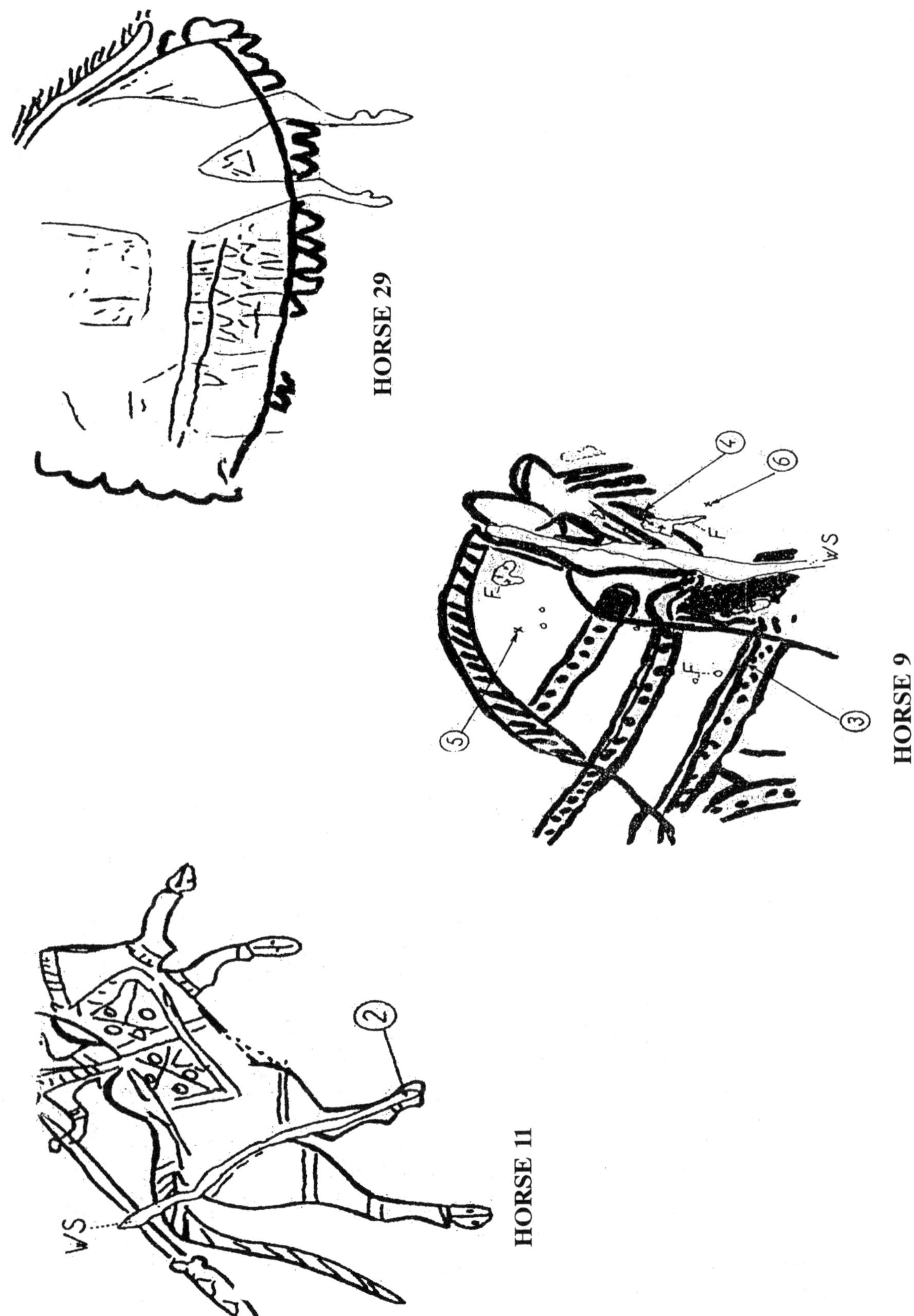

Fig. 25. Rock-shelter No. 10 successive revolution of horse riders.

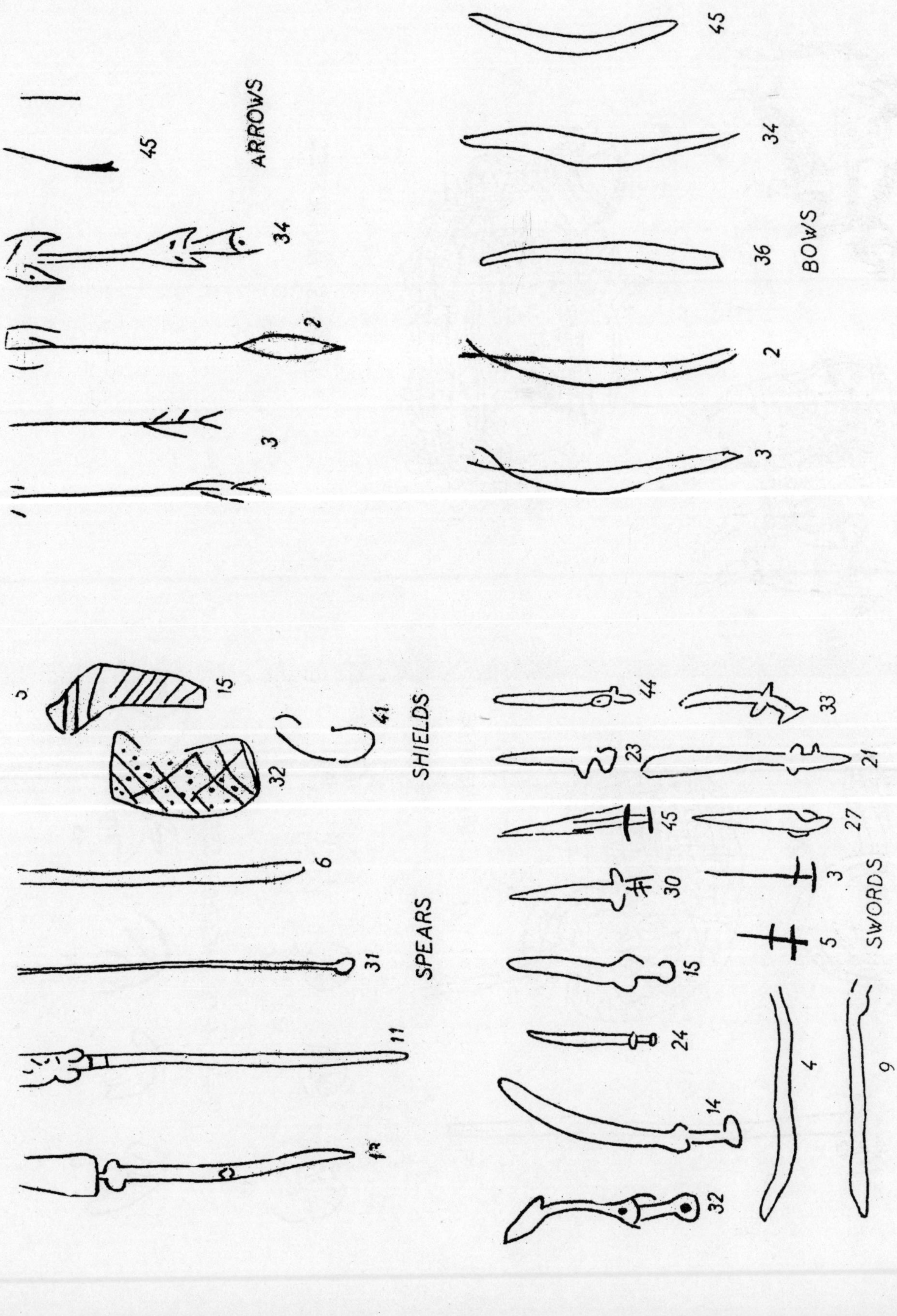

Fig. 26. Rock-shelter No. 10 Typological study of weapons.

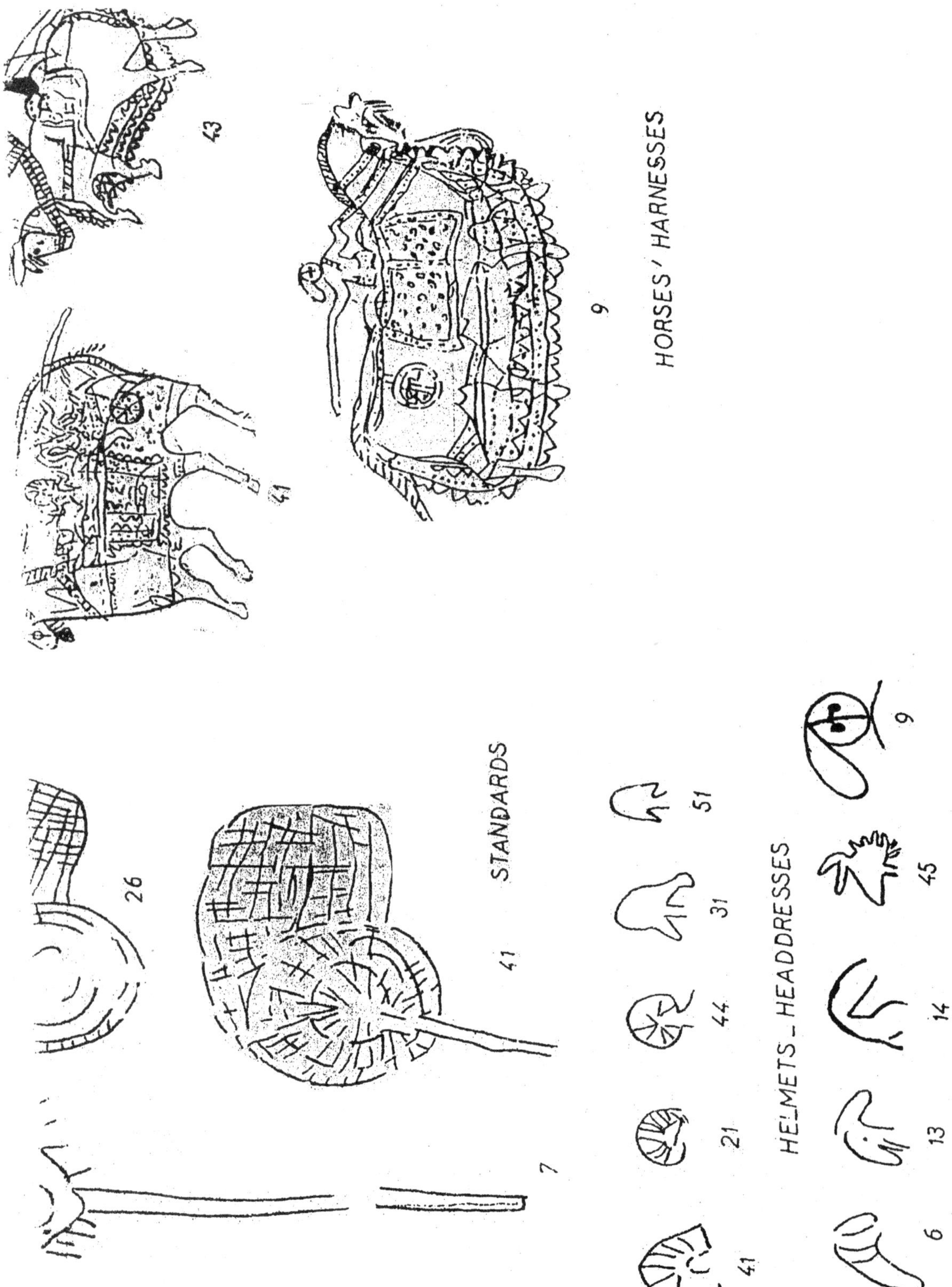

Fig. 27. Rock-shelters No. 10 Panel A3 standards, helmets and head-dresss and hornessed horses.

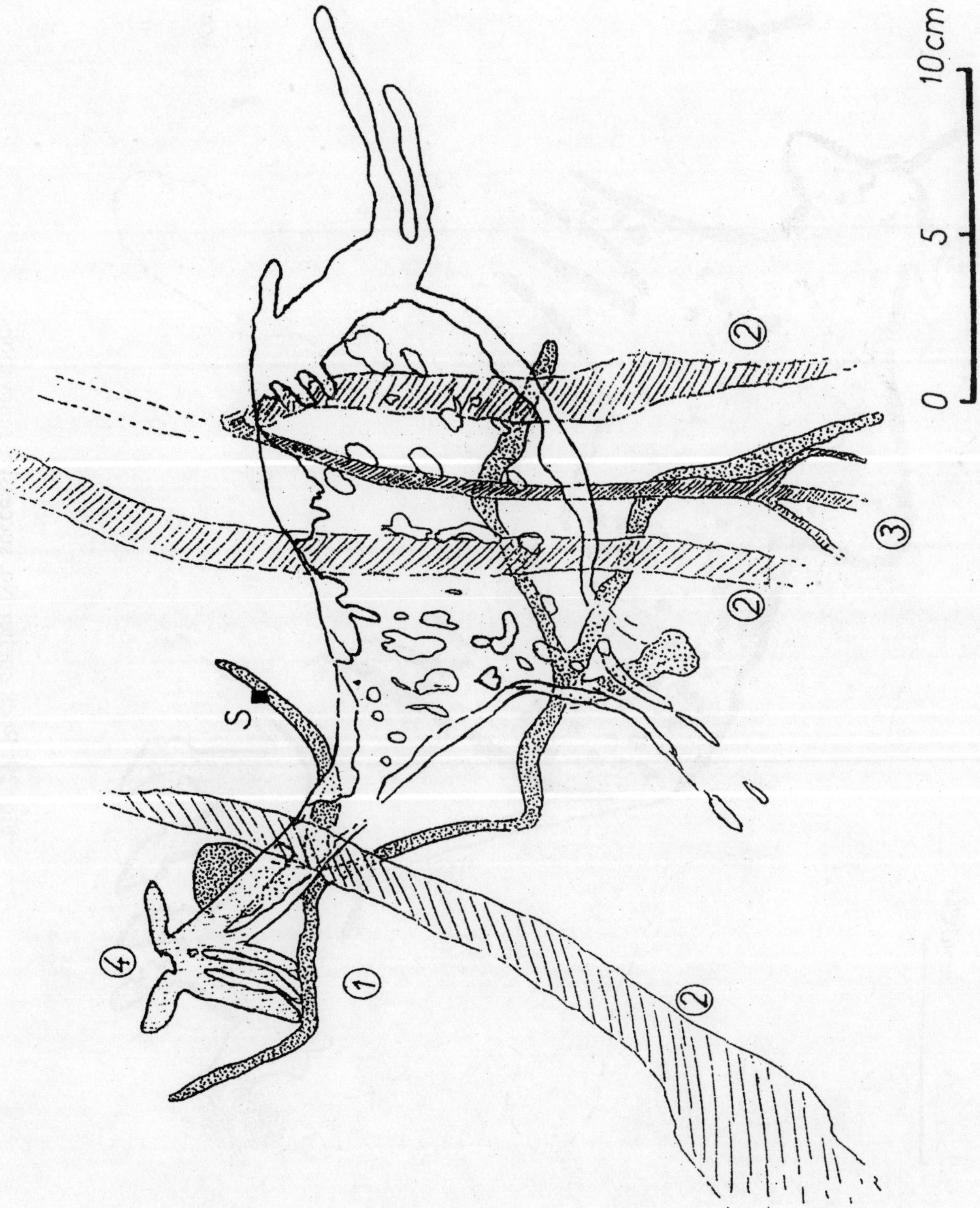

Fig. 28. Rock-shelter No. 9 Green pigments of a human figure.

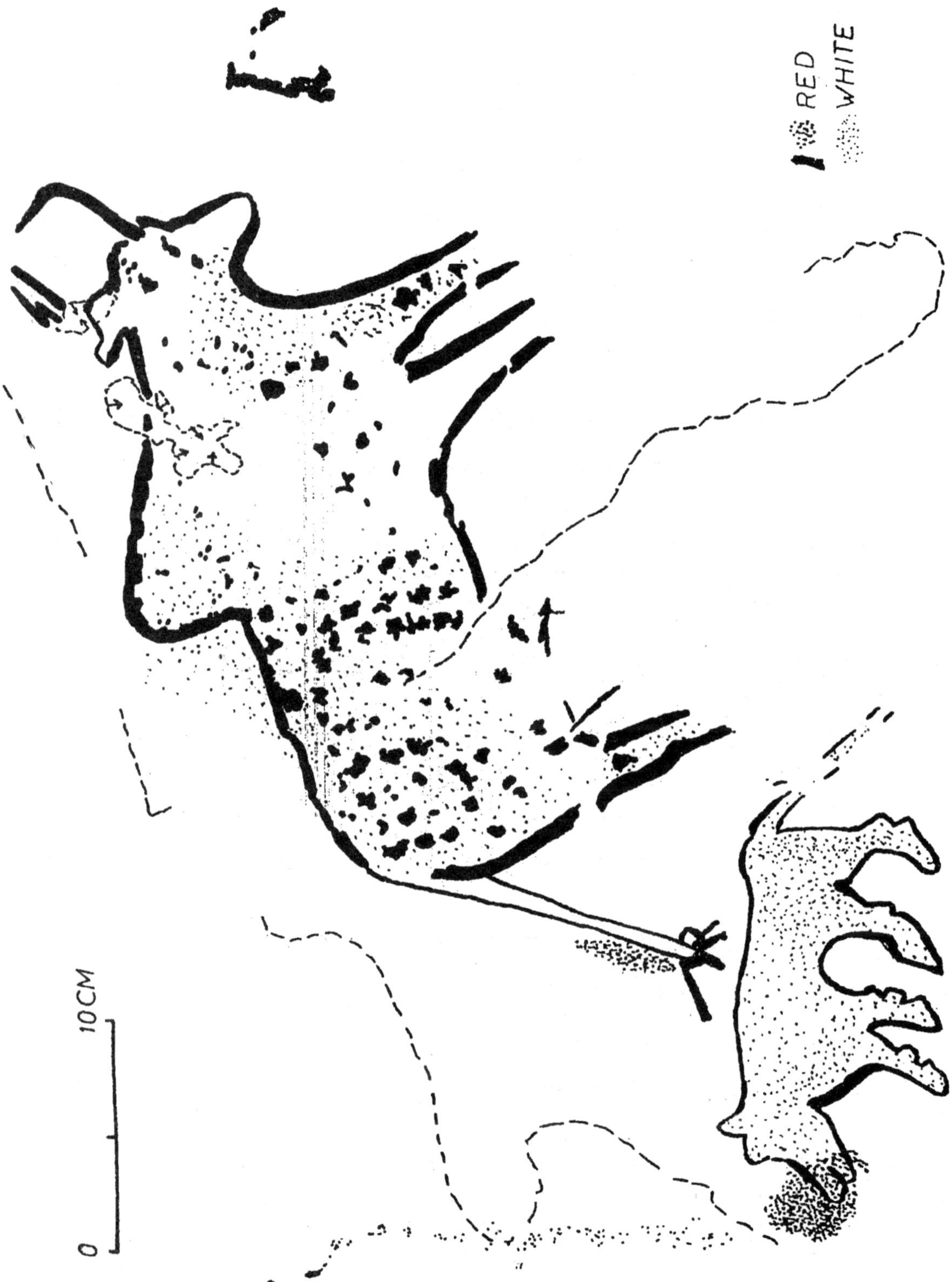

Fig. 29. Rock-shelter No. successive renovations.

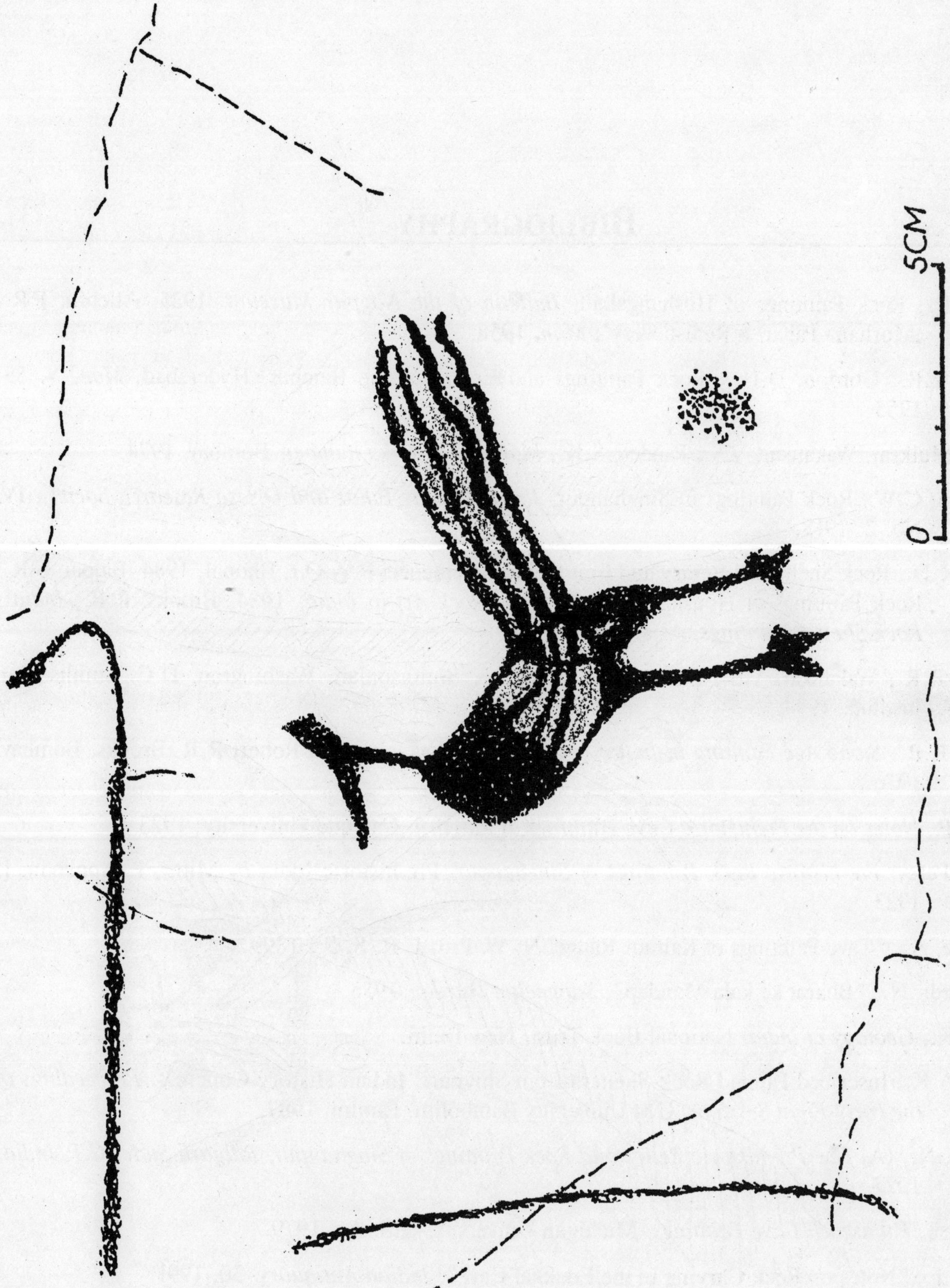

Fig. 30. Rock-shelter No. 10, Panel B2. Recording of a red small bird, (peacock).

BIBLIOGRAPHY

Abrew, D., Rock Paintings of Hoshangabad, *Bulletin of the Nagpur Museum,* 1925. Allchin, F.R., 'Morhana Pahar: a Rediscovery', *Man,* 1958.

Allchin, F.R., Gordon, D.H., 'Rock Paintings and Engravings in Raichur, Hyderabad, *Man,* V. 55: 1955.

Anand, Mulkraj, Wakankar, V.S., Pandey, S.K., *Marg: Bhimbetka number,* Bombay, 1974.

Anderson, C.W., Rock Paintings in Singhanpur, *Journal of the Bihar and Orissa Research Society,* IV. No. 2: 1918.

Bajpai, K.D., Rock Shelters: Literary and Epigraphical Evidence, R.A.O.I. Bhopal, 1984. Bajpai, S.K., Rock Paintings of Houshangabad District, *Rock Art in India,* 1984. Brooks, R.R., *India's Rock-Shelter Paintings.* Asia, 31-44, 1973.

Brooks, R.R., Wakankar, V.S., *Indian Rock Paintings,* Smithsonian, Washington, D.C. Smithsonian Institute, 1974.

Brooks, R.R., *Stone Age Painting in India;* by Vishnu S. Wakankar and Robert R.R. Brooks, Bombay, 1976.

Brown, P., *Notes on the Prehistoric Cave Paintings at Raigarh.* Calcutta University: 1923.

Brown, Percy, *Pre-historic Rock Paintings of Singhanpur,* Pre-historic India *by* Mitra, P. Appendix I, 1923.

Carlleyle, A., "Cave Paintings of Kaimur Range. N. W. Pro. J. R. S. S., 1899.

Chaturvedi, N., "Bharat ke kala Mandap", *Sammelan Patrika,* 1958.

Dey, A.K., *Geology of India,* National Book Trust, New Delhi.

Dubey, A.K., Inscribed Painted Rock-Shelters from Shivpuri: Indian History Congress. *Proceedings of the Forty-Eight Session,.* Goa University Bambolim, Panjim, 1987.

Dutta, A.N., (A) *Few Pre-historic Relics and Rock Paintings of Singhanpur, Raigarh State. C.P. India,* 1927.

Dwarikesh, *Pahargarh Cave Paintings,* Michigan University, U.S. A., 1979.

Fawcett, F., "Notes on Rock Carving in the Edakkal Cave", *Indian Antiquary,* 30, 1991.

Garrod, Dorothy A.E., The Nutufian Culture: The Life and Economy of a Mesolithic People in the Near East, *Proceedings of the British Academy* (London), 1957, Vol. XLI1I.

Ghosh, A.K., "Significance of Rock Art in the light of Ethnographic Parallels", *Rock Art in India,* 1984.

Ghosh, M. R., *Memoirs of Archaeological Survey of India, V. 24,* 1932.

Gordon, D.H., ME. Gordon, (The) Rock Engravings of the Middle Indus *J.R.D.S. of Bengal,* letters, V. VIII, Article No. 7, 1941.

Gordon, D.H., Allchin F.R., Rock Paintings and Engravings in Raichur, Hyderabad, *Man.* V. 55: 1955. Gordon, D.H., Indian Rock Paintings. *Science and Culture,* Calcutta.

Gordon, D.H., (The) Rock Paintings of Kabrapahar, Raigarh State, *Science and Culture,* V. S. No. 5, 1939.

Gordon, D.H., 'Rock Paintings of the Mahadeo Hills', *Indian Arts and Letters,* 10, No. 1, 1936.

Gordon, D.H., Indian Cave Paintings, *J.R.A.S. of Bengal,* V. IX, 1943.

Gordon, D.H., (The) Rock Engravings of Kupagallu Hills, Bellary, Madras *Man*, V. 51: 117-19, 1951.

Gordon, D.H., *Pre-historic Background of Indian Culture,* Bombay, 1960.

Gordon, D.H., *Mystery of'Mahadeo Hills,* III. Lon. N., 1935.

Gordon, M.E., Gordon, D.H., (The) Rock Engravings of the Middle Indus, *Royal Asiatic Society of Bengal.* Letters, V. VII, Article No. 7, 1941.

Gupta, Jagdish, *Pragaitihasik Bharatiya Chitrakala,* Delhi, 1987 (Hindi).

Gupta, S.S. and Banerji, K.D., A note on the Dating of the Rock-Shelter Paintings at Jinghiri, *Rock Art in India,* 1984.

Gupta, J. P., *Bharatiya Kala Ke Pad-Chinha.* 1960 (Hindi).

Hunter, G.R., Excavations at Pachmarhi. *Nagpur University Journal,* 1934.

Hunter, G.R., Rock Paintings of Pachmarhi Hills. *Congress of Pre and Proto-historic Sciences,* 1932.

Hunter, G.R., 'Note on Adamgarh Paintings', *Nagpur University Journal,* 1936.

Jain, J. P. 'Rock Paintings of Shivpuri'" *Rock Art of India,* Bhopal, 1984.

Jacobson, J., Microlithic Context in the Vindhya Hills of Central India, *Ph.D. Thesis Columbia University,* 1970.

Joshi, M.P., 'Rock Paintings in Kumaon', *Man and Environment,* V.II., 1978.

Joshi, R.V., Prehistoric Caves and Rock-Shelters in India, *Uttar Pradesh,* Lucknow, 1963.

Joshi, R.V., and Khare, M.D., "Microlithic Bearing Deposits of Adamgarh Rock-Shelters", *Studies in Prehistory (R.B. Foote Memorial Volume)* Ed. Sen and Ghosh, 1966.

Joshi, R.V., Late Mesolithic Culture in Central India, *La Pre'histoire (Problems aet Tendencies)* Editions due centre National de la Recherche Scientifique, Paris, 1968.

Joshi, R. V., *Stone Age Cultures of Central India.* Pune, Deccan College, 1978.

Joshi, R.V., Significance of Chemical Tests of Cultural Deposits from Pre-historic Rock-Shelters, *Rock Art in India,* 1984.

Kathuria, R.P., Primitive Rock Paintings in Bhopal. *Prachya Pratibha,* Bhopal, V. 3, No 2:1975.

Kesri, Arjun Das, *Shail Chitra Guha Chitra.* (Hindi).

Khare, M.D., Rock-Shelters of Ahamadpur Hill, Vidisha, *Journal of Madhya Pradesh Itihas Parishad,* Bhopal, No. 10, 1976.

Khare, M.D., *Painted Rock Shelters,* Bhopal, 1980.

Khatri, A.P., Stone Age and Pleistocene Chronology of the Namada Valley (Central India). *Anthropos,* vol. 56, 1961.

Khatri, A.P., Rock Paintings of Adamgarh (Central India) and their Ages, *Anthropos,* Bd. 59, S. 759-769, Panlus Varlag, Freiburg Scheweiz, 1964.

Mathpal, Y.N., Pragaitihasik manav ke karyakalap shail-chitron ke darpan me. Lucknow, *D.N. Majumdar Museum of Folk Life and Culture Ethnographic and Folk Culture Society,* 1987. (Hindi)

Mathpal, Y.N., Rock Paintings of India: *An ornithographical Bulletin of the Deccan College Research Institute,* Pune, V. 35, Nos. 3-4: 1976.

Mathpal, Y.N., Rock Art of India: *Journal of Indian History, Trivandrum,* V. 54, Part I: 1976.

Mathpal, Y.N., Baya aur Patani Ki Pahari ke Chitrit Shalishraya, Manav. Lucknow, *Ethnographic and Folk Culture Society,* 4-11:1976 (Hindi).

Mathpal, Y.N., Patani Ki Pahari: a Pre-historic Art Site, *National Herald,* Lucknow, May 22, 1977 (Hindi)

Mathpal, Y.N., (The) Technique of Reproducing Rock Paintings. *Bulletin of the Deccan College Research Institute,* Pune, V. 37: 1978.

Mathpal, Y.N., How to Date a Rock Painting, *Rock Art of India,* Delhi, 1984.

Mathpal, Y.N., *Pre-historic Rock Paintings of Bhimbetka,* Central India, New Delhi, 1984.

Michael Lorblanchet, (ed.) *Rock Art in the Old World,,* IGNCA, New Delhi, 1992.

Misra, V.N., Ecological Adaptations during the Terminal Stone Age in Eastern and Central India. In K. A. R. Kennedy and G. Possehl (eds.), *Ecological Backgrounds of South Asia Pre-history,* Cornell, Cornell University: 1976.

Misra, V.N., Archaeological and Ethnographic Evidences for the Hafting and use of Microliths and related tools. *Puratattva,* 7: 1974.

Misra, V.N., (The) Evolution of Black Element in the Stone Industries of Bhimbetka, Central India. In R.K. Sharma (ed.) *Indian Archaeology: New Perspectives,* New Delhi: 1982.

Misra, V.N., Pre-historic culture sequence of Bhimbetka. *Pre-historic Man and his Art in Central India,* Pune: 1970.

Misra, V.N., Bhimbetka: Pre-historic Man and his Art in Central India; by Virendra Nath Misra, Yashodhar Mathpal and Malti Nagar. Pune, *Bhimbetka Souvenir Committee,* 1977.

Misra, V.N., Mathpal, Y., *Bhimbetka Excavations.* Pune, Deccan College, 1976.

Negi, R.S. and Mathpal, Y., Pre-historic Rock Paintings at the Site of National Museum of Man on Shyamala Hills, Bhopal, *Rock Art in India.*

Neumayer, E., *Pre-historic Indian Rock Paintings,* Delhi, 1983.

Neumayer, E., *Lines on Stone,* Delhi, 1993.

Pandey, S.K., Naryavalli ke Gauhar Chitra (Hindi) *Madhya Pradesh Sandesh,* Gwalior, 1962.

Pandey, S.K., Madhya Pradesh ke Kuchha Mahatvapurna Gauha Chitra (Hindi) *M.P. Sandesh,* Gwalior, 1963.

Pandey, S.K., Sagar Jile Ki Shailgrahin Chitra Kala (Hindi) *Madhya Bharti,* 1965 to 67, Sagar University.

Pandey, S.K., Problem of Dating the Indian Rock Paintings, *Madhya Bharti* 1965-66, Sagar University.

Pandey, S.K., Hunting Scene in Indian Rock Paintings, *Bul. I.H., Cul. & Archy,* Vol. I, Sagar University.

Pandey, S.K., Painted Rock-Shelters in Madhya Pradesh, Ph.D. Thesis, 1969.

Pandey, S.K., Bundelkhand Ki Shail Garhin Chitra Kala, *Maithili Sharan Gupta Centenary Volume.*

Pandey, S.K., Pre-history of Indian Rock Paintings, *Prachya Pratibha,* Vol. III, No. 2, Bhopal, 1975.

Pandey, S.K., Indian Rock Art and its Problems, *Rock Art in India,* 1984.

Pandey, S.K., Central Indian Rock Art, *Rock Art in the Old World,* ed. M. Lorblanchet, IGNCA- New Delhi, 1992.

Pandey, S.K., *Indian Rock Art,* New Delhi, 1993.

Rajaguru, S.N., Mineralogy and Palaeoenvironment of Bhimbetka Rock Shelters, Madhya Pradesh *Rock Art in India,* 1984.

Sankalia, H.D., *Pre-historic Art in India,* New Delhi, 1978.

Sankalia, H.D., Navadatoli Dancers, *Antiquity 29* (113), 1985.

Sankalia, H.D., *Pre-history and Proto-history of India and Pakistan,* Pune, 1974.

Silberrad, C.A., Rock Paintings of the Banda District, *Journal of the Royal Asiatic Society of Bengal* No. 3, Calcutta, 1907.

Singh, R.L. (ed.) *India, A Regional Geography,* Varanasi, 1971.

Sonavvane, V.H., An Important Evidence to Date Rock Paintings of Mesolithic Period, *Rock Art of India,* New Delhi, 1984.

Sundara, A., Further Notices of Rock Paintings in Hire Benakal, *Journal of Indian History,* Trivandrum, V. 52: 21-332.

Sundara, A., Some Selected Rock Paintings from North Karnataka, *Rock Art in India,* 1984.

Supekar, S.G., *Some Aspects of Pleistocene Stratigraphy and Pre-history of the Central Narmada Basin,* Poona, 1968.

Tiwari, Shankar, Rock Paintings at Chiklod. *Prachya Pratibha,,* Bhopal, V. 3, No. 2: 1975.

Tiwari, Shankar, Jaora- the Shelter of the Largest Rock Painting in India. *Prachya Pratibha,* Bhopal V.3,No. 2: 1975.

Tiwari, Shankar, Painted Rock Shelters of 'S-Belt' and the Chalcolithic Cultures of Betwa Source Region, *Prachya Pratibha,* V. IV, No. 2 Bhopal, 1976.

Tiwari, Shankar, Twenty Five Years of Rock Paintings Exploration in the Betwa Source Region, a Re-appraisal, *Rock Art in India,* 1984.

Vajpeyi, K.D., Abchand ke Gavhar Chitra. *Bharti,* V. 2, 1962 (Hindi)

Verma, R.K., The Rock Art of Southern Uttar Pradesh with Special Reference- to Mirzapur, *Rock Art in India,* 1984.

Wadia, D.N., *Geology of India,* London, 1939.

Wakankar, V.S., Rock Paintings of the Bhopal Region, *Rasa,* Bhopal, 1972.

Wakankar, V.S., Pre-historic Rock Paintings of the Chambal Valley, Paper delivered at the All India History Congress, 1955.

Wakankar, V.S., Rock Paintings of Narsinghgarh, M.P. *Sandesh,* Gwalior, 1972.

Wakankar, V.S., Rock Paintings of the Chambal Region, Paper delivered at the All India History Congress.

Wakankar, V.S., and Robert R.R. Brooks, *Stone Age Paintings in India:* Bombay, 1976.

Wakankar, V.S., Bharteeya Shailashrayeen Chitrakala Aur Uska Kal Nirnaya. *Manav,* Lucknow, Ethnographic and Folk Culture Society, 1-1: (Hindi).

Wakankar, V.S., Bhimbetka, the Pre-historic Paradise; *Prachya Pratibha,* Bhopal, 1975.

Wakankar, V.S., Bhimbetka Excavations, *Indian Historical Quarterly,* V. I & II, Trivandrum, 1973.

Wakankar, V.S., Painted Rock Shelters of India. Pune University, Pune 1972.

Wakankar, V.S., Techniques of Pre-historic Paintings and Engravings, *Rock Art in India,* 1984.

Wakankar, V.S., Bhatnagar, V., *Dawn of Indian Art.* Ujjain, 1978.

Wakankar, V.S., Brooks, R.R., *Stone Age Painting in India,* Bombay, 1976.

INDEX

C

D

Q

R

S

✧✧✧

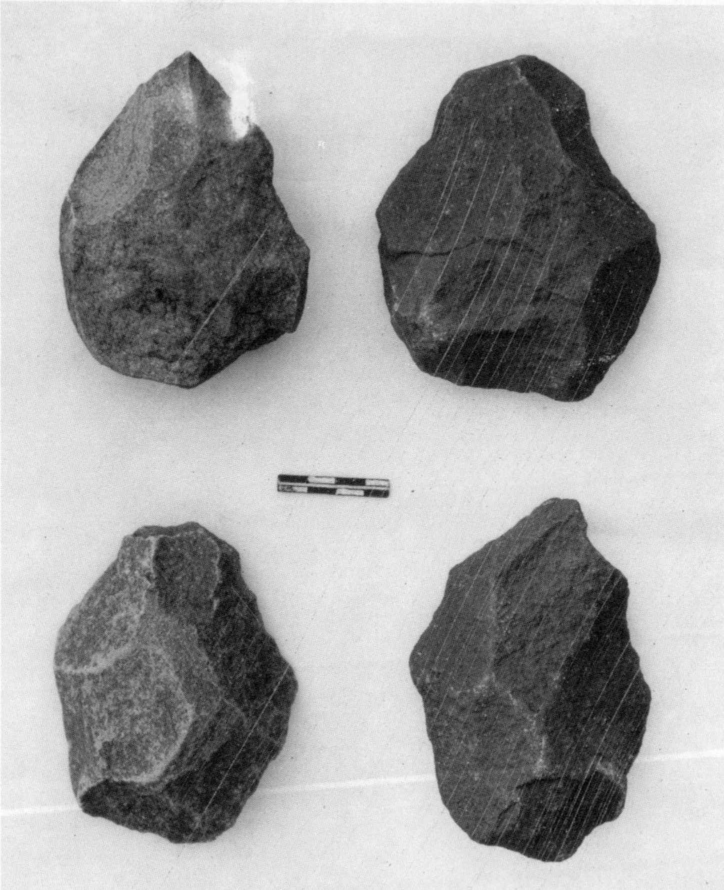

Pl. I. A-Early Stone Age tools.

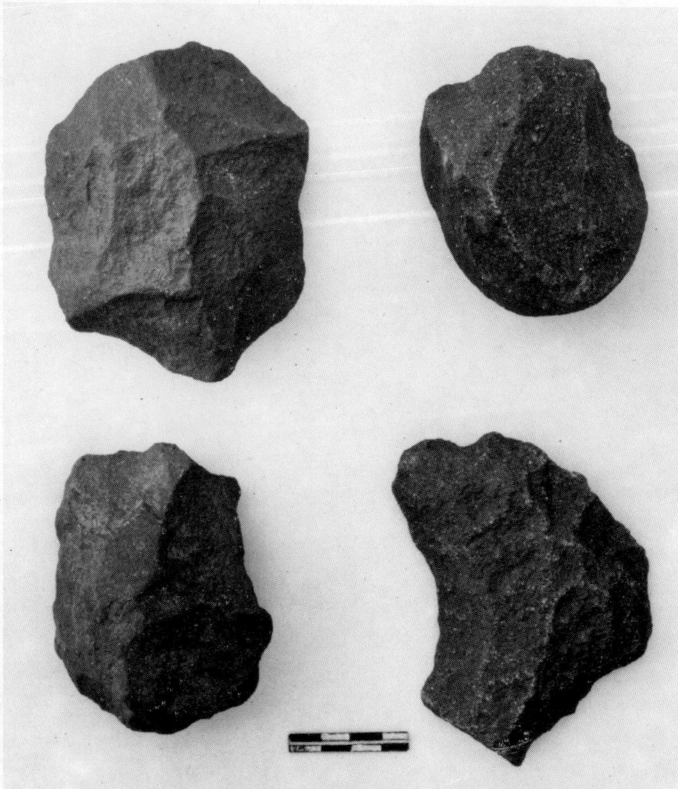

Pl. I B- Middle Stone Age tools.

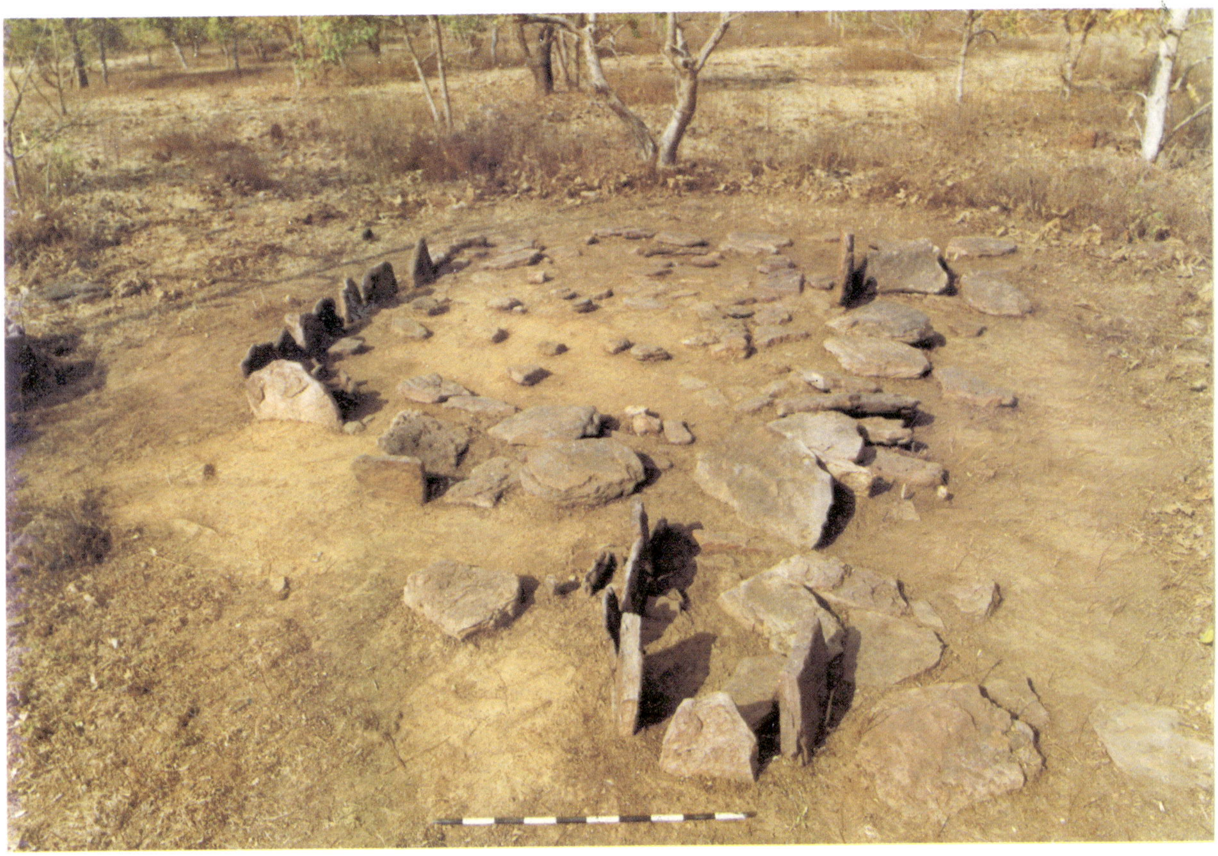

Pl. II. Megalithic site.

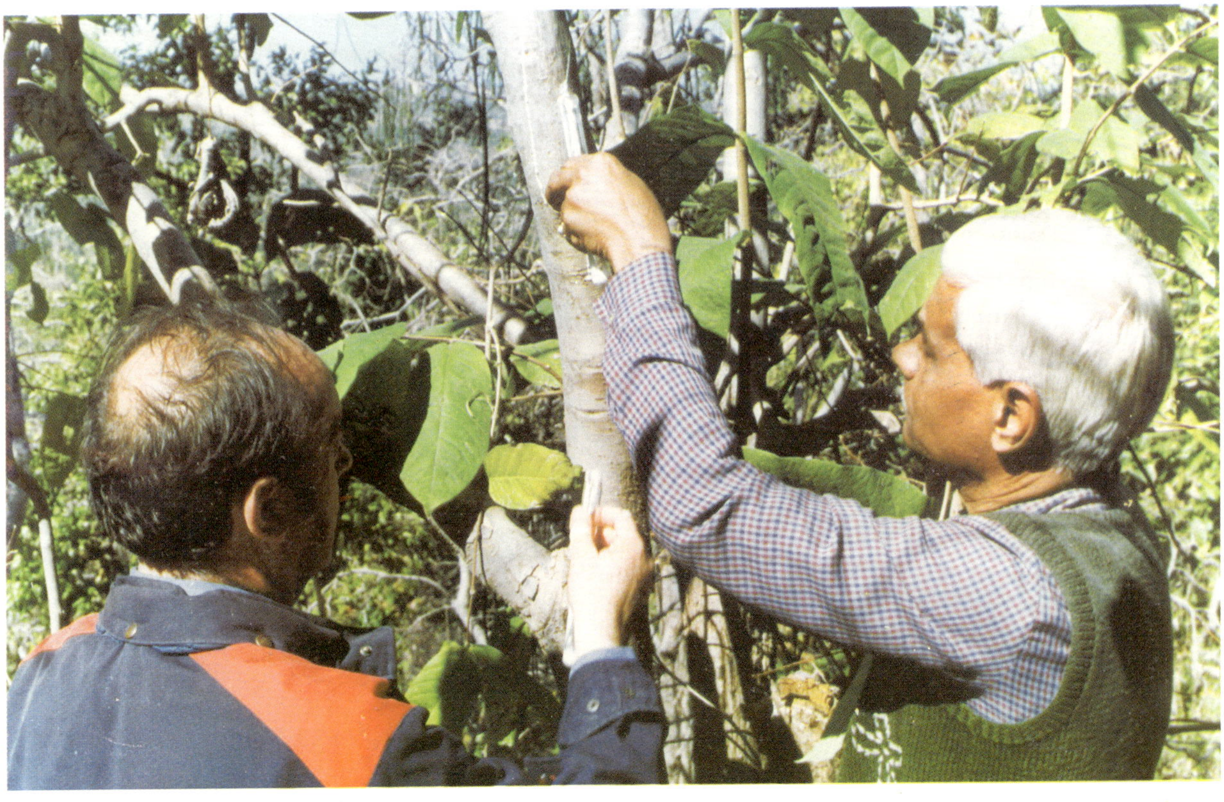

Pl. III. Collecting the binding material.

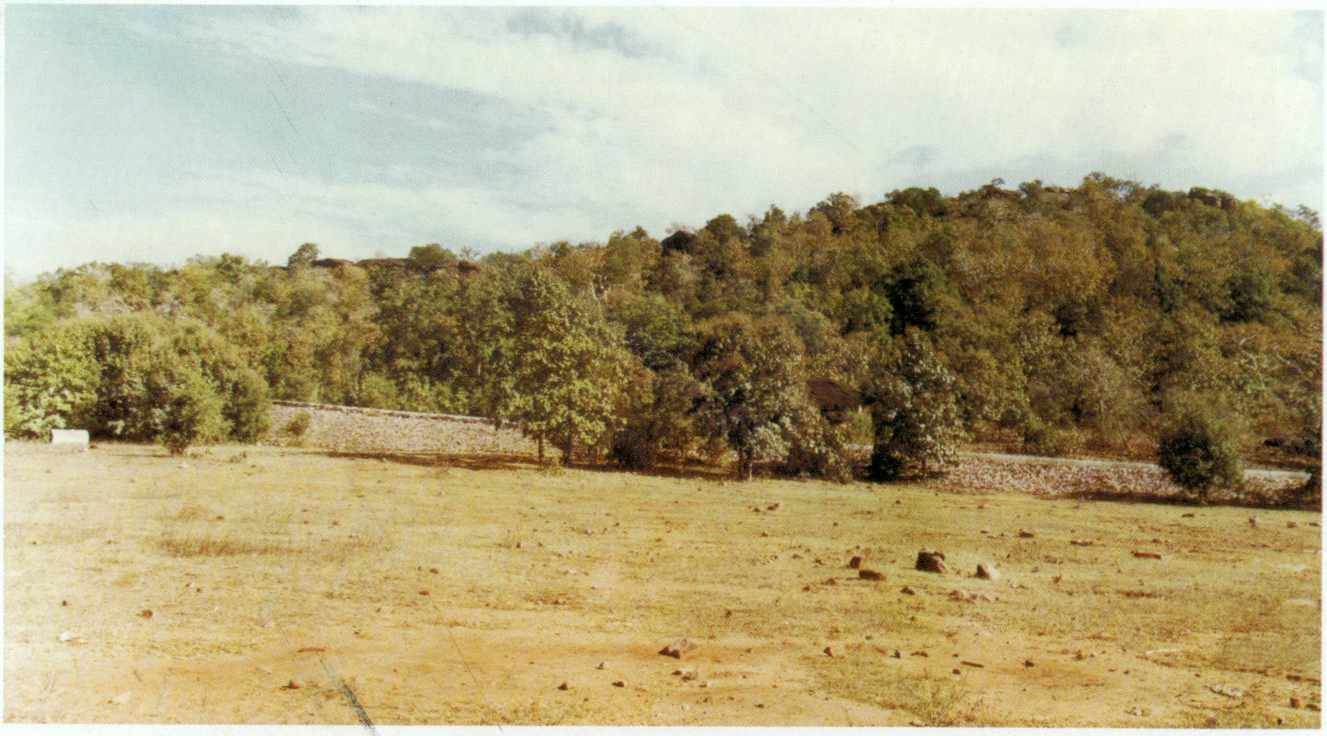

Pl. IV. General view of Jhiri hill.

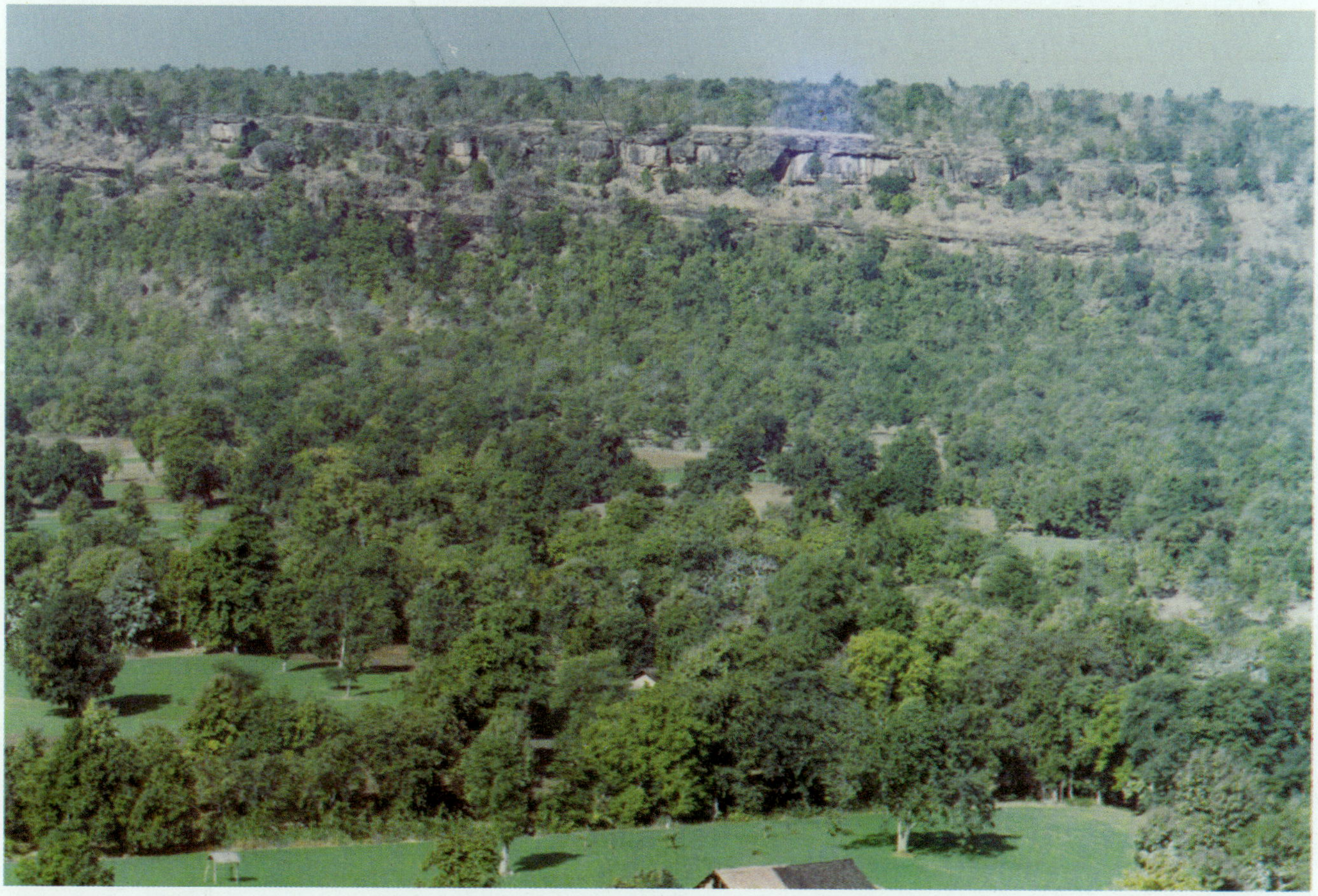

Pl. V. General view of Kathotia rock-shelters.

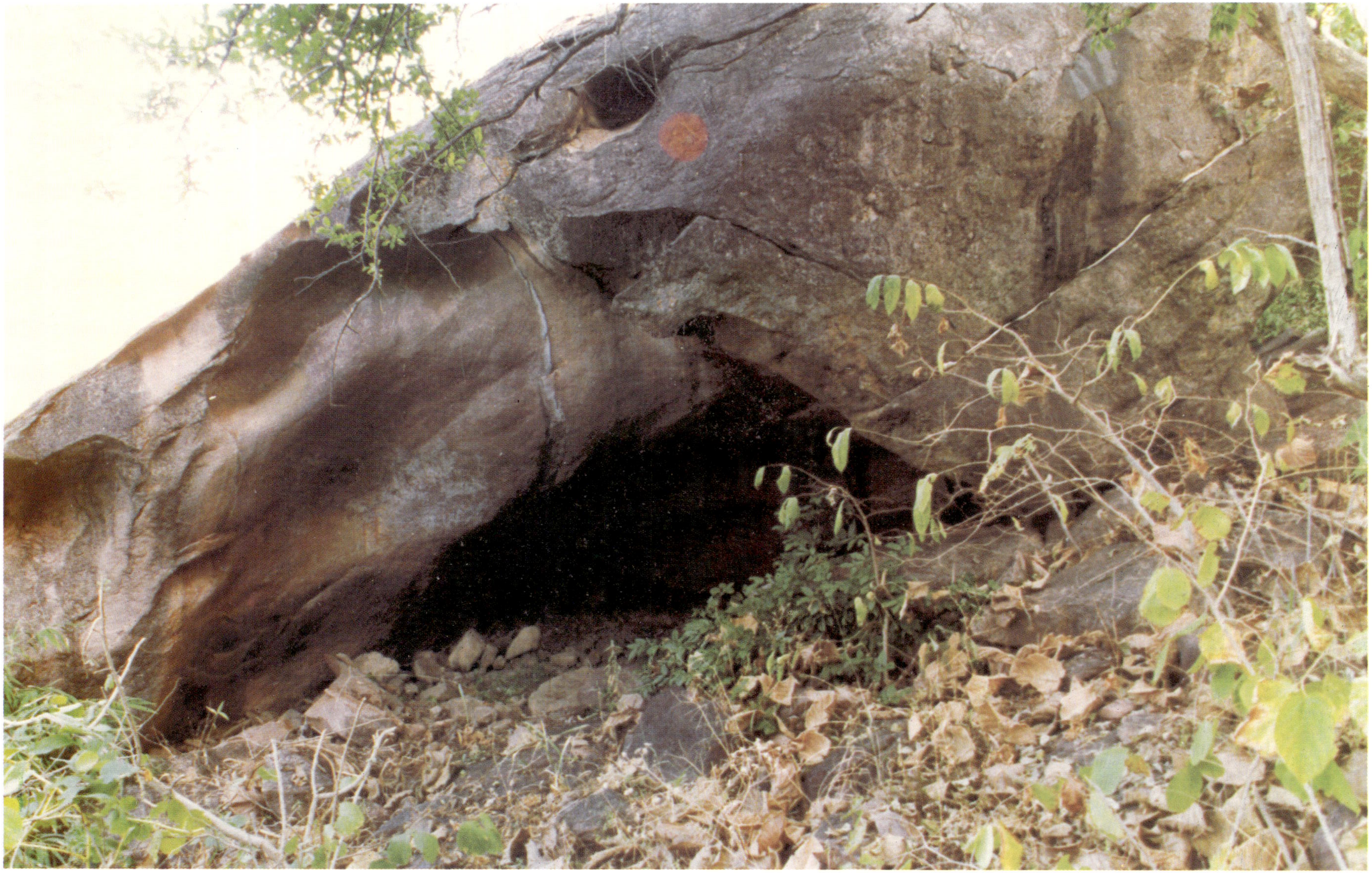

Pl. VI.R.S. No. 17- View from south.

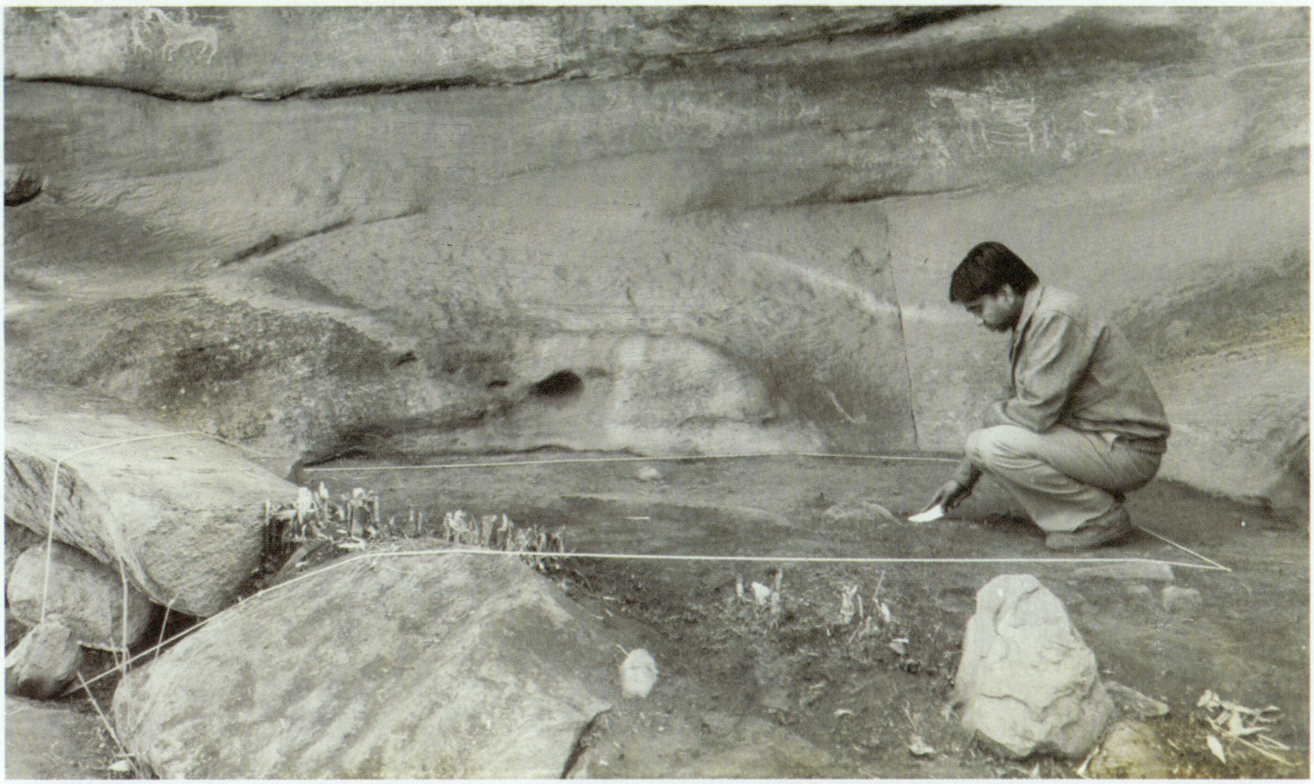

Pl. VII. R.S. No. 6- Habitational area and painted surface.

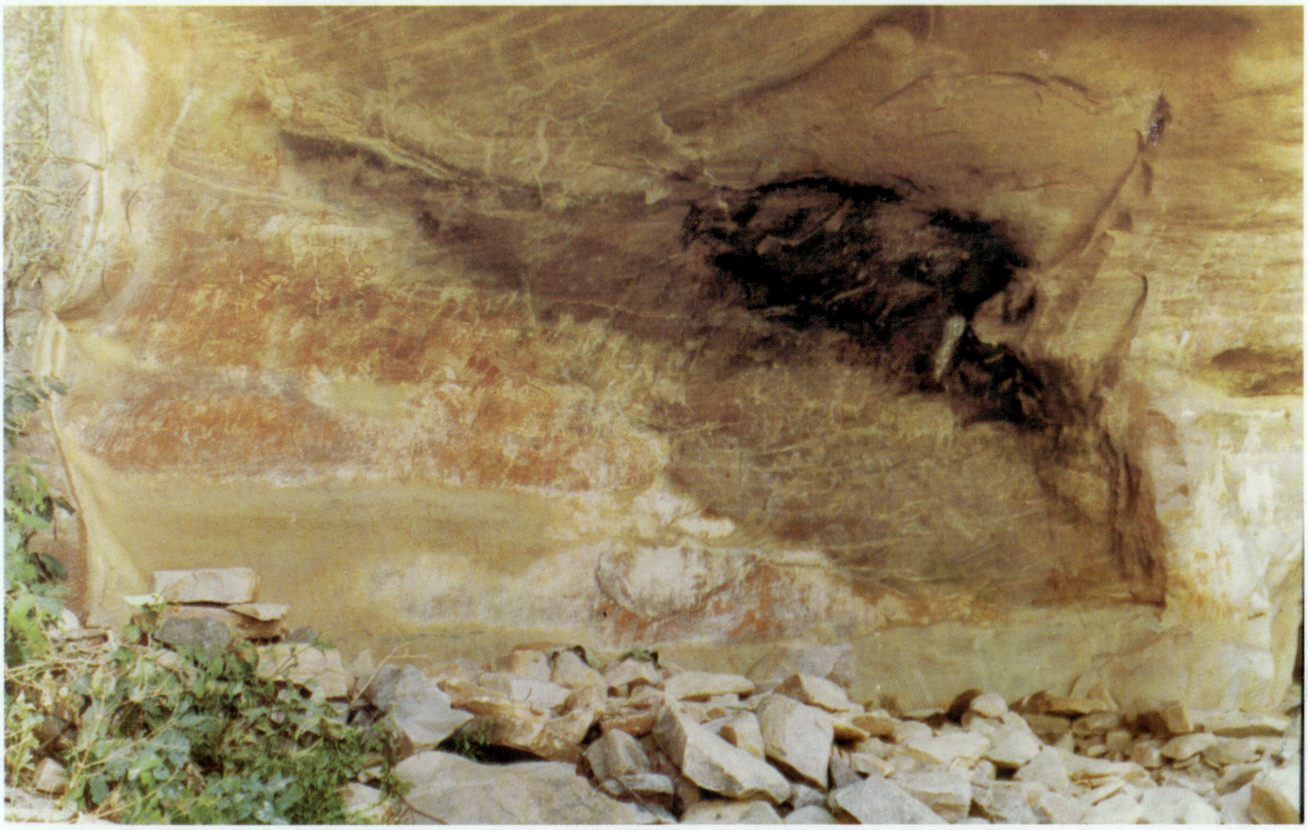

Pl. VIII. R.S. No. 13- Habitational area and painted surface

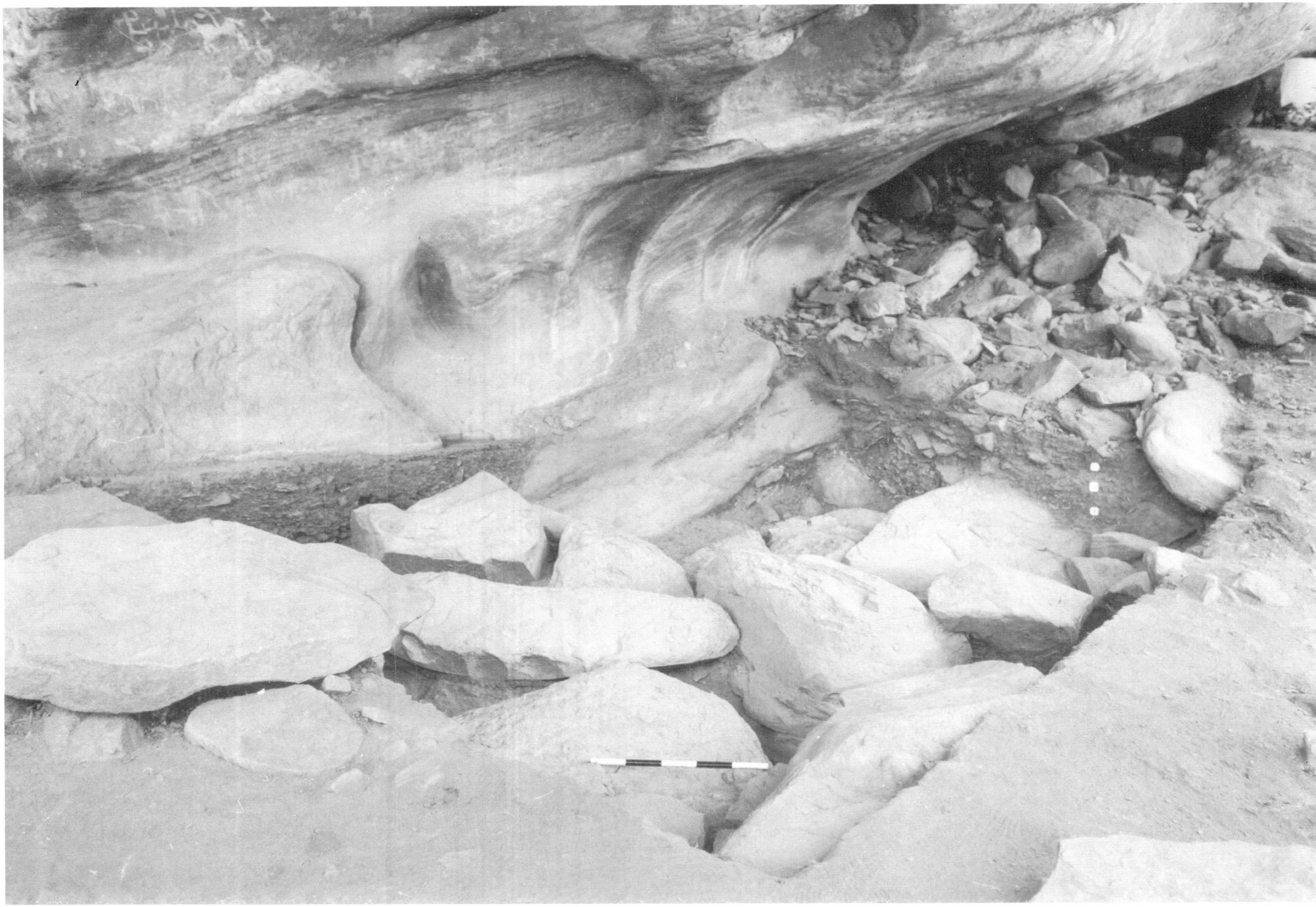

Pl. IX. Depressions with paintings.

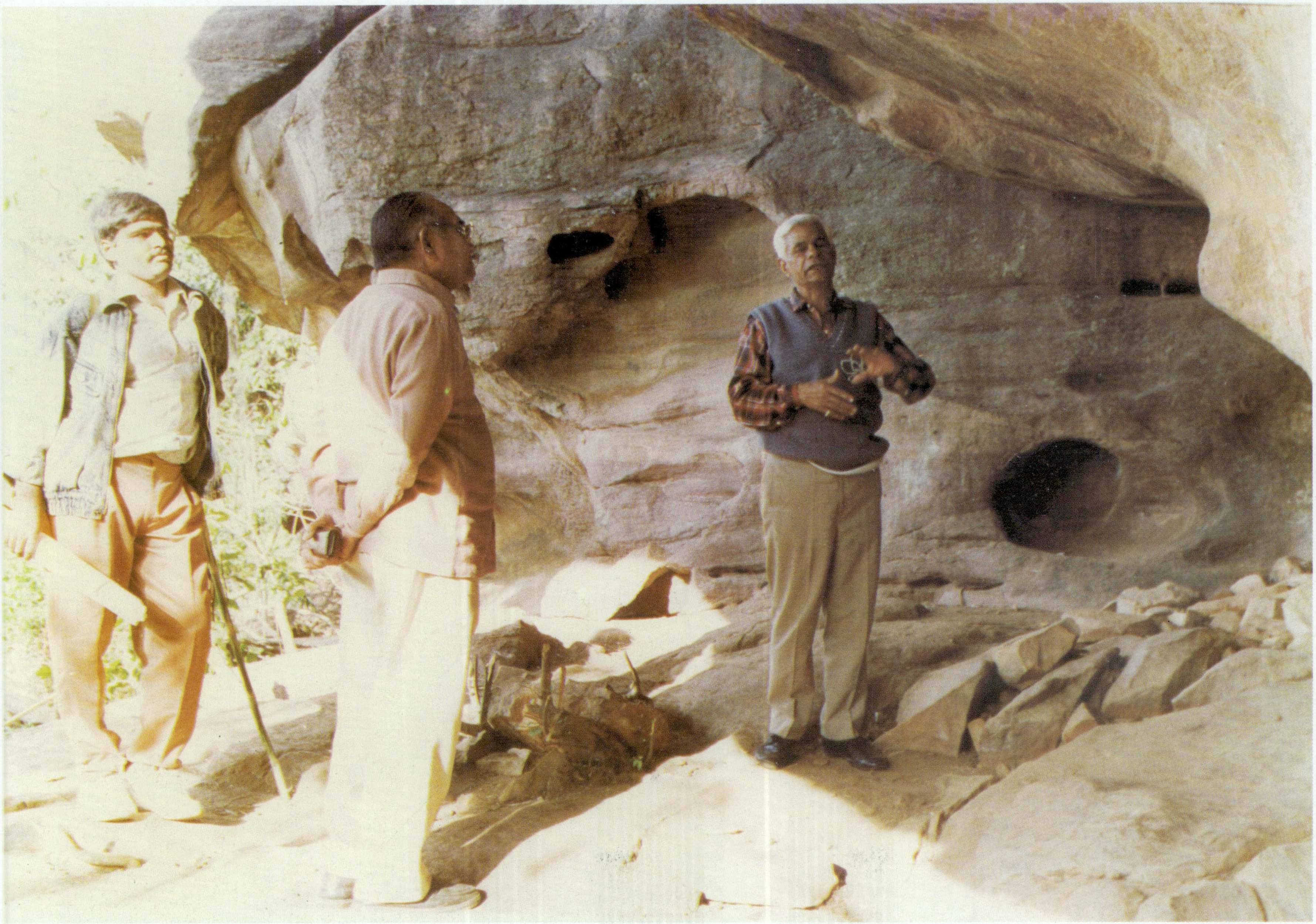

Pl. X. General view of R.S. No. 3.

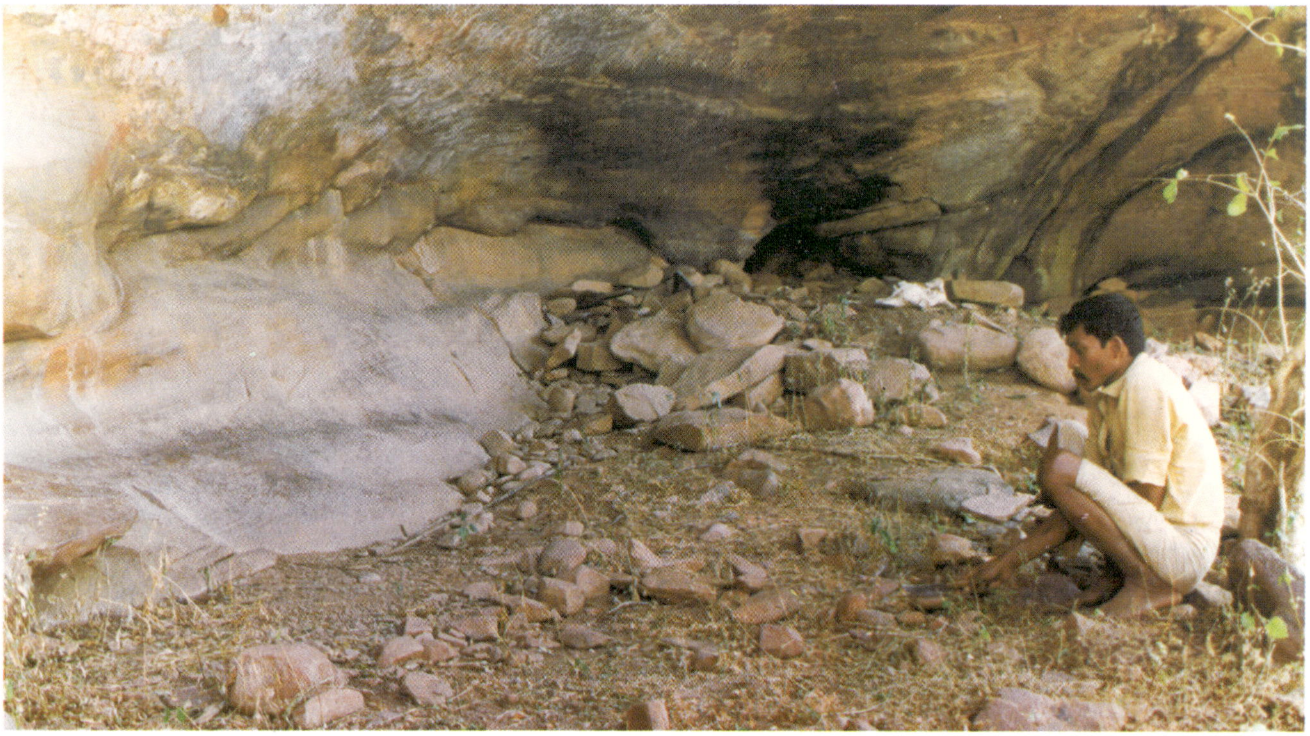

Pl. XI. R.S. No. 3- Before excavation.

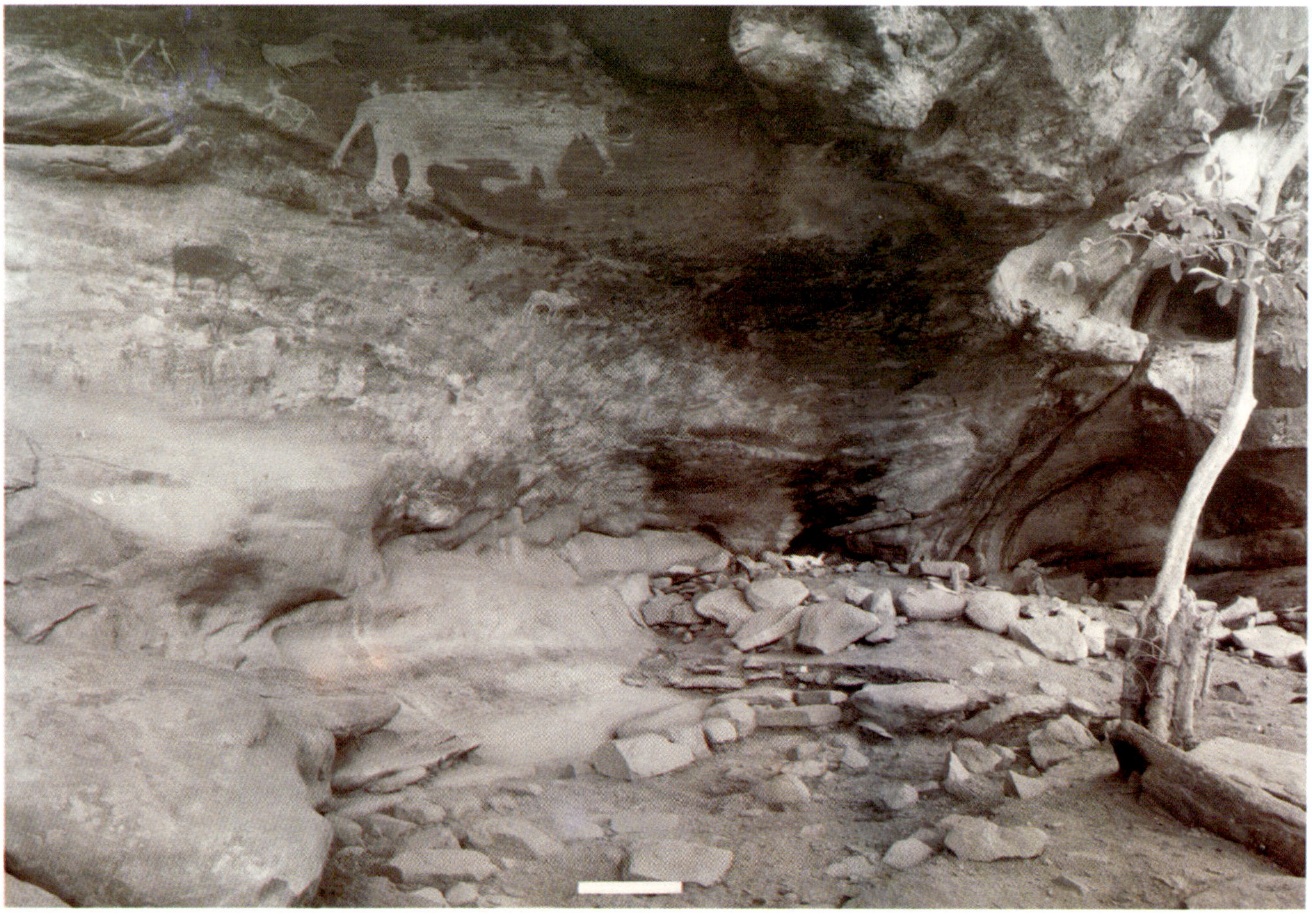

Pl. XII. R.S. No. 3- Trench showing rectangular structure and fire place.

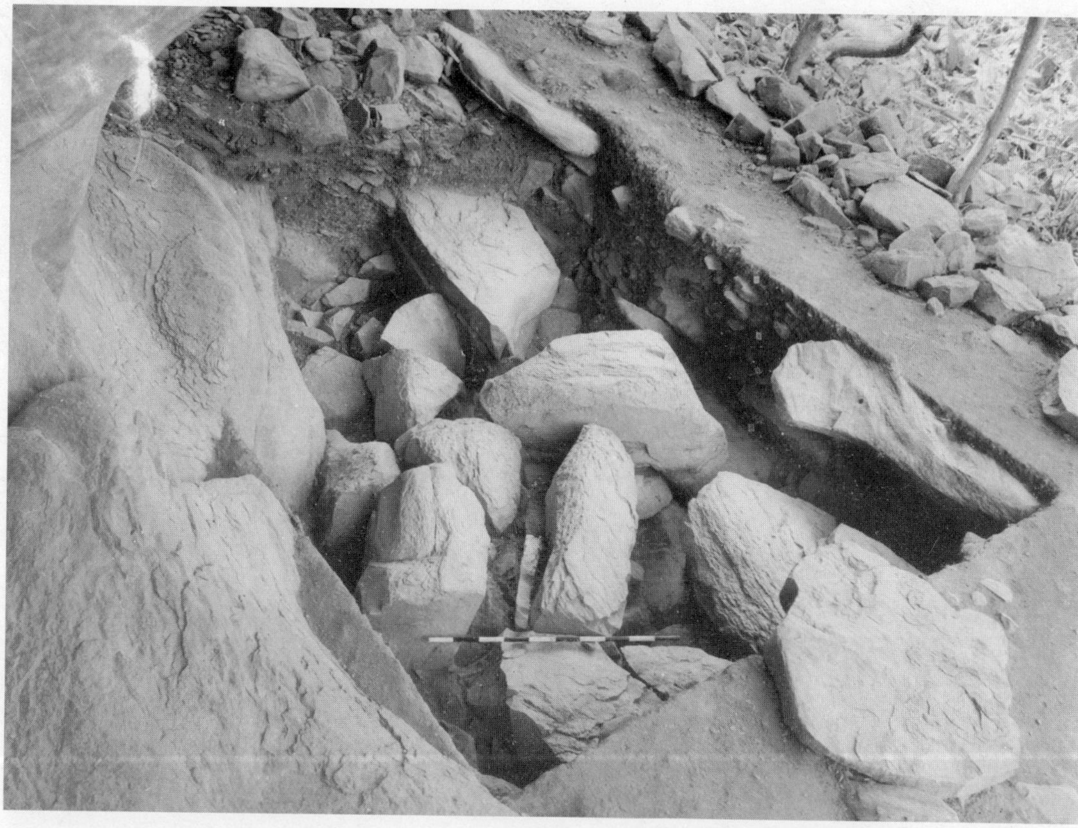

Pl. XIII. R.S. No. 3- Close view of structure and fire place.

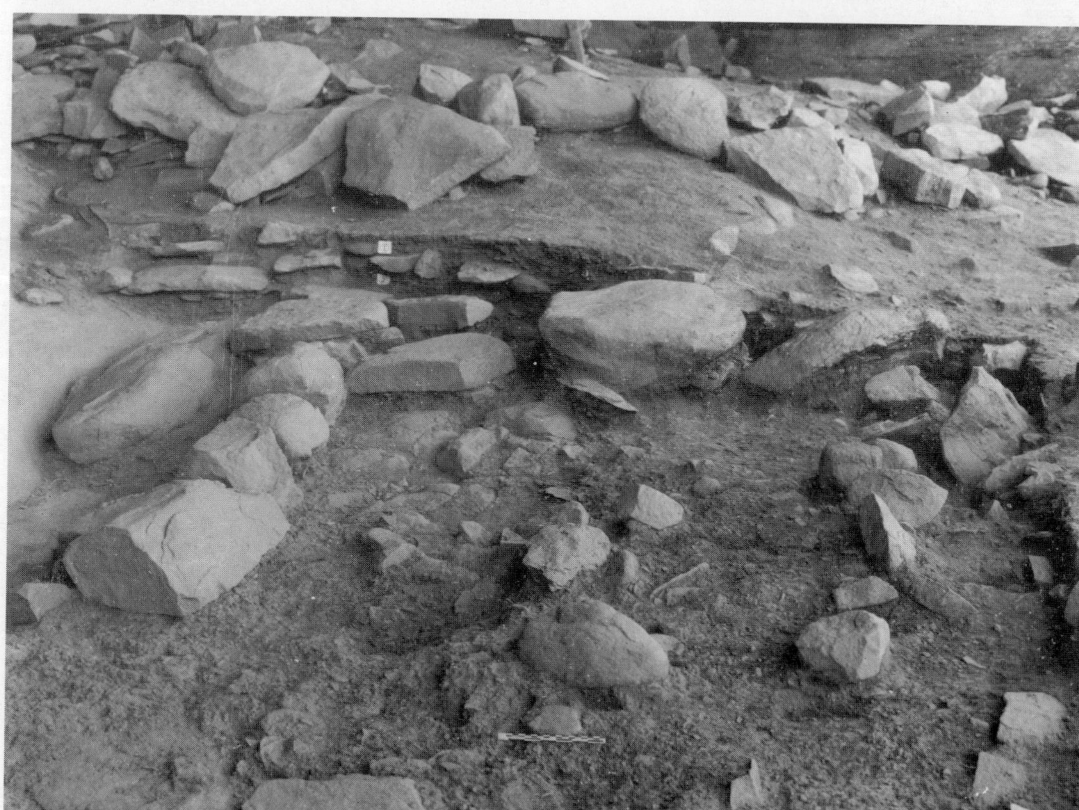

Pl. XIV. R.S. No. 3- Habitational deposits.

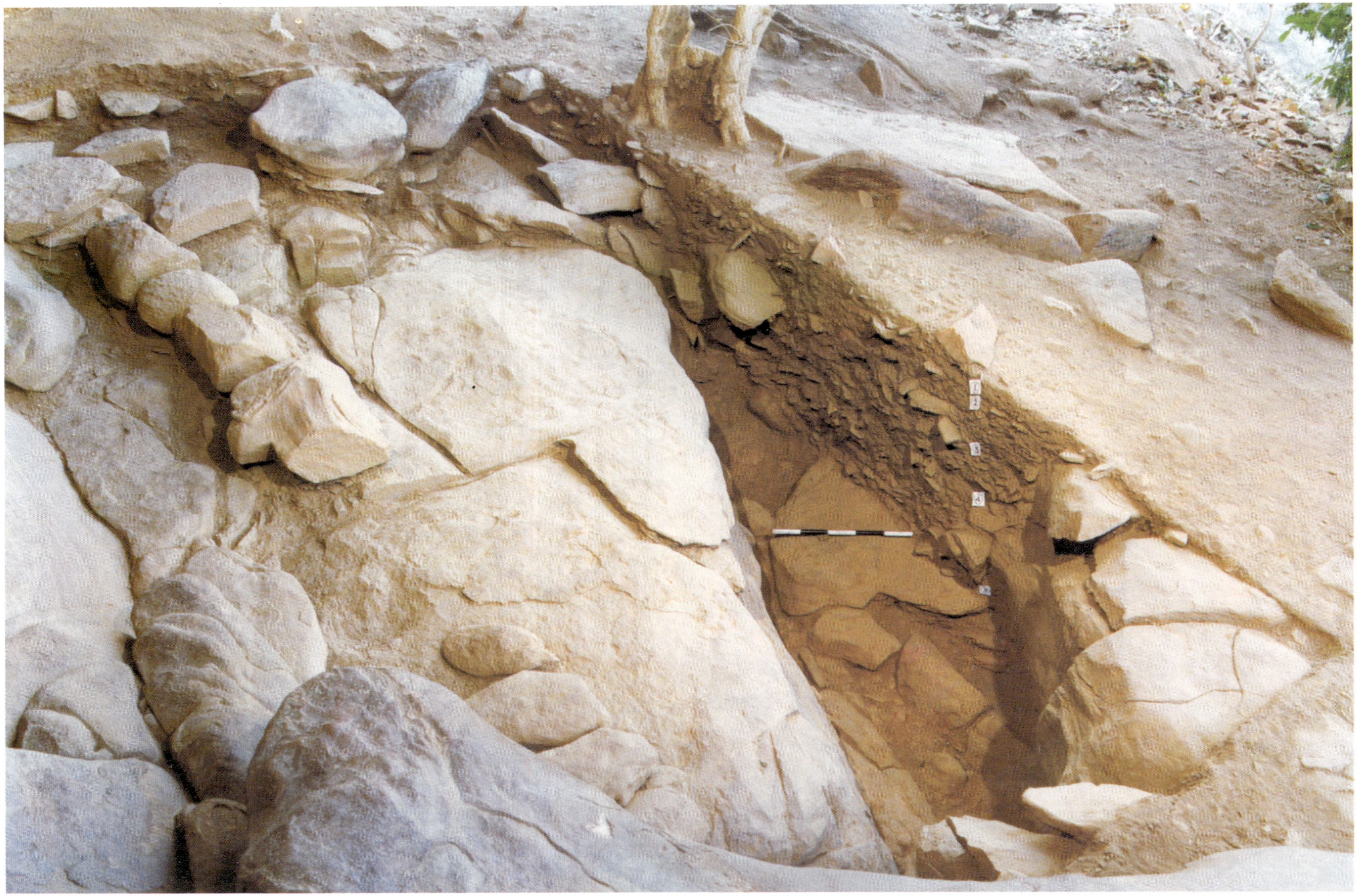

Pl. XV. R.S. No. 3- Habitational deposits viewed from north.

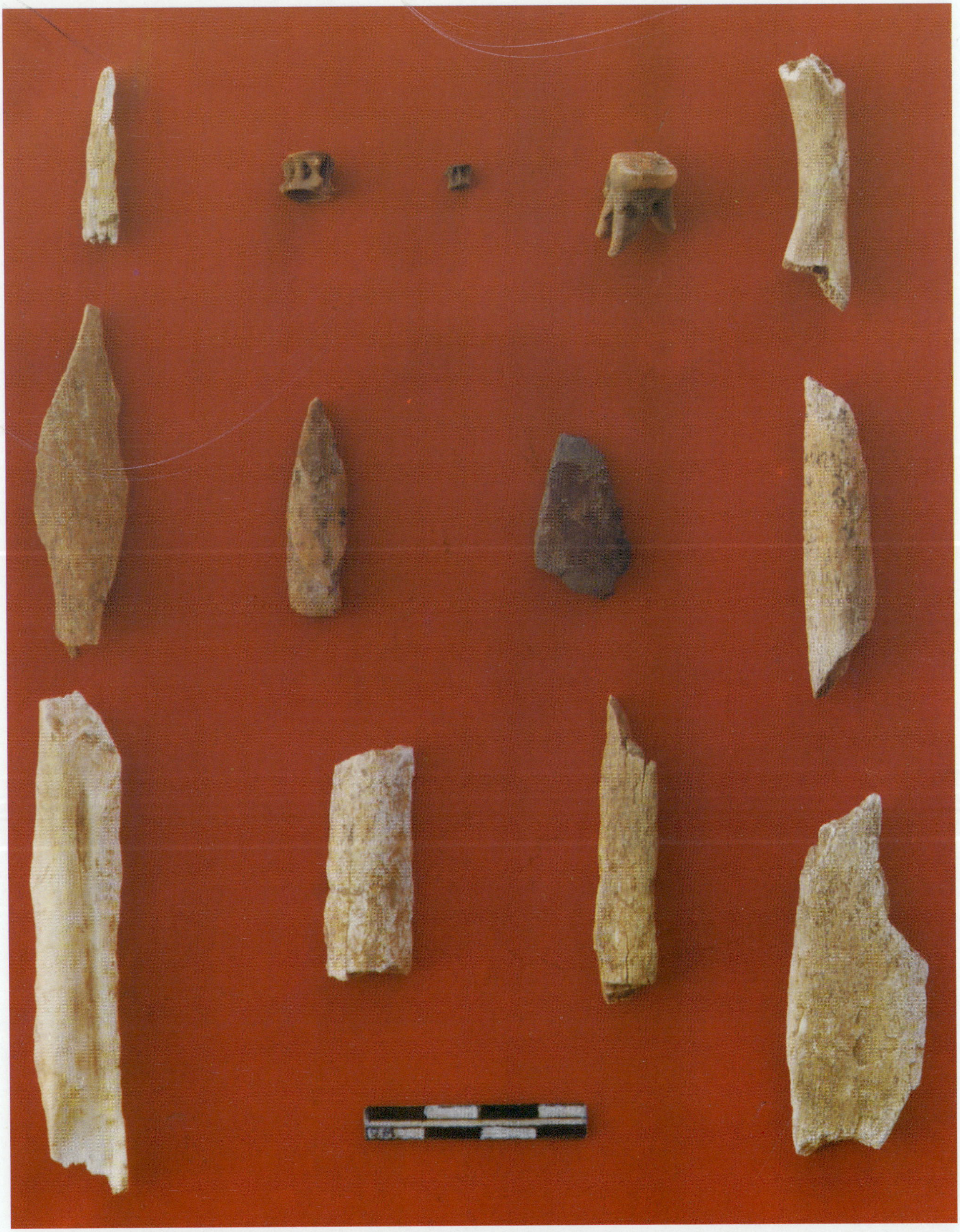

Pl. XVI. Bone fragments.

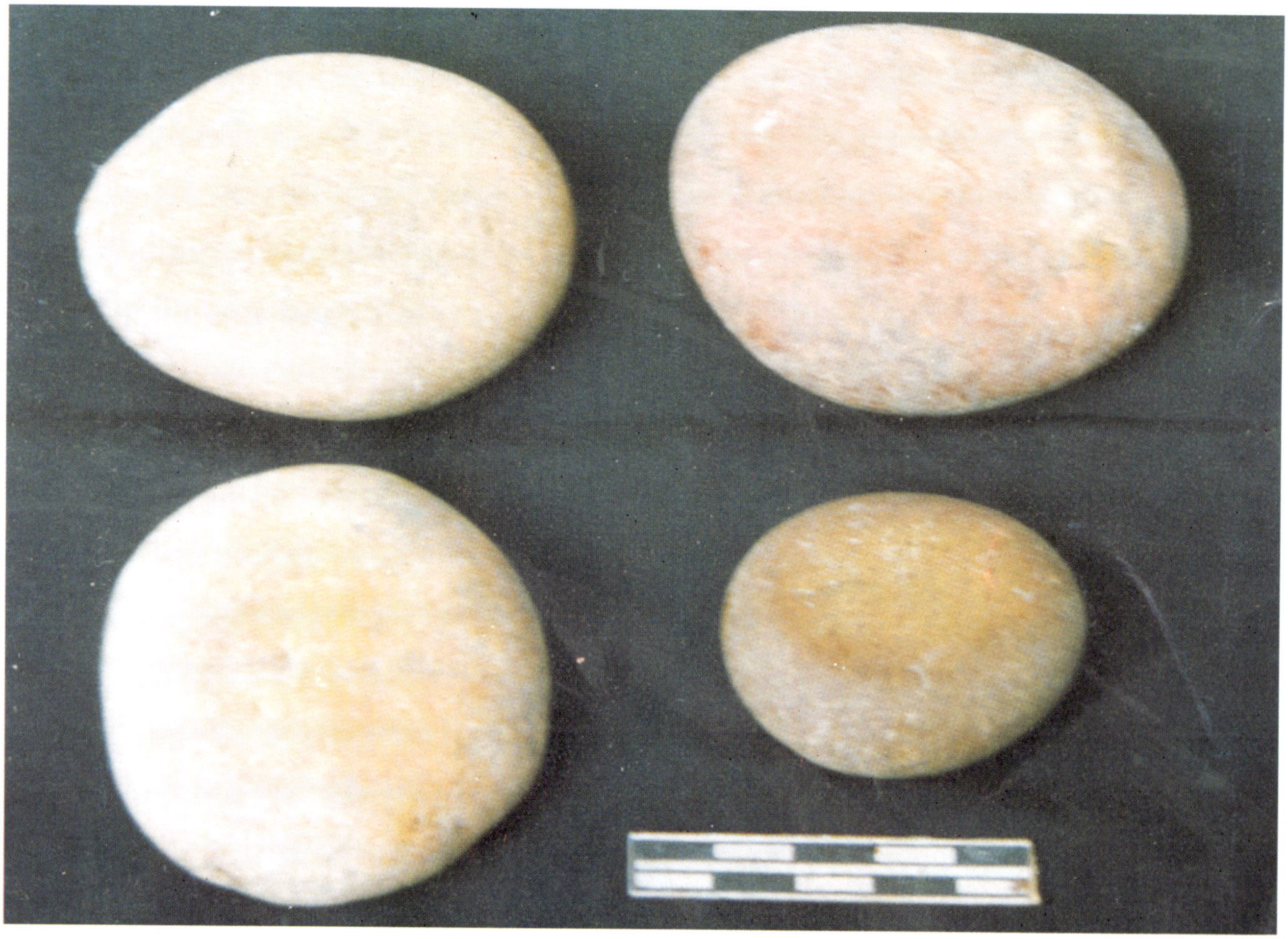

Pl. XVII A. Hop-scotches.

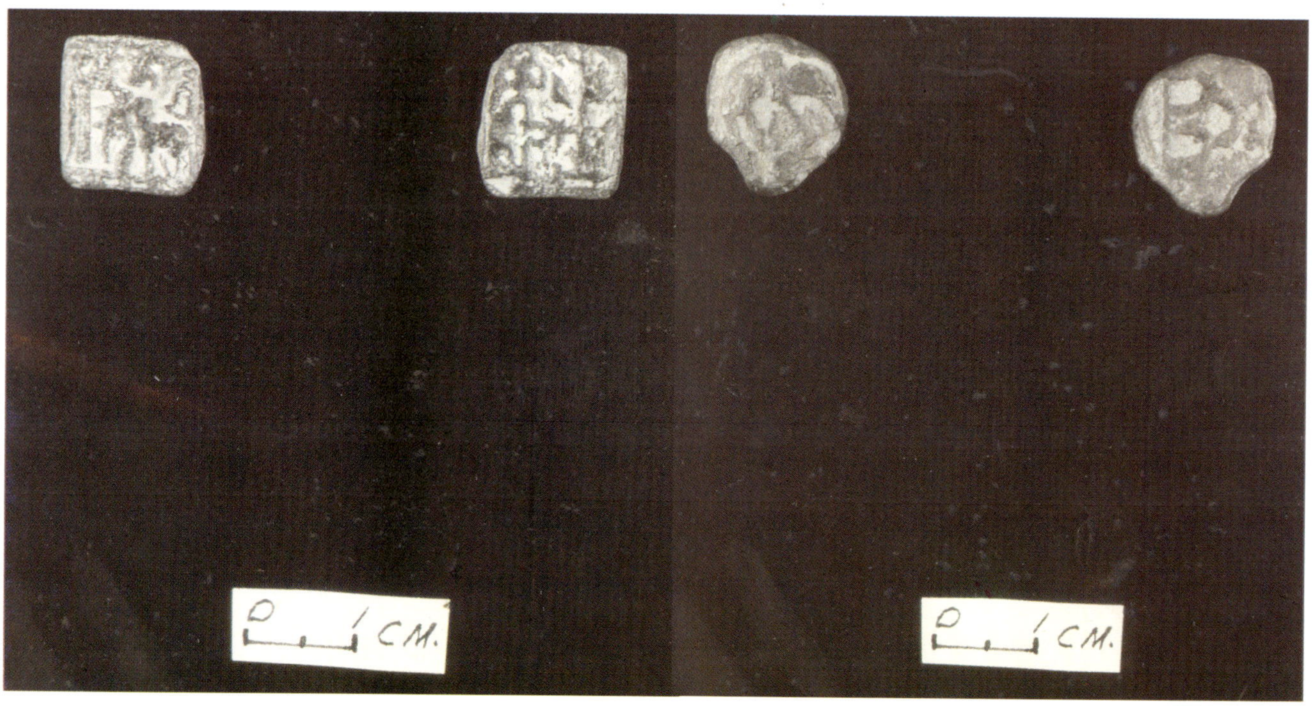

Pl. XVII B. Copper coins.

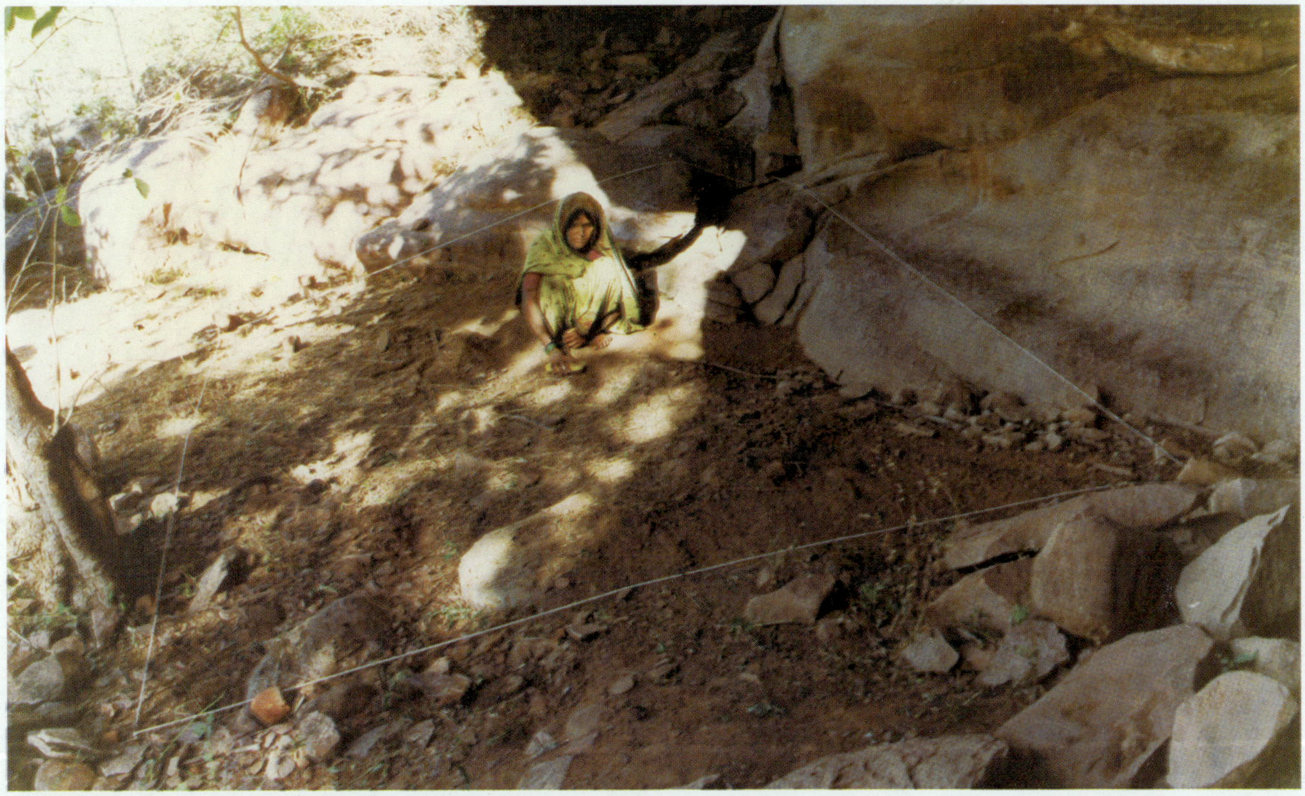

Pl. XVIII. R.S. No. 8- General view

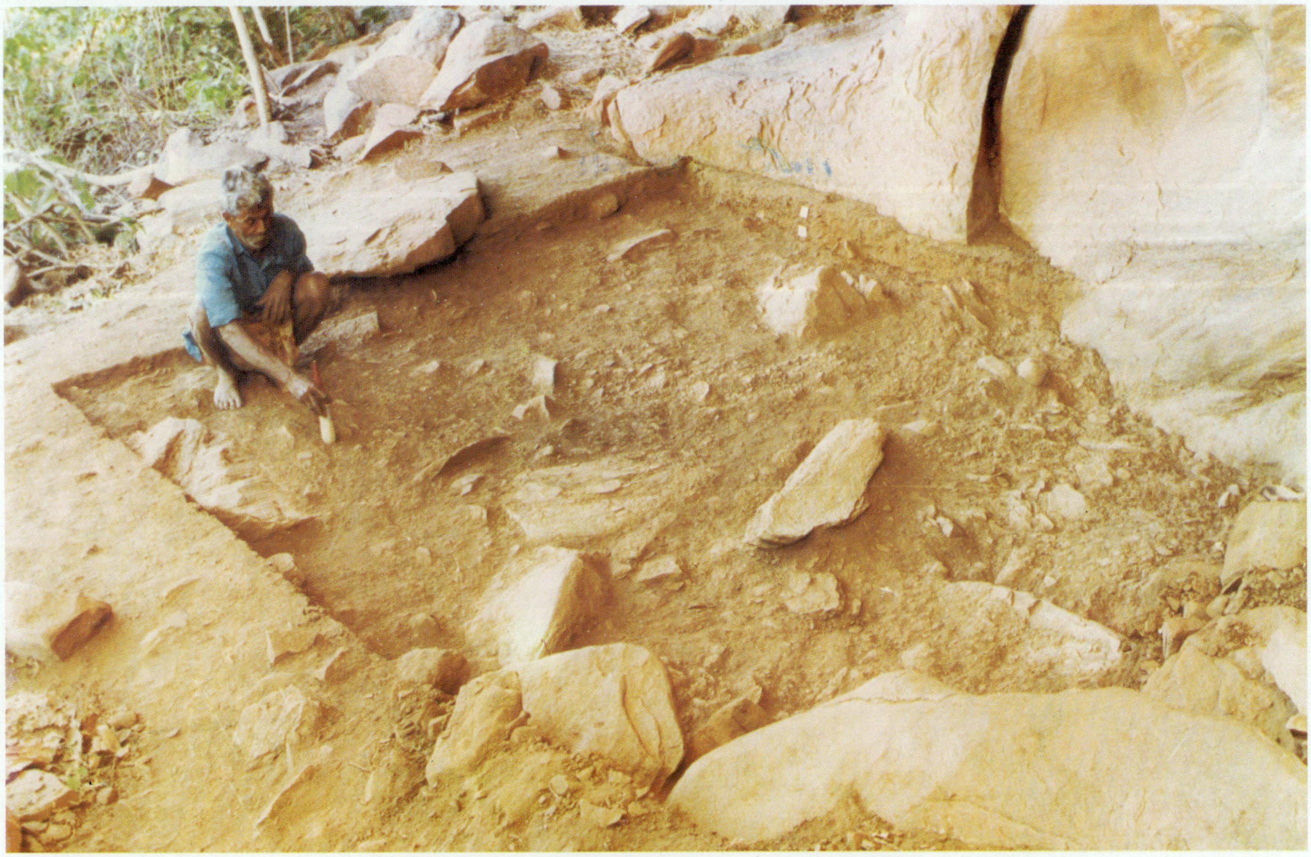

Pl. XIX.R.S. No. 8-The trench with fire place.

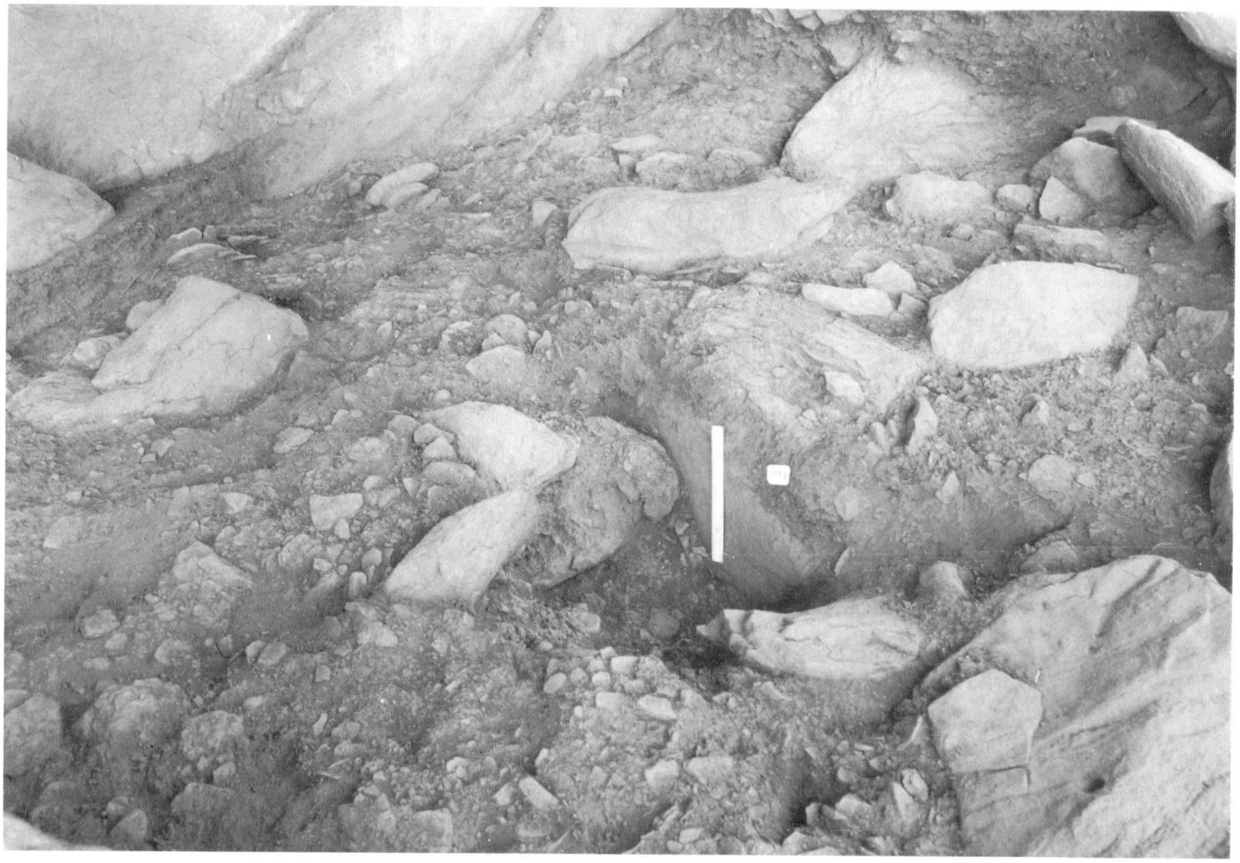

Pl. XX. R.S. No. 8- Fire pit.

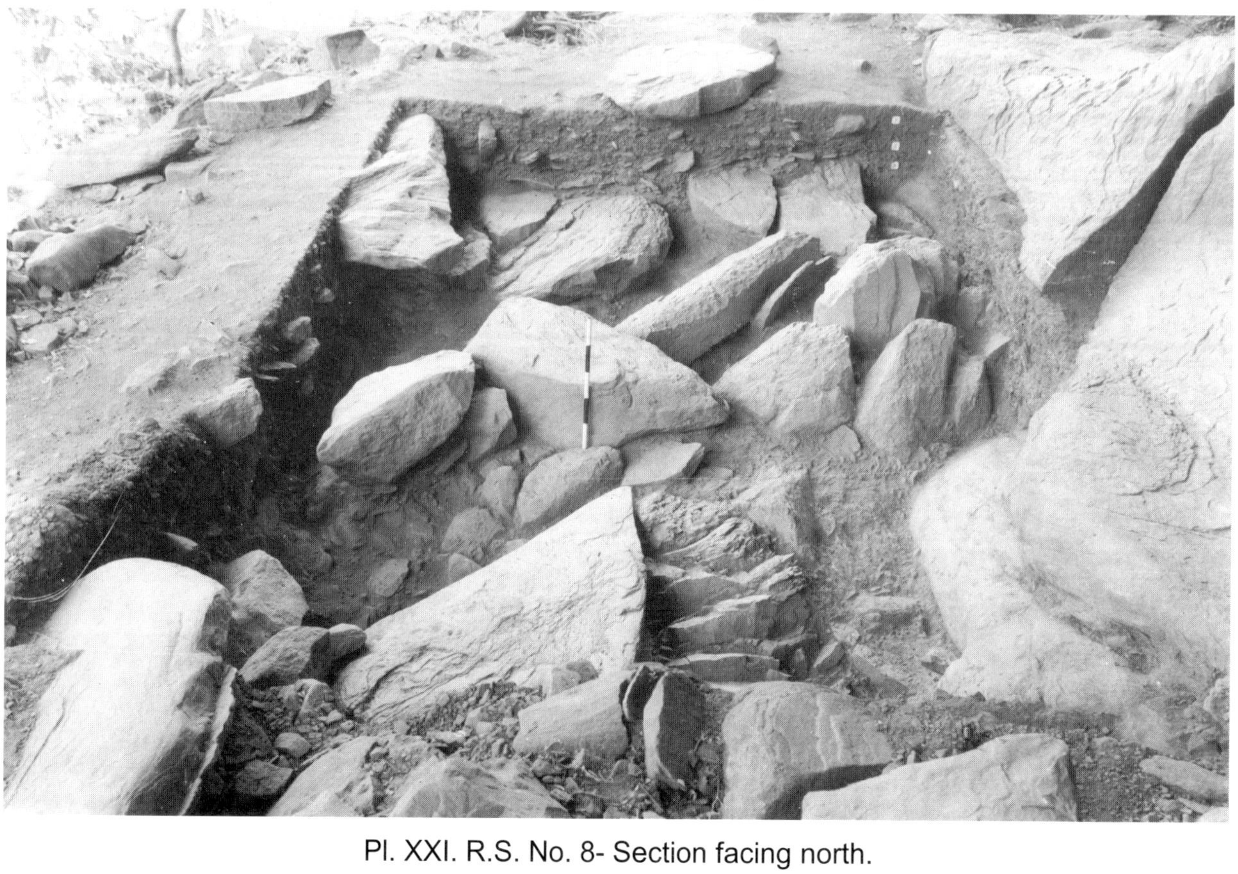

Pl. XXI. R.S. No. 8- Section facing north.

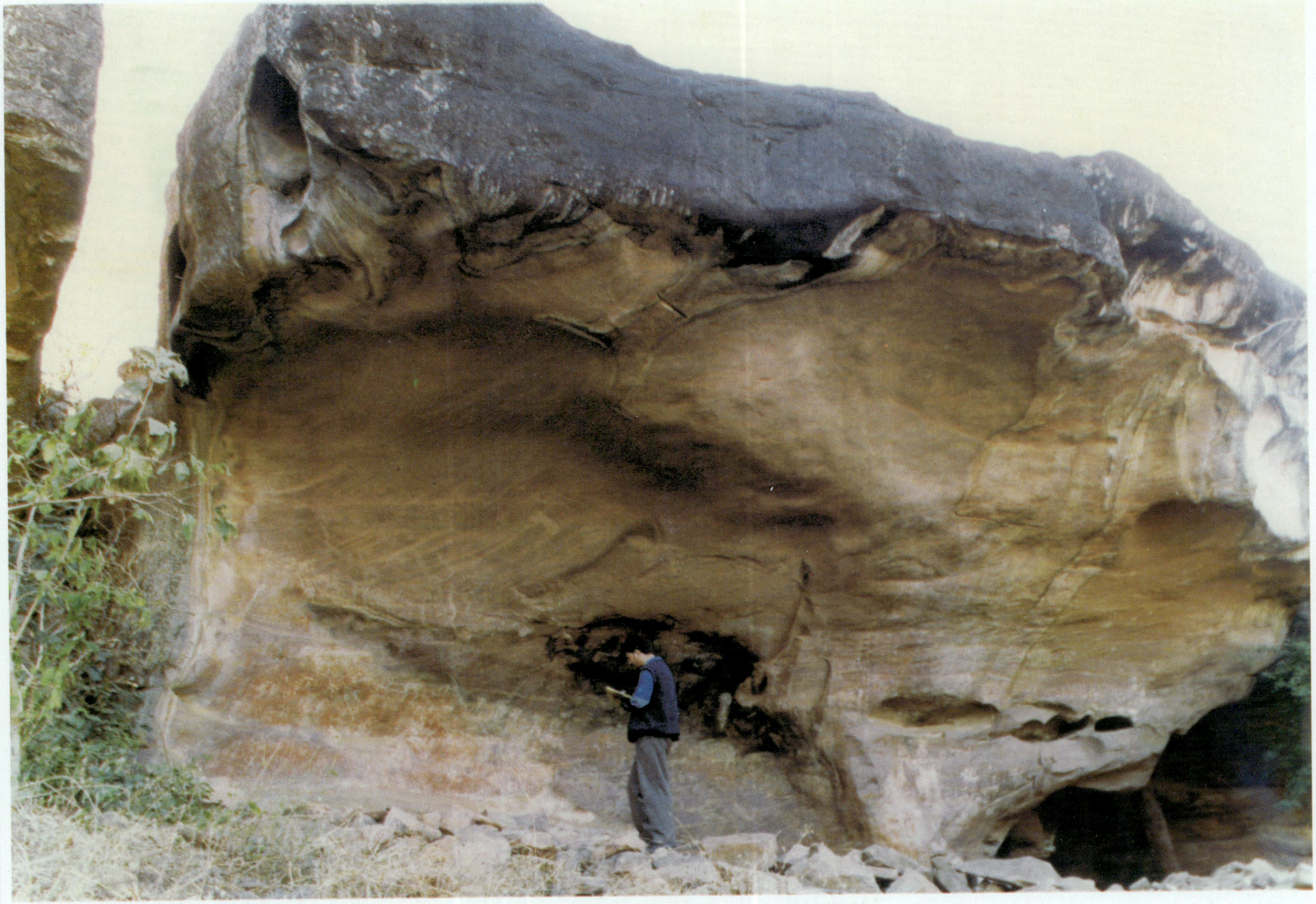

Pl. XXII. R.S. No. 10-General view

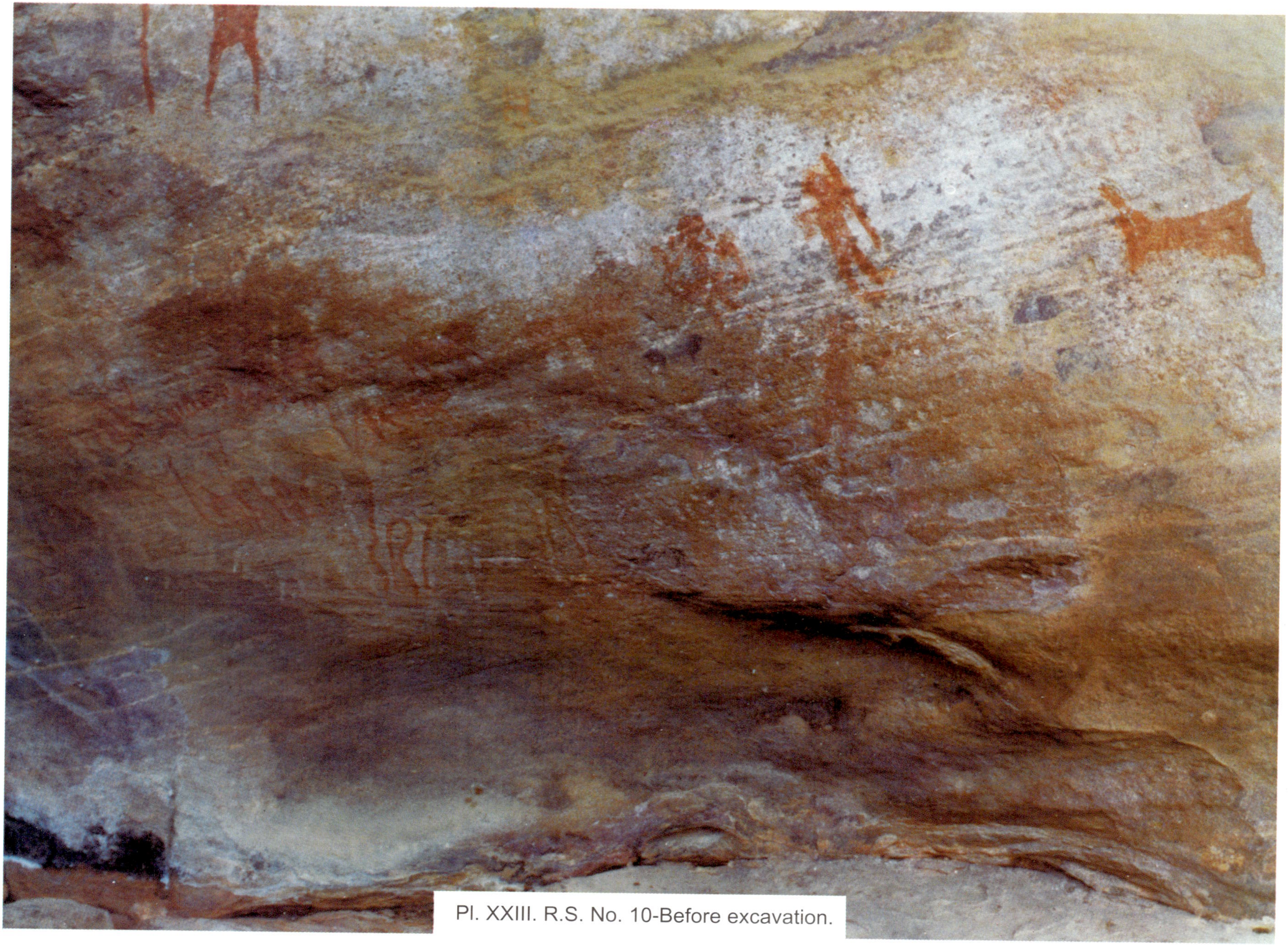

Pl. XXIII. R.S. No. 10-Before excavation.

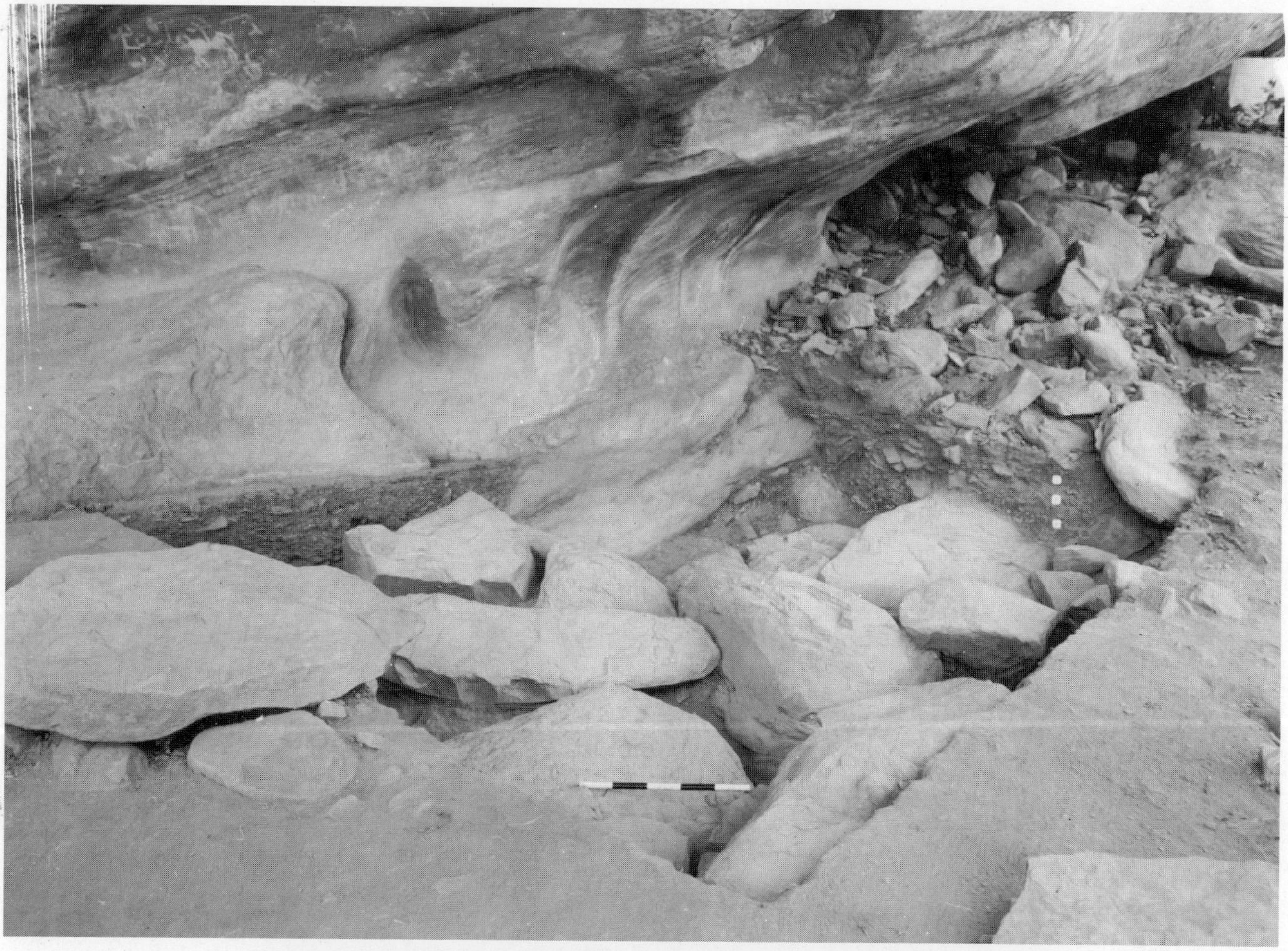

Pl. XXIV. R.S. No. 10- View showing the excavated area.

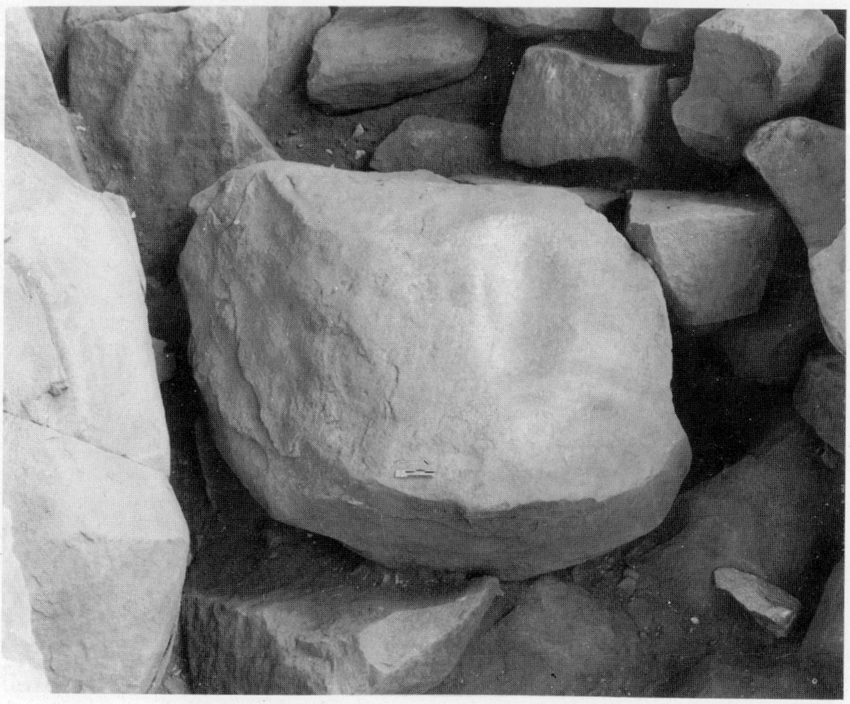

Pl. XXV. R.S. No. 10- Grinding stone.

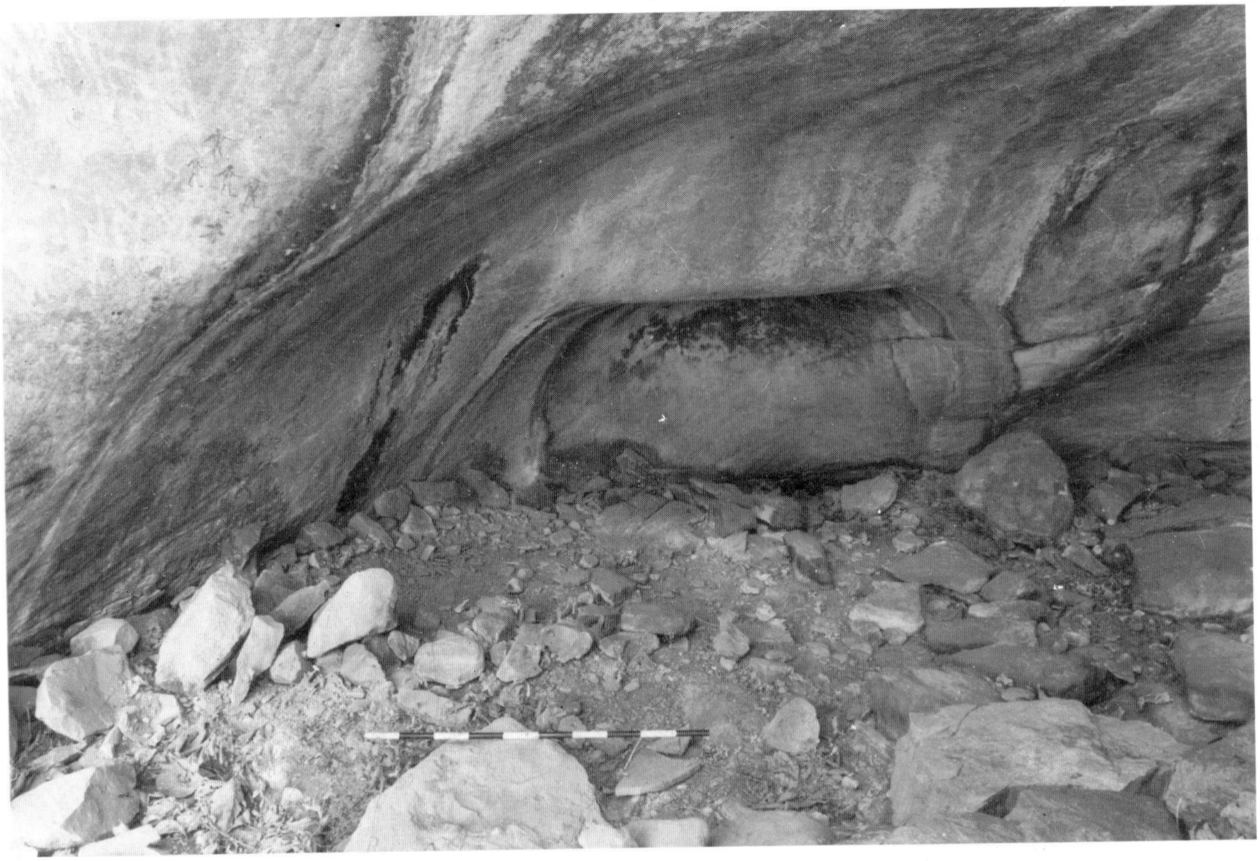

Pl. XXVI. R.S. No. 17-Before excavation.

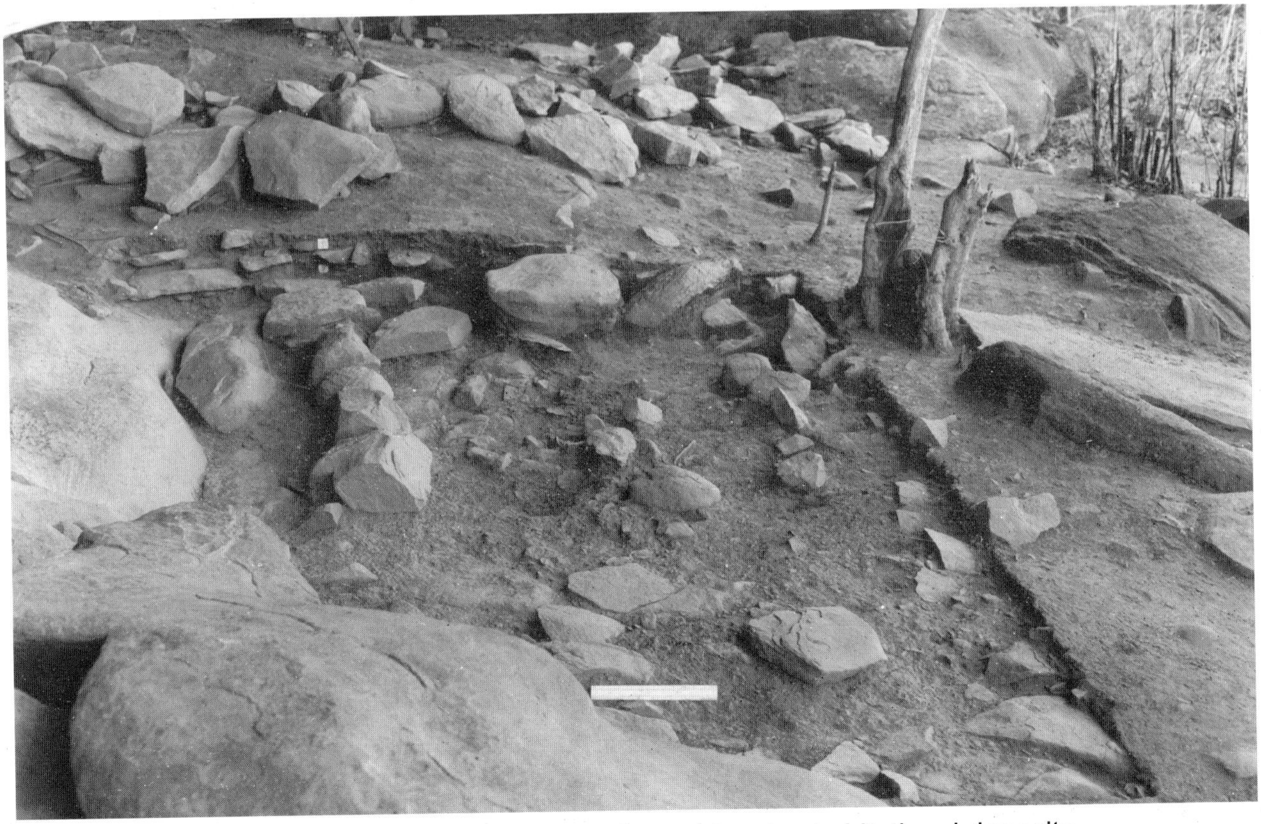

Pl. XXVII. R.S. No. 17- Excavated area showing habitational deposits.

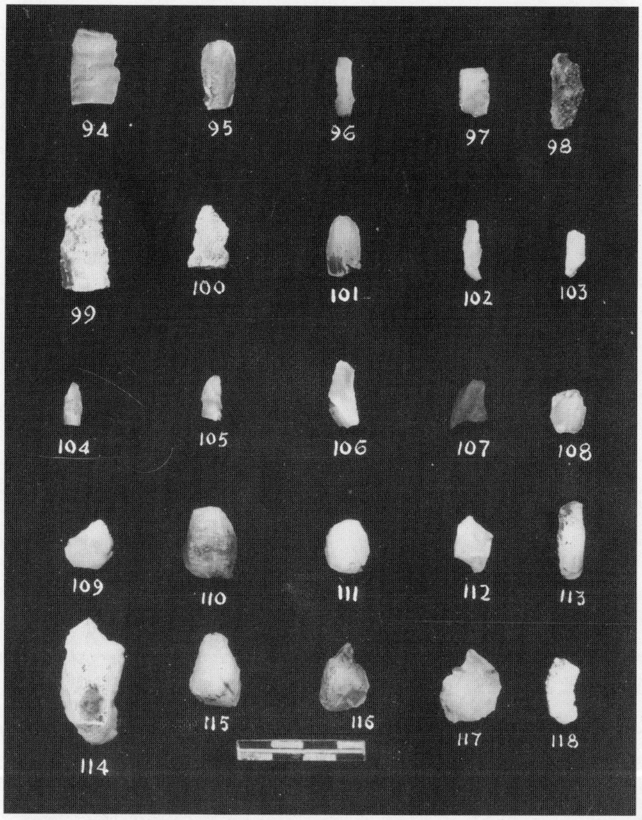

Pl. XXXII. Microliths R.S. No. 8.

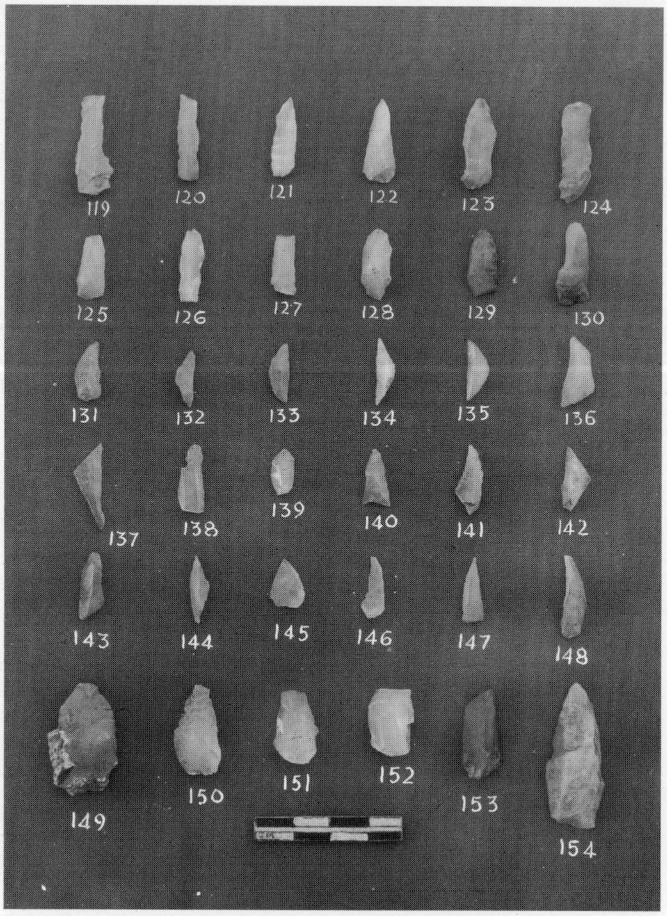

Pl. XXXIII. Microliths R.S. No. 17.

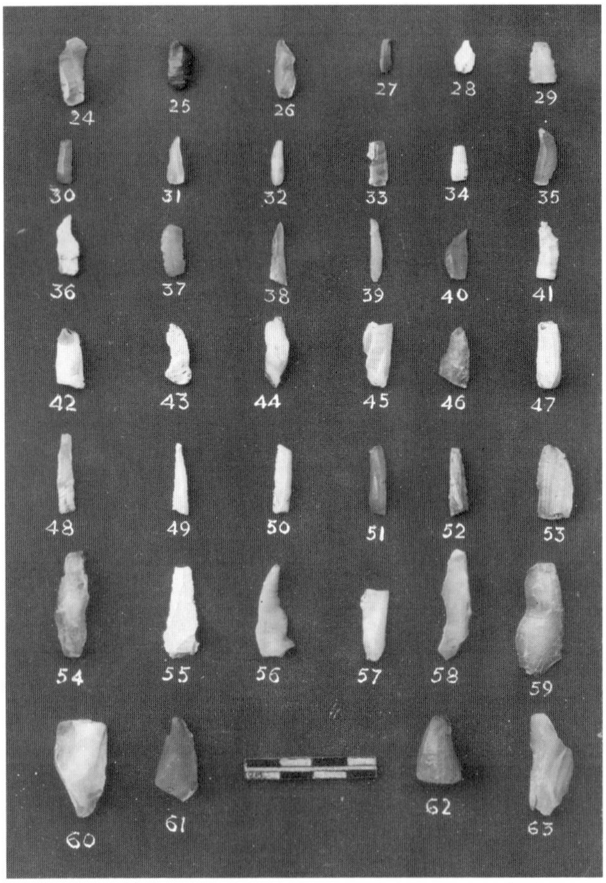

Pl. XXX. Microliths R.S. No. 3, Layer 2. .

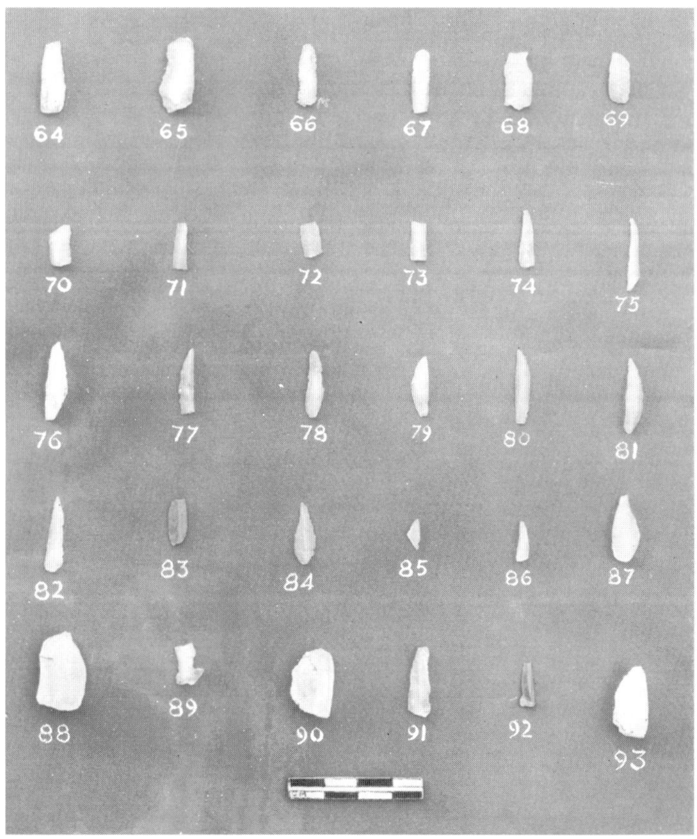

Pl. XXXI. Microliths R.S. No. 3, Layer 3 and 4.

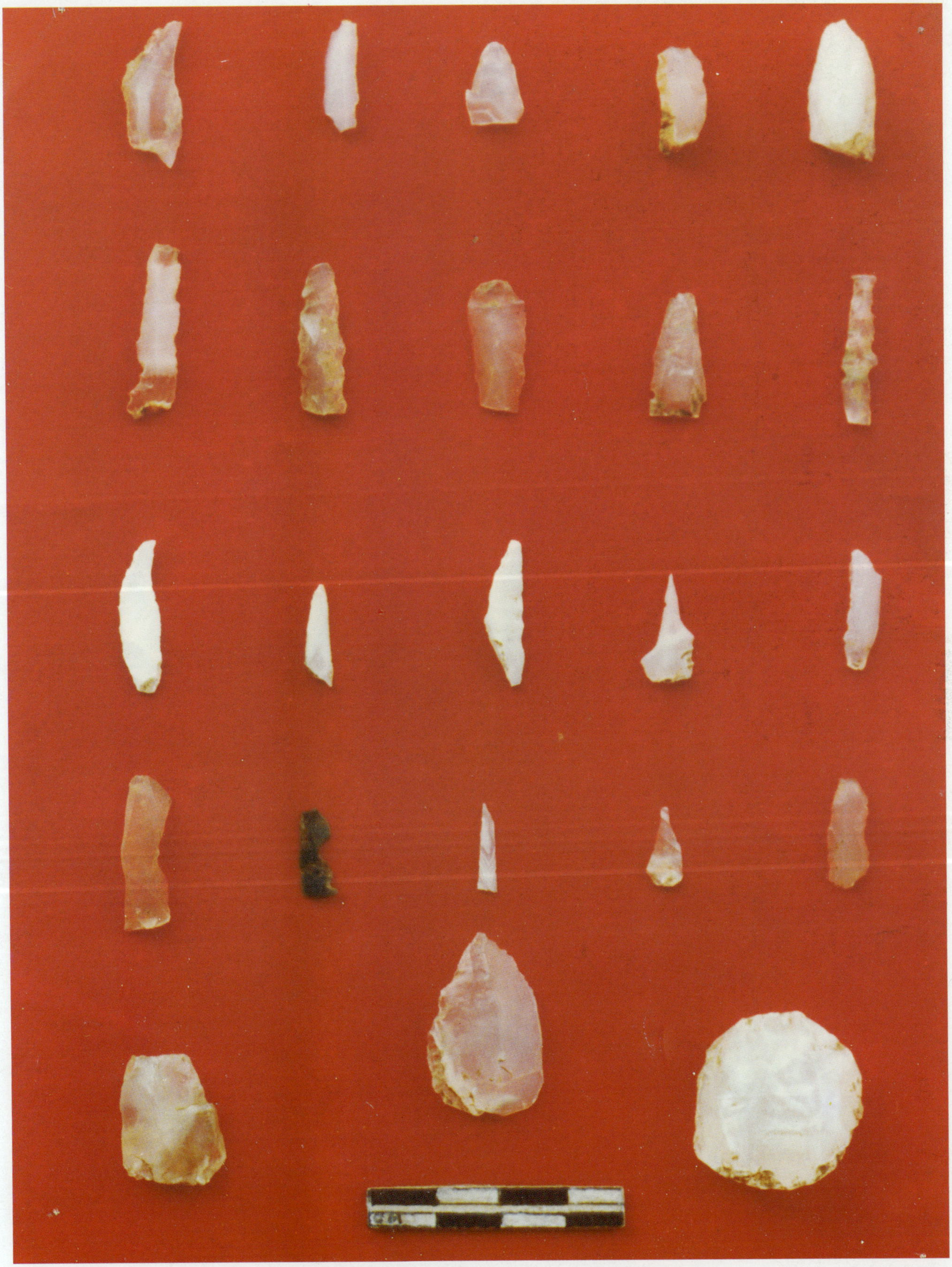

Pl. XXIX.Microliths R.S. No. 3, Layer *2*.

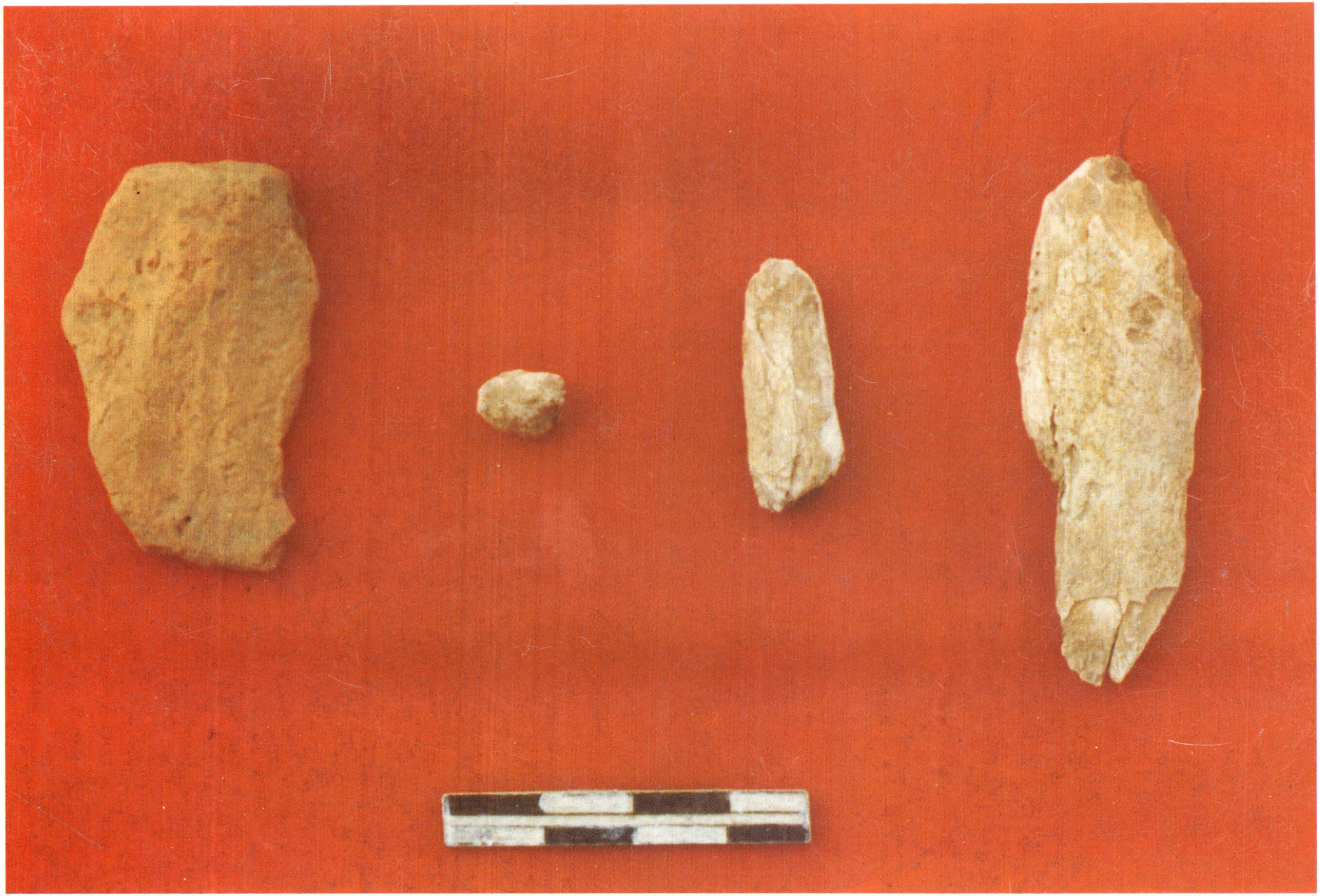

Pl. XXVIII. Colour Pigments.

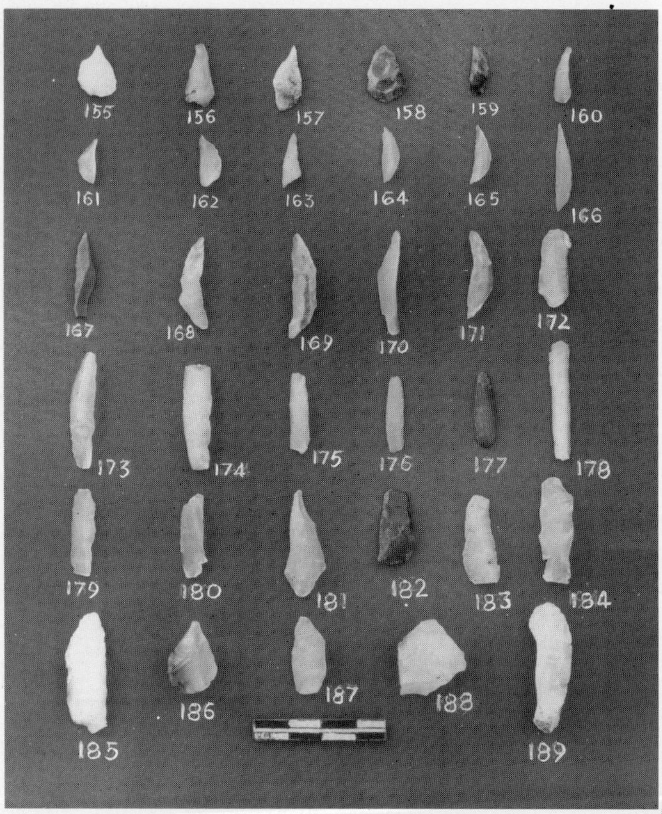

Pl. XXXIV. Microliths R.S. No. 17.

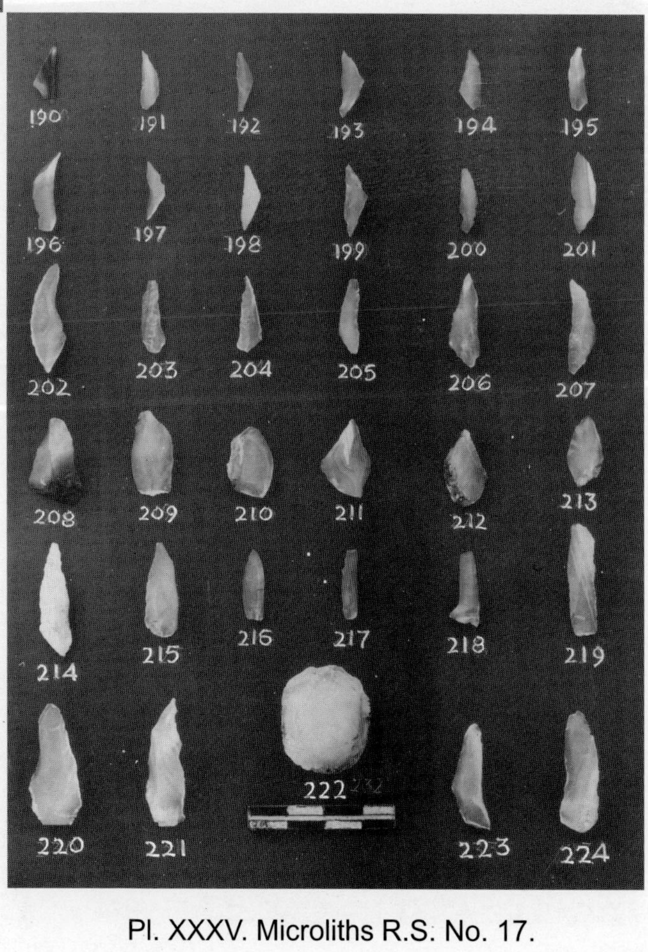

Pl. XXXV. Microliths R.S. No. 17.

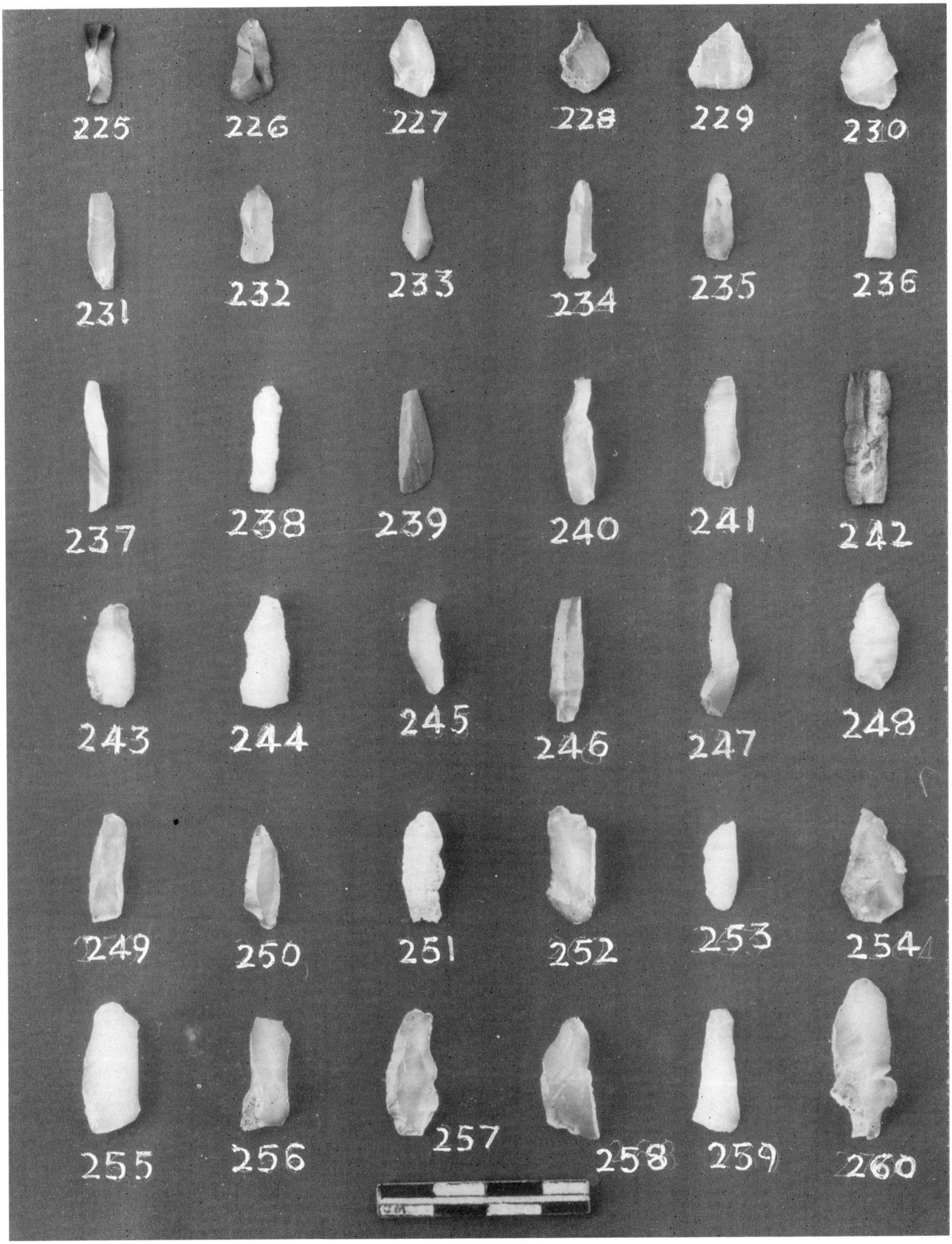

Pl. XXXVI. Microliths R.S. No. 17.

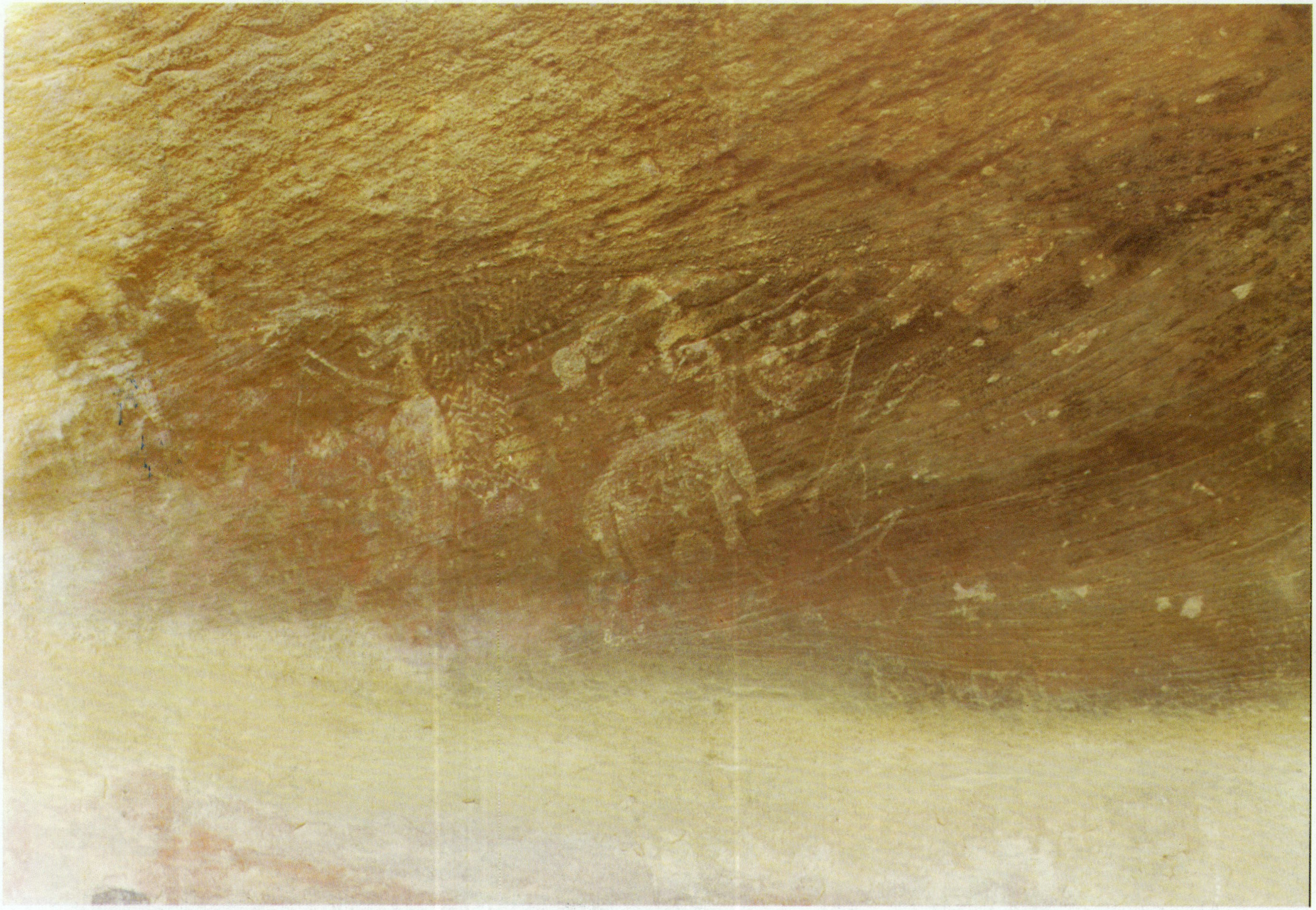

Pl. XXXVII. Paintings in R.S. No. 10 depicting harpoons.

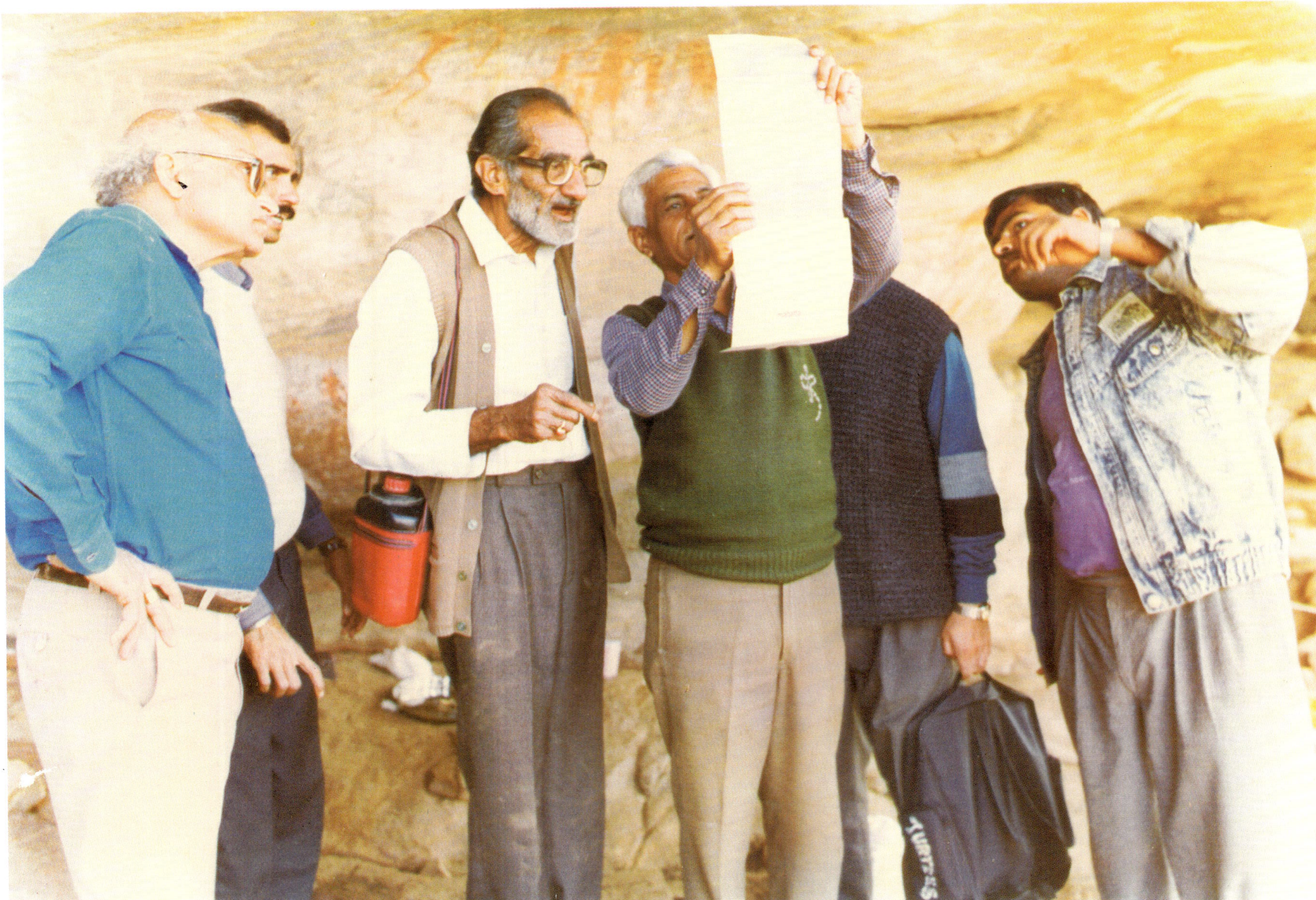

Pl. XXXVIII. Experts Checking the results in the field.